STOP SCHOOL FAILURE

Other Gesell Institute Books

STOP SCHOOL FAILURE

LOUISE BATES AMES, ASSOCIATE DIRECTOR

CLYDE GILLESPIE, CHIEF CLINICAL EXAMINER

JOHN W. STREFF, DIRECTOR OF VISUAL RESEARCH

Gesell Institute of Child Development

HARPER & ROW, PUBLISHERS
NEW YORK, EVANSTON, SAN FRANCISCO, LONDON

Grateful acknowledgment is hereby made for permission to reprint the material specified:

Norman E. Silberberg, Kenny Rehabilitation Institute, for the material quoted in Chapter 9.

Excerpt from "My Life Story," on page 187, by Sheila Greenwald. Copyright © 1966 by Harper's Magazine, Inc. Reprinted from the July, 1966 issue of *Harper's Magazine* by special permission.

Poem on pages 115–116 by Kaye M. Innes. Reprinted by permission of the author.

The card picture "Cow" (Fig. 13) copyright © 1949 by L. L. Tillery. Reprinted by permission of Optometric Extension Program Foundation, Inc.

Ready or Not? The School Readiness Checklist, on pages 110–111, by John J. Austin and J. Clayton Lafferty. Published by Research Concepts, 1368 East Airport Road, Muskegon, Michigan 49444.

Alan Gartner for permission to reprint the quotation in Chapter 11.

Excerpts from "The Slow Learner," on pages 218–220, by Dr. Albert O. Rossi, which appeared in the *New York State Journal of Medicine*, 1968, Vol. 68.

Ray C. Wunderlich, M.D., for permission to use quotation in Chapter 11.

The poem on pages 270–271 by Marlin S. Werner is reprinted by permission of the author.

Paul E. Mawhinney for permission to quote excerpts from "Why We Gave Up on Early Entrance" in Chapter 10.

FIRST EDITION

STANDARD BOOK NUMBER: 06-010114-8

LIBRARY OF CONGRESS CATALOG CARD NUMBER: 79-181603

To our colleagues

Frances L. Ilg, M.D.
Richard J. Apell, O.D.
Richard N. Walker, Ph.D.

CONTENTS

STOP SCHOOL FAILURE

CHAPTER I

INTRODUCTION

"I just hate school!"

"The reason my boy can't recite is that his mind goes blank. . . ."

"He could do the work all right if he really wanted to. He just doesn't try."

The day is far distant when no *child* will complain that he hates school, when no *parent* will struggle for a plausible explanation of her child's inadequate performance, when no *teacher* will feel that some of her pupils fail simply because they are not trying.

But all of us—teachers, parents, child specialists—can hasten that day, or at least reduce the number of school failures, if we can understand more than some of us now do about why children fail in school.

There are probably as many parents anxious and alarmed and uncomfortable about their children's progress and performance in school as there are parents who feel secure and satisfied with the way things are going.

Can we help anxious parents to feel a little more secure? Can we actually change matters so that children will do better in school?

We think we can.

One of the most important things anyone can do in this direction is to try to stop the assignment of blame. Some people feel that blame for most school failure rests on the children themselves, because so many of them are not "motivated" and do not "try." Others blame teachers for not understanding the children or for not doing a good job of teaching. Still others blame the parents for providing a home atmosphere that is not conducive to good health and study habits, or that is not adequately stimulating. But *blaming* has not turned out to be a useful expedient, either in explaining or in remedying school failure.

Diagnosing school difficulty, just as one might diagnose a physical ailment, is something else again, and seems far more effective than merely attempting to assign blame. If we are to help those children who are having trouble do better in school, we must find out, first of all, what it is about each special child—or what is wrong for him in the school situation to which he is being exposed —that is causing failure.

Two important things that most parents wish for their young children—good health and school success—have more in common than many parents realize. If your boy or girl is seriously ill, you go to the doctor and find out what is wrong. If things are seriously unsatisfactory in school, over any prolonged period of time, you should also go to the specialist—the teacher, principal, guidance person, psychologist—and find out where the main source of difficulty lies.

If an illness is serious, you do not as a rule merely apply a lot of homemade remedies. You don't urge your child to try his best to get well. Similarly, when there is serious trouble in school you should not, though many do, simply redouble your own efforts to help or motivate or encourage your child to try harder. As one little girl so admonished replied, "I'm trying as hard as I can right now."

Few parents if any ever say to us, "My child has been sick for years. In fact he never has been really well. I sometimes wonder if I shouldn't take him to the doctor and find out what is wrong with him." But parent after parent does say to us, "My child has never done well in school. He hates it and he gets terrible grades. Sometimes I think I should take him to a child specialist and find out what is wrong with him."

2

Parents think they should, but they so seldom do!

The purpose of this book is twofold. First, if things are not right for your boy or girl in school, we would like to urge you to do your very best to find out why. And, second, we'd like to tell you about the more common causes of school difficulty and failure, suggest ways to get help in identifying them, and discuss some of the things that can be done to set matters right. For, unless you are very lucky or unless the problems are minor ones, diagnosis needs to precede effective treatment, for school problems as for physical illness.

The present book is a companion volume to an earlier publication, *Is Your Child in the Wrong Grade?* by Ames (Harper & Row). That book invited parents to check on their children's grade placement and to consider the possibility that any given child might conceivably be overplaced in school and trying to do the work of a grade whose demands are beyond his capabilities. This unfortunate, but common, situation often exists because most school systems still enter children in school, and subsequently promote them, on the basis of birthday age rather than of behavior age, which we consider a more effective criterion.

The present book goes beyond the scope of the earlier volume in that, whereas *Wrong Grade* talked chiefly about incorrect grade placement, this book discusses the many other possible causes of school failure. It also stresses the importance of diagnosis, pointing out that it may take a specialist to determine the cause or causes of school failure, and insists that unless one knows the reason for failure it is most difficult to prevent or stop it.

Finding out what is wrong is, obviously, only the first step toward remedying matters. An effective child behavior clinic should be able to help any parent take not only this necessary first step but also the further remedial steps that must then follow. We diagnose not merely so that we can label. We diagnose so that we can know what must be done to correct failure and bring about success.

If professional help is not available, hopefully the things we tell you in this book may help you and your school to help your child, if he is having trouble, to a more effective, successful, and happy school adjustment.

There's every reason to assume that any boy or girl *can* succeed in school. He may not go to college. He may not get As and Bs. He might not even be able to manage in an ordinary class in what we think of as the regular stream of education.

But there should be, somewhere in an educational system like our own, a school, class, or teacher to help every child (with perhaps a very few exceptions) to learn successfully and happily at his own level of performance. There should be available for every child a school situation that he can accept, where he will be comfortable and reasonably successful, and in which he can perform in a way that will enable his parents to feel comfortable.

Individual differences among children, and differences in ability and aptitude, are so very great that this will not be an easy thing to achieve. Fortunately, if things are explained to them clearly and sympathetically, most parents do help, in those cases where a special type of schooling is needed, by accepting the child's need for slower progress or for a smaller class or a special class or otherwise different type of school situation.

In order to achieve all this, we need, first of all, to know a great deal more than we now do about individual children and how they learn. Second, we need either such small classes that each teacher can respond to and adapt to individual differences, or a great many different *kinds* of classes. We shall need, in any case, to provide many more different kinds of curriculum than are now available. We will discuss some of these possibilities later on in this volume.

Though a child specialist can usually help, we must not lose sight of the fact that sometimes children fail in school for perfectly ordinary, everyday, commonsense reasons. There are some children, for instance, who don't like their teacher, and some teachers who don't like certain children. A personality conflict can result in either case, leading to school failure—which can often be remedied simply by moving the child to a different teacher's room.

There are children who fail simply because they are mad at the world and disenchanted with the Establishment. We see this frequently in inner-city schools. The problem in such cases, though understandable, is considerably beyond the scope of a book like this.

Sometimes, though admittedly the phrase has been overused, a child is indeed, as his parents fondly hope, "just going through a phase." There are times, especially at the often inwardized and sometimes unhappy ages of thirteen and fifteen, when it seems as if about all the energy a child has goes into growing, with very little left for schoolwork. Happily, more often than not the child actually does "snap out of it," and returns shortly to more effective functioning.

Or sometimes poor schoolwork can be the result of a child's own special reasoning. There are a few bright, quick little girls who very early discover that too-good school performance does not make them particularly popular with boys, so they soft-pedal their activities even to the point of getting less good grades than they are capable of. Occasionally, the same kind of wish for popularity influences boys as well. Jim, for instance, was admittedly a very bright boy. Neither school nor parent could understand his poor academic performance. Finally, along in sixth grade he suddenly did much better, starting to bring home grades that fitted what was considered to be his true ability level. Asked what had brought about this change, he explained to his mother, "Kids don't like you if you do too well. But now I think they like me okay, so it's safe to do better."

All this means is that before seeking help from school or psychologist about what is considered a child's poor performance in school, any parent should at least use his own common sense in trying to figure out what things he thinks *might* be causing the difficulty.

There Is Always a Reason

Though we cannot always spot it, it's safe to say that there is always a reason for poor schoolwork. One cannot, for instance, agree with Charley's teacher's evaluation of Charley's poor schoolwork: "He refuses to do his work in school for some mysterious reason that he refuses to divulge."

That Charley refuses to divulge the reason, we can well believe. Most children do not *know* why they are failing in school except that the work is "too hard." But that the reason for his poor schoolwork was mysterious is unlikely. Careful diagnosis nearly always reveals clearly the reason why *any* boy or girl is doing poorly in school.

And though home and school, as we have suggested, can and sometimes do unwittingly contribute to a child's school failure, more often than not *the answer lies in the organism.* The Gesell point of view holds that, though the child's environment—and especially that part of the environment made up by his teachers and parents—must do everything it can to provide the best circumstances possible for growth and learning, the basis for every child's behavior lies primarily in his own body.

Behavior is a function of structure. To a large extent we behave as we do because of the way our bodies are built. Dr. Arnold Gesell expressed this notion clearly when he commented that "environmental factors support, inflect and modify but they do not generate the progressions of development (34)." Each child behaves as he does chiefly because of the kind of body and brain he has inherited and the stage in his development he has reached, even though of course his behavior at all times is influenced by the circumstances in which he finds himself.

A good child behavior clinic takes into account both the child and his surroundings in reaching its diagnosis. After diagnosing his potentials and problems, it then helps to alter or arrange the en-

6

Introduction

vironment in order to provide the support and help he needs. But, obviously, we can't know what he needs until we know quite a lot about what he is like. Each child's needs are special and to some extent unique to his own organism.

Not every parent, worried about his child's performance in school, will have the opportunity to take him to a behavior clinic or child specialist. And not every school system today can furnish all the special and different kinds of school opportunity needed by all the different kinds of children who attend. This book, hopefully, will share with parents who cannot consult clinic or psychologist, or whose school system does not offer the very latest and most refined kinds of special classes for those children who need them, some of our own clinical findings. Or it can assist those parents who may be able to consult a clinic or psychologist to discover some of the ways in which they can be expected to help. It will also give suggestions as to why a child may be having trouble in school as well as suggestions as to what can and cannot be done to help him.

Information and advice given here are based primarily on our own clinical experience. However, nowadays an increasing number of psychologists and of physicians are looking at child behavior problems from what we consider a sound biological point of view. Thus we present here suggestions from writers other than ourselves whose findings have proved useful to us and, we hope, will also prove useful to you.

This book is written primarily for parents. But we hope it will also be of interest to the educator and the child specialist.

For the educator, information given here may be useful in setting forth the main reasons which a child behavior clinic finds to be at the basis of the majority of school failures we have encountered in over a decade of clinical practice. The educator will also find that we strongly support and appreciate both what the schools are accomplishing and the difficulty of their task.

Child specialists, most of whom have their own effective tests and their own theories and findings as to why children fail in school, may be interested to know what tests we have found most useful in diagnosing the causes of the school problems we have treated. They may also be interested in finding out what causes, in our experience, most often lie at the basis of trouble in school.

Schools Without Failure is the title of a recent popular book on education by psychiatrist William Glasser, first known to the American public through his brilliant, non-Freudian book for parents and professionals titled *Reality Therapy*. In this second publication (1969) Glasser has turned his attention to the schools. He gives his own suggestions for changes he would like to see made —elimination of grades, of rote learning, of tracking—and then proposes the application of his sensible type of reality therapy in order to promote mental and emotional well-being of all school-children.

We, too, support the idea that schools should be concerned with the mental and emotional, as well as the academic, welfare of students. We, too, would like to see certain changes in the schools. Less optimistic than Dr. Glasser as to the prospect of substantial change in the near future, we have turned our concern primarily to things that can be done to prevent or remedy failure within the system more or less as it exists today.

Our proposals in some ways supplement, in some ways offer alternative possibilities, to those recommended by Glasser. Hopefully if any boy or girl is having problems in school, there is a good chance that some of the suggestions given in this book can help him toward greater success.

CHAPTER 2

TEN CHILDREN IN TROUBLE

Let's say your boy or girl is having trouble in school. Trouble comes in many different guises. Some parents consider it trouble if their child gets Bs instead of As, or Cs instead of Bs. Others don't worry about grades but do worry if a child behaves so badly that teacher or principal complains. Still others worry less about grades and school behavior than that their boy or girl dislikes school, is miserable and mopey, overfatigued, or even ill as a result of the school's demands.

Without knowing your own child and his particular problem, his strong points and his weak ones, we cannot tell you for sure *why* he may be having trouble in school. But we *can* tell you about children we have known who suffer in school even as your own boy or girl may be suffering, who fail as your own particular child may be failing.

The problems of children described in this chapter* do not represent all the different possible kinds of school problems, but they are typical of children in enough trouble to make their parents seek professional help. It is our hope, if your own child is having school difficulty, that among the children described here there may be one (or several) whose problems are the same as those of your own boy or girl. It is our hope that the problems suffered by these children may offer clues that will lead you to a better understanding of the difficulties your own boy or girl may be experiencing.

Whether you see your own child here or not, take our word for

* This chapter need not be read straight through in one sitting. If you get tired of children in trouble, go right on to the rest of the book.

it—if he is having trouble in school or is failing in school, there is a good reason for this trouble or failure. *Persist until you find it.*

Bad, Bored, or Overplaced?

Was five-year-old Billy, a complete kindergarten disaster, bad, bored, or overplaced? Opinions differed. Billy's father and the neighbors thought he was bad. His mother felt that her bright little Billy was bored in kindergarten and that that was why he was so disruptive. The teacher, having had considerable experience in these matters, believed that he was simply overplaced.

Diagnosis here, as always, was essential since, if Billy was bad, hopefully some sort of disciplinary techniques both at home and at school might help him to be better. If he was bored, a more stimulating and more demanding school situation would need to be provided. But if he was overplaced, then he would need to be taken out of kindergarten and put back into nursery school.

The school's complaint, with which even his mother reluctantly agreed, was that Billy was a disruptive influence on others. He walked on counters and tables, tried to take over all lessons, grabbed books from the teacher or other children. He crept around the floor and would not sit still unless he was the center of attention. He was extremely aggressive with other children.

Billy, according to his teacher, acted more like a three-year-old than a five-year-old. He demanded her constant attention, liked to sit in her lap and suck his thumb. He became very belligerent when any of the other children were given a chance at anything, insisting, "I'm the teacher's partner—only me." He liked to kiss his teacher and the girls. His attention span was *very* short, although he reportedly was a bright little fellow who could count (with a little help) to one hundred, could print his name, and was interested in reading.

10

A thorough Behavior Examination* given in December, when he was five years and one month old, clearly showed why Billy was having such a hard time at school. (Or at least why he was giving the school such a hard time.) This examination showed that Billy at this time was not suited for kindergarten. His age alone might have warned of this, since he did not turn five till mid-November, after starting school in September.

With the exception of his motor behavior, which rated at a good five-year-old level, Billy's responses to our tests were merely at a four- to four-and-a-half-year-old level. He succeeded in copying a four-year-old square, but needed help in making a four-year-old gate with the cubes. He failed the five-year-old demand of copying a divided rectangle. His completing of the Incomplete Man Test was at a delightful four-and-a-half-year-old level. He added long fingers, long hair down under the chin, a large, round belly button.

On the Lowenfeld Mosaic Test (a test made up of a box of little chips or pieces of different colors and shapes, with which the child is asked to "make something" on a sheet of white paper), he put several large triangles together in a sloppy approximation of a four-year-old hexagon. His response to the Rorschach Inkblot Test (a very special test that presumably tells us how the child experiences or what the world looks like to him and what his personality is like) was definitely preschool, with a level of accuracy of perception no better than a three-year-old.

He behaved in the examination situation like an extremely out-of-bounds four-year-old, climbing on the table, wandering around the room, grabbing objects out of the test cabinet, turning off the lights, asking to go to the bathroom, saying he was *through* and wouldn't do any more. He was extremely difficult to examine even with good preschool techniques.

Though Billy gave the impression of being a good, bright boy, because of his extreme immaturity, restlessness, and short attention

* All tests mentioned in this chapter are described in full in the appendix.

11

span he did not do himself any sort of justice on an intelligence test. On the WISC verbal he rated only an I.Q. of 94. On the pre-school WPPSI Test his verbal score was 91, his performance score 111, averaging 101.

There was thus no question whatever in our minds about Billy's developmental level. He behaved like a four- to four-and-a-half-year-old child, and, except for his motor behavior, there were no hints as yet of a five-year-old type of response. In no way suited for kindergarten, he would fit best in a good four-year-old nursery group, on an alternate-day attendance plan. By another fall, hope-fully, he will have matured enough and calmed down enough to make kindergarten attendance possible, though even then he may well be one who will need some time off—perhaps every Wednes-day.

As to intelligence level, Billy's case is a good example of the fact that there can be many adverse factors (such as short attention span and inability to stay with *any* task for long) that can prevent a child from expressing what is probably his full potential. We ex-pect that Billy will be able to make a more adequate response to an intelligence test—and thus come closer to expressing this potential —later on. This will not mean that his actual intelligence will have increased, since the potential was presumably there all along. Changes in measured I.Q. do tell us something, but they should not be taken *too* seriously. Billy's low I.Q., however, gave warning that if continued in kindergarten and subsequently promoted, he pre-sumably would not be able to function in school in a way that would do justice to what we (and his mother) believed to be his true potential.

Billy's case is a simple and clear-cut illustration of the fact that overplacement in school can mean disaster, even at the kinder-garten level. It illustrates as well the fact that developmental level, and overplacement if present, are clearly demonstrated and easily evaluated, especially at the earliest ages. Later on a *bright* imma-

12

ture child may be doing so well academically that the school may unfortunately tend to overlook immaturity.

Early evaluation of behavior level is thus to be recommended for two important reasons: (1) it is easily accomplished; (2) when it comes at the beginning of the school career it can, if made in time, prevent the school failure that might occur without it. Since it comes first, such failure can be disastrous in that it produces in the child's mind the notion that school is a difficult, unhappy place to be.

HE COULD DO BETTER IF HE WOULD

"You'll *have* to do something about Bob," complained Bob's third-grade teacher to his mother. "He could do the work all right if he would try, but he's so lazy. He doesn't begin to work up to his true potential."

Bob's teacher was obviously out of patience. She admitted that his oral work was passable, but the same could not be said of anything that required writing.

His mother was even more discouraged about the boy than was his teacher. Her report to the behavior clinic to which the school referred Robert indicated that her son was rebellious, loud, bossy, demanding of attention, fresh, and nervous at home. He was also, at eight and a half, still wetting his bed at night. As his mother expressed it, "I am in a constant state of tension with this boy. I find it hard to be loving with such a difficult child. I hope to find out more about his personality and to get advice about what in his behavior can be encouraged and what overlooked."

A careful clinical examination showed that Bob, like so many others, was too immature for the grade he was in. Though of course each schoolchild has his own individual special bad points, as well as good ones, many weaknesses are shared by most of those in trouble. Immaturity is one. Not every single child who is having trouble in school is immature for his age and grade, but it's safe to say that the majority are.

Another weakness that Bob shared with the great majority of boys and girls failing in school was that he had a severe and easily discernible visual problem.

Unlike many school problem children, however, Bob had a good, strong, measurable intelligence, well above average. This was very probably the reason his teacher felt that he could do better if he would. Too many teachers, for too long, have judged their pupils' academic potential by their intelligence alone. They seem to figure that any child with an average or above average I.Q. *can* do the work. They ignore the obvious consideration that *much more than the child's I.Q. goes to school.*

But, average I.Q. or not, Bob had one behavior characteristic that psychologists are increasingly coming to recognize as a severe handicap to academic success. His levels of ability for different functions were widely *scattered.*

A wide scatter of abilities or of potential, even though some of these abilities may be at or even well above performance expected at the child's birthday age, tends to present a real problem for the child in question. Some psychologists even think that extreme scatter may be a clue to at least minimal brain damage. If some abilities are way up and others way down, it often seems difficult for a child to find a level at which he can organize and proceed to function. He gets lost, as it were, between his own highs and his lows.

Since this wide scatter of abilities was Bobby's major problem, though by no means his only one, let's take a look at the boy's unusually *uneven* endowment.

Even his adequate intelligence showed an uneven base. When tested with verbal tests, he rated an I.Q. of 100. When tested on performance tests, he rated a strong 113. These two averaged out at I.Q. 107, but this in itself did not tell the true story of a very modest verbal ability but good performance.

On the Gesell behavior or developmental tests, Bob showed himself responding to different parts of the test battery all the way from a preschool level up to close to his actual age, a range from four and a half years to eight years, too wide a span for the boy's poor organizational abilities to master or pull together so that he could find a level on which to function effectively. His total performance averaged no better than seven years of age, though he came close to his birthday age on both Single and Double Commands for identifying right and left and on the Monroe Visual III Test. Teething, too, was close to an eight-year-old level with the complete eruption of his lateral incisors.

But Copy Forms was considerably below his chronological age. His circle started at the bottom instead of at the top, as would be normal for an eight-year-old. His organization of forms on the page was poor—they were not arranged in a horizontal row, as one would expect—and he failed to get the diagonals of the divided rectangle across the center line, as would be expected of even a five- to five-and-a-half-year-old. And his diamonds were poor (see figure 1).

One of the most revealing and most discouraging parts of Bob's test performance was his response to the Lowenfeld Mosaic Test. All Bob could do with these chips was to scatter single pieces on the paper, like a three-year-old. (He did not seem discouraged or disappointed at this poor performance but, rather, seemed cheerfully satisfied that he had made something.)

On so-called achievement tests, Bob did not do too badly. In fact, considering his somewhat low and highly scattered abilities, he showed that he *was* trying. Here at the beginning of third grade (he was seen at our clinic in late October), oral paragraph reading scored at grade 2.9; reading of single words, at grade level 3.0. His reading *seemed* actually worse than it scored since he read without

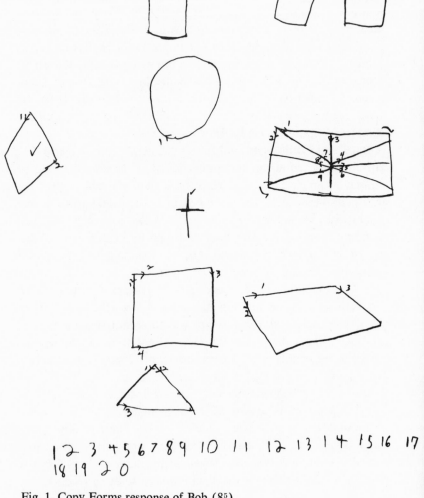

Fig. 1. Copy Forms response of Bob (8^5)

expression and apparently without getting much meaning from what he read. (Asked, after reading a paragraph, if he believed what it said, he replied, "I don't know. I wasn't listening.") Arithmetic process was only at second-grade level.

His response to the Rorschach Inkblot Test was limited, inaccurate, immature (in many ways like that of a preschooler), and showed his marked tendencies toward stubbornness and opposition. Correctness of form* was only 63 percent, about what one would expect of a three-year-old. His response to this test suggested that Bob had barely begun to respond to the world in a way that might be either comfortable, rewarding, or rewarded.

And now for Bob's vision, an area of activity that is very often poor, in one way or another, whenever a boy or girl is having trouble in school. At the least, it is safe to say that *whenever there is school difficulty, vision should be checked.*

Bob was no exception to this general rule. In his case, though he had good acuity in each eye, his focusing system seemed out of phase or discoordinated. He did not localize objects well in space, which interfered with such tasks as reading and writing, and he also showed inadequate eye motility. There was great stress in all near-point functions such as fusion and depth perception—they were a strain for him to perform.

So, what can be done for Bob? One very specific area where help could be given at home was for his problem of bed-wetting. To be able to stay dry at night would not make him a better reader or writer, but it would make him feel better about himself, and would make his mother feel better about him. Most child specialists now agree that, when there is nothing medically or physically wrong with a child (and Bob's parents had checked this out with their

---

* Though there are no definitely "right" or "wrong" responses on the Rorschach, some responses look to the examiner or to an outside, objective observer better, or more like what is shown on the blot, than others. These are scored $+$. If what the child reports doesn't seem in any way to resemble what the examiner, or an objective observer, thinks the blot might look like, they are scored $-$.

own doctor), when an older child does not stay dry at night it is often because of an immaturity in his functioning. He has not quite made that last step that would permit him to wake and go to the bathroom when his bladder is full.

Help has been given many by use of a simple conditioning device. The child lies on a special sheet, a sheet so treated that when it is dampened by urine a buzzer rings, waking the child. Normally, by the time a child is four or five years of age, a full bladder alone wakes him. But when he has not matured to this level, if it can be arranged that a bell ring every time his bladder is so full that he starts to wet, gradually the connection is made in his nervous system so that he does wake just *before* he wets and thus before the bell rings.*

Now for school itself. Even though he was a good-sized boy well into eight years, Bob needed to be replaced at once into second grade. He also needed much structure of environment and much individual attention from his teacher. And both at school and at home Bob needed a humorous but firm approach from someone he believed had faith in him.

It is easy to see from this examination, which revealed Bob's tremendous low points as well as his high ones, why he was not doing as well as his teacher thought he could. His wide scatter or range of abilities made him a difficult boy to plan for. But his strong points were numerous enough—an above-average intelligence, a behavior endowment that averaged not too much more than a year below his chronological age, good visual acuity, and best of all a personality that did not seem to have been too entirely warped by three years of overplacement in school and much nagging both at home and at school—that one could hope for a smoother school and home career in the future than in the past.

* Good conditioning devices can be purchased at a reasonable price from Dry-O-Matic Company, 10055 Nadine, Huntington Woods, Michigan 48070; from Westec, Inc., P.O. Box 322, Lewiston, Idaho 83501; or in many cities from a local medical supply house.

Visual help in the way of lenses (glasses) should improve both his sustaining power and his ability to do effective written work. Any possible perceptual or visual training could be postponed for the time being, though it might be needed later.

"I JUST HATE SCHOOL!"

"I just *hate* school!" Eight-and-a-half-year-old Timmy scowled and clenched his fist.

"You do? Why?"

"Because it's so long! It takes so long to get in and so long to get out."

We didn't, at first, know why school seemed so long and so hateful to this normal-looking and rather handsome little boy. Was his failure, and subsequent hatred of school, *his* fault? His parents' fault? The school's fault? Necessarily anybody's fault?

Fortunately, we did not have to make do with guessing. A careful diagnostic examination, such as the one we gave Timmy, brings to bear the skills of the several child behavior specialists customarily available at a well-staffed child behavior clinic. Thus, hopefully, some one of the several different kinds of evaluation and examination such a clinic can make will reveal the reason for any child's school difficulty and will help the parents and the school understand why the child is having the kind of trouble he is.

A diagnosis, of course, is not a cure. But until you have the diagnosis, until you know why the boy or girl is having the trouble he is experiencing, it is hard to correct that trouble.

So what we needed to know was why Timmy hated school. Why, when he appeared to be of normal intelligence and normal, ordinary personality, came from a good home, started first grade at the usual age of six, had he failed first grade in the first place and failed again a second time around? And why, at eight, having failed

19

first grade twice, was he just starting second grade still unable to read or to work out even the simplest arithmetic problems?

His teacher complained that he was lazy and restless and that his attention span was short. She felt that he could do better school-work if only he would try and would pay attention.

The school psychologist, in this case a young man new at his job, had tried to find a solution to the problem by giving Tim an intelligence test. Tim's I.Q., according to this psychologist's inter-pretation of responses, was 107. Nothing wrong with that.

And so the psychologist took one of those great big leaps which unqualified specialists sometimes do take. He reached the totally unwarranted conclusion that, since Tim's intelligence was above average (not actually true as it later turned out), he *should* be able to do his schoolwork, and that the reason he was failing in school must be because his mother yelled at him at home and otherwise treated him badly. Therefore, he prescribed, both she and the father should have some therapy. This presumably would make them happier and better adjusted, they would then treat Timmy better, and then Timmy would do better in school.

If you haven't run into this sort of thinking it may sound very strange to you. But for many years mental hygiene clinics insisted that almost anything wrong with almost any child was the fault of his parents. The parents had done something "wrong," and that is why they got bad results. So the recommendation that all too many made was that if a child was in trouble, his parents should receive therapy.

Tim's mother would have gone along with this. Like most mothers, she would have done almost anything if she thought it would help her son. Fortunately, his father, a bricklayer and a very down-to-earth, sensible man, refused to go to the clinic for therapy.

What to do next? Neither school nor parents gave up—though Timmy may be assumed to have done so some time back. Tim was referred to a behavior clinic, staffed to give a multiple diagnosis and to search for possible reasons for school difficulty other than parental disharmony. And, like most any such adequately staffed clinic, it did find the reasons.

To begin with, since, though by no means the most important thing we need to know about a child, his I.Q. is important, we checked this. It turned out to be not the substantial 107 that had been identified, but a treacherously low 88. This would mean, in our estimation, that Tim might do better in a special class for 75- to 90-I.Q. children.

A somewhat low intelligence, however, turned out to be the very least of Tim's liabilities.

A simple developmental (or behavior) examination, aimed at determining the age of Tim's behavior—was he behaving as a total organism like the eight-and-a-half-year-old he was by birthday age, or was he, perhaps, behaving like a somewhat younger child—showed him to be at a six- to six-and-a-half-year-old level. This nice and basically normal little boy was behaving, in a general way, more like a six- to six-and-a-half-year-old than like the eight-and-a-half-year-old child he was by birthday age.

Since what we expect of the typical child of any age is merely an average, and to get an average some must, inevitably, be a bit above and some a bit below that level, it is not unusual to find many normal children behaving a little ahead of or a little behind our expected average of what a six-, seven-, or eight-year-old child "should" do. But two years behind the theoretical average makes real trouble. In Tim's case it meant that now at eight and a half he was ready, not for second or third grade, but merely to begin first grade. It was no wonder that during the two previous years, when his behavior age had been only four to four and a half, and five to five and a half, he had totally failed first grade. No mystery there.

If a wobbly I.Q. (only 88) and serious and substantial immaturity were the sum of Tim's problems, he would have been a boy in trouble. Unfortunately, there must have been more evil fairies

21

than good present at his birth, since he had one further severe problem. He had a perceptual difficulty that caused him to see, or at least to recognize, only small parts of any given visual stimulus and even those incorrectly. Thus, when and if he *did* put the pieces of anything together, the whole that resulted was not accurate, since it was made up of inaccurate pieces. At least it did not resemble the things the rest of us see.

Visually, Tim showed a low but measurable amount of hyperopia (farsightedness) and a definite need for plus lenses to improve his visual acuity at both far and near. These lenses were prescribed. Also, because of his confusion with right and left directions, it was felt that his left eye should for a time be patched when he reads. Depending on his response to lenses and patching, further visual recommendations, probably for some amount of perceptual training, will be made later on.

So here's a little boy with three strikes against him: a low intelligence, marked immaturity, and a perceptual disability. Small wonder that Timmy was having trouble in school.

When we interviewed his parents, his mother admitted that she had had much the same kind of perceptual and learning difficulties when she was young. She remembers her own mother setting her down in front of a clock and trying to teach her to tell time. When she failed to learn, her mother claimed she wasn't trying, didn't love her parents, didn't want to learn (all those things we say to children when they fail to live up to our often unreasonable expectations!).

Now, what's to be done with Timmy? There's only one fair answer. This is a boy who desperately needed help with the way he was seeing and interpreting things. Glasses will do for a start, probably to be followed with some amount of perceptual training. And he needs to be in a very special class. Not so much a class for children of low intelligence (Tim's intelligence may be potentially considerably higher than it presently rates) as a special class for children with perceptual problems. He is not suited to regular class-room attendance at any level, most certainly not at the second-grade level.

If such a class is not available, his perceptual problems will have to be dealt with, so far as they can be, by the visual specialist alone. And a probably already overburdened regular classroom teacher will have to add very special attention to Timmy to her other burdens.

What grade he should be in, if it must be an ordinary regular classroom, is very hard to say. It should be no higher than first grade. That's where he would belong according to his behavior level *if* his I.Q. were just a bit higher and if he did not have a severe perceptual problem.

But could school, parent, and Timmy agree to his spending a third year in first grade? Starting school too soon, though it might not at first glance seem such a dreadful thing to do, can present problems like this that follow a child for years to come—problems whose solution becomes increasingly difficult with each successive year of overplacement.

Whatever academic solution is decided upon, Timmy's academic future does not look rosy.

A PSEUDO SLOW LEARNER

Any slow learner presents a serious problem, not only for himself, but also for his parents and his school. That child whom we call the *pseudo slow learner* is in some ways even more unfortunate a problem than the true slow learner. The pseudo slow learner is the child who, admittedly, is learning slowly in the situation in which he finds himself but who—correctly placed in school—need not be a slow learner.

A clear example of this is Lawrence, a seven-year-and-one-month-old boy from an unusually brilliant family. When referred to us in January, Lawrence was failing second grade.

This boy had unfortunately started kindergarten when he was only four years and nine months old, entering first grade at five years and nine months, and second grade at six years and nine months. Thus by age alone he was, at least by our figuring, too young for the school situation in which he found himself.

His kindergarten teacher reported of him that he worked with the group only when he was interested, had very poor speech, often had a bowel movement in his pants. He was a poor listener, couldn't sit still, and interrupted often. She felt he was not ready for kindergarten.

His first-grade teacher reported that he was sloppy in his dress and had many undesirable physical habits. His attention span was short. He still could not sit still. His coordination was poor, his speech not always clear. He took part in class activities only when it pleased him, and his work was by no means up to grade level.

Second grade was no more satisfactory. The school considered him to be not only unready for second grade but a slow learner. Reading was only at a beginning first-grade level.

A behavior examination made it clear, in unambiguous terms, why Lawrence was having trouble in second grade—needless trouble, it would seem, in view of his very high I.Q. (verbal I.Q. 123, performance, 138, full-scale 133). Seven-year-old, second-grade Lawrence was behaving at the time of examination (in January), on most of our behavior tests, at a six- to six-and-a-half-year-old level. There was considerable scatter. His Incomplete Man response was no better than five and a half years (see Figure 2). On Copy Forms he used one entire sheet of paper just to copy the circle and cross, like a preschooler. But response to Single and Double Commands (right and left) was at age. In spite of this scatter, his behavior rating probably was most fairly placed at six to six and a half years.

Signs of immaturity could not be overlooked. The boy was not

Fig. 2. Lawrence (7¹): Incomplete Man at a 5½ year level

a second-grader. In addition to the striking immaturity shown on the behavior examination, Lawrence gave himself away in answers to some of the routine questions posed in the WISC intelligence test. Thus, when asked what he would do if a much smaller boy tried to get into a fight with him, he said he would call his mother. When asked what he would do if he saw a train approaching a broken track, he said he'd tell his mother to stop it. During the course of the visual examination he referred to a train as a "choochoo," unusual for a second-grader. His general response to the behavior examination also shrieked of immaturity. He wiggled. He tired. He wanted to leave the room and constantly inquired, "How much more?"

That school and even life itself was no great treat for Lawrence was suggested by the fact that, when asked what he liked to do best at school, he replied, "Go to the bathroom." When asked to complete the sentence, "We had fun when . . . " he replied, "We had fun when we sleep." And a spontaneous drawing that he made for the examiner suggests that all is not too right with this boy's world (see Figure 3).

In school, Lawrence was achieving at a fair mid-first-grade level with his math, but his math was considerably ahead of his reading. He showed himself as one who reaches out for new territory and performance before he has organized and consolidated the old, so that the performance is not solid or well integrated. Yet, and this cannot and must not be overlooked, the boy, as noted, scored an I.Q. rating of 133. Throughout the test situation he showed himself to be of potentially very superior caliber.

For instance, on the Sentence Completion Test, in spite of much wiggling and some fatigue, he gave such answers as the following:

Most girls *like to have privacy.*
Brothers are *two boys that have been born together.*
When I saw what they were doing *I stayed out of their way.*
My father *doesn't play around at work.*

26

Fig. 3. Spontaneous drawing of Lawrence (7[1]).
"The airplanes came to rescue the cars, but they started to fall apart in the air so they're going to crash into the cars. The pilots fell out of the planes and they're sitting on the wings. The ambulance came to help out but pieces fell off it and pushed into the cars. If the cars keep going they will all crash into the tree."

Why would anybody *steal things? When they can buy them. If they work.*

My mind *tells every part.*

Lawrence was indeed a boy who was learning slowly, but he was in no fair sense a slow learner. Admittedly he *was* slow for a second-grader, since he was functioning at pretty much of a first-grade level. However, he was *not* slow for a six- to six-and-a-half-year-old, which was what he was, behaviorally speaking.

The discrepancy here was not between what Lawrence was behaviorally as a total functioning organism and what he was doing in school as a learner. Rather, the discrepancy was between the level at which he was functioning and the grade in which he had been placed by the school.

Once grade placement has been adjusted on the basis of be-

27

havior level, one predicts that Lawrence will be not a slow learner but very probably a most effective one. Lawrence is not at fault in this instance. The fault if any is in a system that determines grade placement on the basis of chronological rather than behavioral age.

In conclusion, just a bit about Lawrence and his mother. When asked to complete the sentence, "My mother doesn't . . ." he replied, "My mother doesn't like me." On the Rorschach Inkblot Test he responded to the one card that some specialists consider the "mother" card with the description, "Something all wrecked up. Real old. Falling apart. All wrinkled. Got no head. . . . Something smiling but you just see the smile, not the person."

This response, to the examiner, suggested that Lawrence did not feel his mother to be a warm, helpful, or supportive person on whom he could depend. When asked how she got on with her son, the mother cried a little and said, "Of course I love him, but I really don't like him very well. Every day when he comes home from school I just clench my fists and think, 'Can I stand it one more day?' He comes in the door either belligerent or crying. I try to be supportive, but it's awfully hard."

Not for a minute must one assume that this boy's problems were caused by his mother. But, admittedly, the way she responded to his problems did make things worse for him. Now, after the examination and a conference with the examiner, she is going to try to make Lawrence feel that she likes as well as loves him, school success or not. (And, of course, hopefully, an adjustment in his grade placement will increase his school success.)

ARE HIS PARENTS TO BLAME?

Lawrence's mother may have been a part of his problem, but at least she was fortunate to escape condemnation from psychologist or clinic. Not so with the parents of a little boy named Tex. The school psychologist put the blame for their son's bad behavior and unsuccessful school career squarely on his parents' shoulders.

Tex, not quite seven, was referred to a child behavior clinic because he was so *bad* in school. In fact, this boy was reported by his first-grade teacher to be so very bad and such a disciplinary problem that the school he had been attending had threatened not to let him come back the following year. He was also failing all his first-grade subjects, but this did not seem to bother the school as much as did his badness. The school psychologist had tried to help, but his findings were for the most part negative: "Tex is a badly disturbed boy. He is full of feelings of hostility and aggression, apparently brought on by poor home treatment. He feels unloved."

The result of this diagnosis was that Tex's mother and father were urged to seek psychiatric help in order that they could treat their son in a more loving manner and thus make him happier. They were reluctant to do this—chiefly on the grounds that they believed themselves to be rather unusually happy and contented, both with each other and with Tex and his brother—but they were not *sure* the school psychologist was wrong. As they told us later, "How can you be certain? It's so hard to know what 'normal' really is. If a psychologist says you're maladjusted and are harming your child, perhaps you are."

Fortunately, before seeking the recommended psychiatric help for themselves, these parents took their son to a normal child behavior clinic, on the faint hope that the reason for Tex's bad school behavior might be something about Tex and/or the school and not merely that they were showing him an inadequate amount of affection at home.

Since you have already read Tim's story, it may come as no surprise that it was not all the parents' fault, but that there *was* something about Tex himself that had caused his serious school difficulties. Tex, like so many children today, had started school too soon and thus was seriously overplaced.

Though he was six years and eight months old when examined in March, toward the end of first grade, and his I.Q. was 119, most of Tex's behavior fell close to a five-and-a-half-year-old level. On Copy Forms and on Single and Double Commands, which tested his understanding of and orientation to the right and left sides of his body, he responded like a five-and-a-half-year-old. The Rorschach response showed him to be a highly endowed but complicated five-and-a-half-year-old, with some responses (as "torn-off leaf" on Card II) way down in the anxious, preschool range. Responses were highly original but there were some indications that Tex, at least in some situations, was actually quite disoriented. Inaccuracy of response suggested at least a slight perceptual problem.

Tex was a boy who tried hard to do what he was asked. But he became so extremely disoriented if the task was too hard for him and his first response turned out to be incorrect that it was extremely important to give him tasks at which he could succeed right away. As long as an examiner or teacher met him at his own level he could respond very nicely. But it must be kept in mind that his level was nearer five and a half than the six and a half he was by birthday age.

The confusion with which Tex responded to too-hard tasks was shown when the examiner asked him, "If John had four pennies and his mother gave him two more, how many would he have?"

Tex opened out all his fingers, looked at them hopefully, and then started to open and close them, one or two at a time, as if he thought the answer might magically appear in some miraculous combination of open and closed fingers. It did not. Small wonder that Tex was failing in arithmetic (as well as in his other subjects).

Tex's responses to the Sentence Completion Test may help to round out the picture of an extremely immature, confused, but potentially quite normal and perhaps even gifted little boy:

> It would be fun to be *a monkey*.
> Sometimes I feel like *going to bed*.
> My mind *when I fail my mind gets mixed up*.
> When I'm alone *I'm scared*.

30

It's not fair that   *I hate people.*
If only I dared to I would   *like people.*
Why would anybody   *laugh at me?*

This story in itself is almost routine: a perfectly nice little boy, started in school on the basis of his chronological rather than his behavior age, is placed in a class one year ahead of the place where he can be expected to do the work. Result: he fails his schoolwork *and* misbehaves. It escapes the routine not simply because the school blamed Tex and was going to expel him for the way he behaved, but because it had nearly pushed a perfectly nice, normal, and reasonably well-adjusted man and wife to seek psychiatric help for themselves—help that so far as could be determined they absolutely did not need.

Happily, this kind of diagnosis, which used to be given out quite freely by mental hygiene and local child behavior clinics, is no longer as popular as it once was. Clinics used to be satisfied to take the all-too-easy (and usually incorrect and inadequate) course of blaming parents when children did poorly in school.

Now more and more clinics are coming to agree with our basic contention that, when there is trouble in school, *the answer more often than not lies in the organism.* That is, in the majority of cases when children have serious trouble in school, the fault lies not in the parents but in some special thing about the child that makes him unable to meet the demands of the school situation as it exists.

What needs to be done, therefore, is not to improve the parents' emotional health or their adjustment to each other and to their child, but rather to do something either to help the child function more effectively in his present school situation *or* to change the kind of school situation. That is, for academic success each child must fit the situation he finds himself in. Sometimes the *child* can be changed a bit. Sometimes the *school* situation can be changed. But, when things are wrong, to right them something has to give. And it is not usually the *parents* who need changing.

31

HER MIND GOES BLANK

Sara Smith's story illustrates the fact that there is always a good reason, in fact often several good reasons, *why* a child has trouble in school. Those mysterious children, like Sara, whose *mind goes blank for no reason that anyone can determine,* always really do have a good reason for their blankness of mind or whatever the manifestation is that the school and family consider the source of difficulty.

It is not that Sara's mind goes blank that causes her to fail in school. The source of her difficulty is whatever it is that *causes* her mind to go blank. And that, one cannot tell until some qualified person has given her a thorough and careful behavior examination.

Nine-year-old Sara is one of those numerous children who have many strikes against them from the beginning. She suffers from a congenital hip disorder, a hearing disability, and a visual problem that has been only partially corrected with glasses. According to her mother, she gets on nicely at home but at school her mind goes blank and she is failing third grade. According to the school, Sara is a large, aggressive child who often disturbs those around her. She has a short attention span and is easily distracted. Also, according to the school, she is "not responding to education." The teacher feels that she is stubborn and does not follow directions "on *purpose.*" Tutoring and special help in both reading and arithmetic have had little effect. She can do only the simplest of addition and subtraction problems, and in reading fits only into a prereading or reading readiness class.

Nobody could figure out *why* Sara's mind went blank so often. The behavior clinic to which she was finally referred suspected that this blanking out of thought was simply a device by which Sara protected herself from academic demands that were much too difficult for her. A careful clinical examination was given to find out why third-grade demands were too much for nine-year-old Sara.

32

As with many (though by no means all) children who have difficulty in keeping up with the demands of their grade, Sara had an intelligence problem. Her verbal I.Q., as measured on the usual Wechsler Children's Intelligence Test, was 69, her performance I.Q. was 97. These averaged to a full-scale I.Q. of 80—not enough, usually, to insure success in anything but a very special class.

As low as Sara's intelligence quotient turned out to be, she had another problem equally serious. By now you can perhaps predict what that problem was. Like most other children failing in school, she was definitely overplaced. It is safe to say that, whereas not every child who is correctly placed in school will succeed academically, *nearly every child who is in serious trouble in school* is *overplaced*. Sometimes overplacement is the outstanding difficulty. Sometimes it is just one of several handicaps.

At any rate, Sara's developmental level (the age level at which she was behaving), if rated very generously, averaged no better than six-and-a-half to seven years. This, at best, was two full years below her birthday age and one year below the usual minimum requirement for third grade, the grade she was in. Not only did her developmental level average very low, but there was the added problem of wide scatter in her performance level for different tests. In some things she was way down at a five-year-old level, while on a rare test she could rate as high as nine years of age.

She could figure out things in arithmetic no better than a five-year-old, and needed to have any command or request repeated and clarified, like a five- to six-year-old. She wrote her name like a five-and-a-half-year-old, and completed the Incomplete Man in a five-and-a-half-year-old manner. She was at the very beginning of reading. She had trouble naming different parts of her body, but could carry out commands involving understanding of right and left like an eight-year-old. And one single ability, her memory for designs, was way up at a nine-year-old level. On the Bender Gestalt perceptual test Sara copied designs like a six-and-a-half-year-old.

The Rorschach personality test showed her to have a very modest, though presumably normal, endowment.

Thus, Sara, beginning the second half of third grade, was placed in school at least eighteen months ahead of where she belonged. She definitely needed to go more slowly, perhaps ideally either in an ungraded class or in a special class, since she seemed not too well fitted for the regular stream of education.

Visually, as in some other respects, she did poorly in an odd way. She showed low visual acuity both at far and near, which could not be accounted for by any such refractive error as nearsightedness, farsightedness, or astigmatism. Rather, the main reason for the low acuity seemed to lie in an inability to localize objects correctly in space.

Visual help—she needed at least a year of visual training and special glasses—should help her academic performance but probably not enough to allow her to remain in the regular classroom.

The wide scatter of Sara's abilities as well as her immaturity and low intelligence, plus the fact that she may indeed be suffering from some sort of glandular imbalance (suggested by the general sluggishness of her response and the fact that she has not responded any better than she has to previous visual help), all add up to a serious educational problem. Her problems will not be easy to solve, even with the best of help, but the stamina with which she has adapted thus far to her physical problems will stand her in good stead. Her advanced performance on a few tests—as, for instance, her memory for designs as shown on Visual III—was a decided plus. Her satisfactory behavior at home, as reported by her mother, was another plus. And the fact that she seemed to be a girl who might respond nicely to visual help was still another.

There is every reason to hope that now that Sara's specific problem areas have been identified, and now that people are no longer satisfied with the amorphous explanation of her problem as simply being that her mind goes blank, school and home, working together, may find a satisfactory solution to her academic problems.

Since no special or ungraded class was available in her community, the school has agreed to put Sara back into second grade, where she at this time belongs, and to place her with a special, individual teacher for at least half of each school day. This, plus the needed visual help and hopefully—if it is indicated as necessary—some degree of glandular help or some type of medication or chemotherapy should at least bring some improvement.

That this immature, not very bright little girl, suffering from various physical problems and very poor vision should be a learning problem and should not, even at nine years, be ready for third grade or able to read, is not surprising. What is surprising is that she has been allowed to "coast along" in a regular public school all this time, with tutoring and with people only *wondering* why her mind goes blank.

"YOU'RE BABYING HIM!"

How many mothers, giving their little boy or girl (and it's more likely a boy than a girl) the help and protection they feel the child needs to shield him in his immaturity, have been told by school or psychologist that they were babying him?

Victor's mother is one of many of whom a school has made this accusation. According to the school, "Victor's mother, who babies him, appears to be one of his greatest handicaps." The school also admitted that Victor, an August birthday boy who had started first grade when just barely six and had signally failed this grade, was a trifle immature. He was examined clinically at his parents' request at the age of seven years and one month, when he had just started a repeat of first grade.

The school hoped that if Victor repeated first grade, and if his mother would "stop babying him," things would improve, since there was "nothing really wrong with him." They did admit, however, that even after a year in first grade he could successfully name

35

only letters A through K, that he really couldn't read at all, and that writing and spelling were equally unsuccessful. His powers of attention were reported to be very poor, and he appeared to take no pride in his appearance.

His mother, who felt that she was not babying her boy but was treating him as he seemed to need to be treated, feared that having him repeat first grade was not going to be enough to solve his problems. She felt that he did have some serious problem, either physical or mental, and this was what she wanted the clinic to determine.

If Victor's mother had not been so astute, her son might have spent a second year in first grade. And from the evidence brought to light in a clinical examination, he very likely would have been no more successful the second time around than he had been the first. (Then those concerned might have come to the erroneous conclusion that, since they repeated Victor and he didn't do any better the second time around, "repeating doesn't work." Repeating does *not* "work" in every situation. Like any other prescription or medicine, it works when it is the medicine or prescription needed. Repeating does not solve the problems of every child who is having trouble in school.)

Victor was one of the saddest-looking little boys imaginable. He was a good example of what William Sheldon has called, with perhaps more objectivity than kindness, "poor protoplasm poorly put together." And his behavior was fully as ineffective as his appearance.

Though his responses to a behavior examination scattered from a three-year-old level up to an occasional response at his actual age level, most of his behavior centered closest to five or five and a half years of age. His responses to the Copy Forms and Incomplete Man tests were squarely at five and a half. Thus gross immaturity was his first and most conspicuous problem. His response to Right and Left Commands, scoring at a five-and-a-half-year-old level, showed marked confusion of right and left parts of his body and real disorientation.

Response to the Bender Gestalt copy forms test showed real disorganization. This test, too, was responded to at a five-and-a-half-year-old level. Poor memory was shown in his response to the Monroe Visual III, a test in which the child copies forms from memory. Here he not only blanked out at times, but showed poor sustaining power, his response becoming increasingly poor as the test proceeded.

Occasionally we find an immature child who still does manage, somehow, to do not too badly on achievement tests. Victor was not such a one. His achievement level in both reading and arithmetic was still at a pre-first-grade level. Here he showed a characteristic that we describe as being *reality-bound,* and which Jensen (60) calls associative as opposed to abstract thinking. He seemed to have almost no ability for abstract thought but needed, instead, to work always with real objects. He seemed to have an unusually restricted, literal personality.

Another strike against Victor was low intelligence. Though he was by no means retarded, Victor's intelligence was low enough to make success in an ordinary classroom situation questionable. His verbal I.Q. scored at 82 and performance I.Q. at 92, giving him a full-scale I.Q. of 85.

As if all these handicaps were not enough, Victor turned out to have serious perceptual difficulties. These showed themselves clearly both on the unstructured Rorschach test and on specific visual examination.

The Rorschach showed Victor to be extremely immature—responding, in fact, at a strictly preschool level—and hinted as well at low intelligence, serious restriction of response, and a serious perceptual problem. Victor's accuracy of form (or accuracy of perception) as shown on this test is only 33 percent, far below an expected two-year-old level. This boy did not see things as others do, but bravely made some sort of stab or guess when presented with a visual stimulus. And unfortunately, on this test as on others, he sometimes gave a fairly good response to begin with and then in his confusion and insecurity denied it and made a less good guess.

On a visual examination Victor showed not so much an atypical visual response as one that was unusually immature. Visual response was more like that of a five-year-old than of a seven-year-old, and was undifferentiated and easily confused. Perhaps his most serious problem here was that, though he needed glasses (plus lenses), he was not able to do any better with them than without.

We have seen this kind of problem in other children, bright ones as well as dull, and it inevitably leads to the obvious questions: Why can't this child respond to the lenses he needs? What about his body makes him unable to accept the lens help he requires? In Victor's case the possibility presented itself, as it sometimes does in such cases, that there might be a possible endocrine problem that prevented his body from functioning as effectively as one might hope.

One final, homey example of Victor's immaturity was that, when asked to take his clothes off in order to have a posture picture taken, he objected, saying that he wasn't sure if he took his shoes off that he could tie them again. In fact, he admitted, he wasn't absolutely sure that he could get them back on the right feet.

Victor was one of the lucky ones. Not lucky in his endowment, which obviously presented multiple problems—immaturity, low intelligence, disorganization, disorientation, poor memory, inability to abstract, serious perceptual immaturity, and the possibility of a glandular problem—but because he had a mother who had, so far as she could, protected him from home and school demands he was unready and unable to meet, and had insisted (in spite of the school's protest that there was little wrong with Victor that an extra year in first grade would not correct) that he receive a thorough behavior examination from a qualified clinic.

The results of this examination indicated clearly that Victor was not at this time a suitable candidate for a regular class in school *at any grade level*. Attendance in a special class for perceptually handicapped children was felt to be essential. (Fortunately, in the state in which Victor lived, if a town or city could not provide such a class, the school district was required to arrange and pay for attendance at a perceptual class in some nearby town.) Help with, or at least a check on, his endocrine problem will also be tried, and, following that, either glasses or special perceptual training as may turn out to be needed.

CAN'T COUNT TO FOURTEEN BECAUSE HE HAS ONLY TEN FINGERS

Can we make you feel the plight of a nice, friendly, sturdy, masculine, hard-working, and highly motivated little boy nearly nine years of age who nevertheless was failing dismally in second grade? Can we make you understand (or can we ourselves fully understand) what it must be like, at nearly nine, not to be able to add eight and six *because you have only ten fingers and thus run out of fingers before the problem is solved?*

Adam was referred to us because he was having difficulty in school. He had repeated kindergarten and failed first grade as well, and he was now, at nine, failing almost completely in second grade. His reading was barely at beginning first-grade level, and his attention span was very short. He was physically very restless in class and had difficulty in staying in his seat and taking part in class activities. His problem was exaggerated by the fact that he had frequently wet his pants in school in first grade, though he was now dry.

He had been variously diagnosed as having a perceptual problem, a severe learning disability, and developmental dyslexia. Parents and school thus had been furnished with plenty of labels to describe his difficulty, but so far no practical move had been made to solve his problem except that, fortunately, his school did have one "special" teacher for the whole school and he was luckily permitted to spend some time each day in her room.

Though he had started kindergarten when he was five years and two months, an age too young for the average boy, he fortunately had been allowed to repeat kindergarten. So he started second grade when he was a respectable eight years and two months, quite old enough, assuming that he was developing at an average rate, to manage second grade swimmingly.

A behavior examination, supplemented with visual and projective tests, showed that Adam was *not* developing at an average rate. Far from it. Our tests, individually or all taken together, made it all too evident why this boy was not succeeding in second grade. In fact they gave evidence that even a regular first-grade situation would probably be too difficult for him.

Adam's endowment was extremely uneven—always a clue to possible functional difficulty. He ranged in age, on different tests, from four up through seven years, clustering fairly well around five and a half to six years of age except in the projective personality tests, to which he responded in a clearly preschool manner.

On our Gesell Copy Forms he gave himself away perhaps most clearly on the divided rectangle. He was unable to get his angled strokes across the midline. Thus his response could be rated no better than four and a half to five years. Response to the Incomplete Man was at a rather good five-and-a-half-year-old level. He managed to add a neck and body line but was not yet ready even to try the tie, as would be expected of the usual six-year-old.

He showed confusion of directionality on the Single and Double Commands of the Right and Left Tests, rating at a five-and-a-half-year-old level. On memory for designs, as measured in the Monroe Visual III, he responded at a six-and-a-half-year-old level, with only six out of sixteen forms accurately reproduced, and performance deteriorating as he proceeded. Adam was not able to stay long at any one task or to take too much of any one stimulus. If required to do so, his behavior went to pieces and he thus lost ground. In fact, if kept too long at one task he tended to become uncertain and might repudiate an original, good response.

Results of intelligence testing were not encouraging. His verbal I.Q. on the WISC was 92 and his performance I.Q. 83, which gave him a full-scale intelligence rating of only 87. His reading was at a pre-first-grade level; he was better at single words than on reading of sentences, and, even when he read merely single words, letters shifted and changed for him, *b* becoming *p* or *d* becoming *b*.

In arithmetic he was in equal difficulty. In fact his arithmetic process was one of the saddest and most appalling things about this big, nice, almost nine-year-old boy. He could add four and two, but, when asked to add eight and six, he said he couldn't do that unless he used his fingers. Asked if he would like to try it, using his fingers, he held out both hands, fingers outstretched, and said simply, "But I don't have enough fingers."

All of this was discouraging enough, but the projective tests (tests that presumably tell us something about what the personality is like and the level of emotional or personal development) showed him to be functioning like a preschooler.

On the Rorschach Inkblot Test, Adam gave three "leaf" responses. ("Leaf" is a response given commonly by preschoolers, seldom by children over four or five.) He also tended to see two different things and combine them together into a single whole, even though the combination was inappropriate. Thus, on one of the cards he apparently saw a leaf and also a monster, so he gave the response "a leaf monster." On another he saw a leaf and also a cat, so he gave the response "a leaf cat."

He gave an equally preschool response on the Lowenfeld Mosaic Test, merely combining equilateral triangles into a series of hexagons, or what we term *four-year-old circles*.

On our Sentence Completion Test he gave an interesting picture

41

of a little boy trying to be nice, like a six-year-old, but who underneath felt a real weight of anxiety and sadness. Thus, in a positive vein he gave the following completions:

I like people who   *are nice.*
I sometimes think of myself as   *a good boy.*
My mind   *is nice.*
Brothers   *are kind.*

But on a more minor and more revealing note he also made the following completions:

Sometimes I feel like   *a dummy.*
If I get left behind   *I feel sad.*
My teacher is   *mean.*
When I'm alone   *I feel sad.*
It's not fair that   *I'm alone.*
I think my friends   *don't like me.*
I would be better looking if   *I was happy.*
I can't understand   *what makes me dumb.*

Adam was obviously a very unhappy little boy, and well he might be, since, in addition to the handicaps already described, he also had both a visual and a hearing problem. On the Wepman Auditory Discrimination Test his response was below that expected of the ordinary seven-year-old, indicating that his auditory discrimination was inadequate for his age.

His visual problem was even more severe. He had reduced near vision, and did not focus effectively at near. Or, as the visual report indicated, "There is limited organization of visual space, particularly at distances within arm's reach."

Adam was clearly in trouble. The school's complaint was well justified, and yet Adam was justified, too. We had every reason to suppose that he was doing as well as he possibly could. Our recommendation, therefore, since the extent of the boy's immaturity made it seem unlikely that he could function effectively in the regular stream of education at any grade level, was that he be transferred to a special class for perceptually handicapped children—not a retarded group, but a class for those children who must learn in concrete terms, who cannot manage abstractions.

Learning needs to be spelled out for him step by step. He will be best motivated to learn when he can understand the value of learning in terms of action and doing—that is, in terms of the effect on himself. He can be helped to learn if the teacher will recognize *his* interpretation of a problem and why he solves it as he does. She must recognize what the problem is for Adam—that is, must appreciate what *he* thinks the given task amounts to. She can then first help him to solve the problem as he sees it, and then help him to see what the problem is as she feels she has presented it to him. He must for the present work a good deal with real or concrete objects, never abstractions, since Adam, like Victor, is one of those boys whom we label *reality-bound*.

Visually he needs quite a lot of help. He should start with low power plus lenses in dual-focus form (with plain glass in the top of each so that he can use his own adequate distance vision). Lenses will help him toward a needed near focus, may help him localize better in space, and should help his visual mechanism to function more flexibly. Later on, specific visual training may be useful, but at present his response is too immature for anything but regular gross motor types of perceptual exercise.

Reading beyond the single-word stage should not be required at this time. In fact, one may have to think of teaching Adam, at least for the time being, in terms of what has been called a "bookless curriculum."

This is a good boy, a good, solid boy. His expressed ambition for the future is to be a carpenter. He may well end up in this or some similar kind of work. If the school can keep the required learning experience from being too utterly defeating and deadening, one's hope for Adam's future can be positive indeed. His family has fully accepted the need for special schooling, and the father admits that his own school experience was much like his son's.

BODY AND BEHAVIOR BOTH IN TROUBLE

Chances are, in our estimation, that whenever a child's behavior is less than satisfactory it is safe to say that one source (if not the main source) of that difficulty lies somewhere in his body. But the close relationship between body and behavior is not always as clearly evident as in the case of nine-year-old James.

Fat, friendless, unhappy, underactive, underachieving, and immature, James did not seem to those who examined him to have very much going for him. Yet the very examination that illuminated this boy's problems and deficiencies also showed the way toward a possible alleviation of his problems.

James had been referred to the school psychologist because of his extremely poor school performance and because he was unhappy at home. The psychologist, according to the parents, had not been "too helpful." But he did say that James was hypoactive, hostile to both examination and examiner, needed to be in a small class with a male teacher, and ideally should be in a special class for children with emotional disorders. The specific diagnosis was that James "appeared to be suffering from a psychoneurotic disorder of the depressive type."

His parents do find him hard to live with and describe him as a boy of high-strung and nervous temperament who shows a general aversion to learning, hostility to his teacher, and opposition to homework. The school reports that his work is below grade level, that he is a loner, and that he has no friends. At the beginning of the school year he complained a great deal of headaches and other pains and used the bathroom frequently. He showed interest in

44

science, but otherwise performed below grade level. It was reported that he squinted frequently, with and without glasses.

James, when we saw him at our clinic, did present a rather unusual appearance. He was 53 inches tall and weighed 134 pounds, about 50 pounds over the usual expectation. Though considerable plumpness would reasonably be expected, since this boy rates a full 6½ in endomorphy,* he is overweight even for a boy of this physical type. He is without question a big, fat, overweight boy, and his obesity cuts down his physical activity, his appeal to other people, his opportunity for making himself "one of the crowd."

Both socially and academically, at school and at home and within himself, this boy faced serious problems. Though the initial psychological examination, when he was seven years of age, had somewhat condemned him, it had offered few positive suggestions (other than that he be in a special class) for a solution of these problems. Nor had school any practical advice to give.

Fortunately, clinic help was sought. A complete behavior examination, supplemented by an intelligence test, projective tests, and a visual examination, gave many clues both as to what was wrong with James and what might be done to begin to set things right.

Like many other children in trouble, James showed himself up clearly, high points and low, on a behavior examination. And, again like many others in trouble, he showed himself not only to be immature but of a highly uneven endowment, strong in some areas but very weak in others.

On the Gesell behavior examination, James's responses ranged from five years (Single Commands, Right and Left) through seven years (Double Commands, Right and Left, and Monroe Visual III memory for designs), to seven and a half in Copy Forms and eight

* Readers not familiar with the theory of constitutional psychology, which classifies people by their body type (endomorphs, mesomorphs, and ectomorphs), are referred to Chapter 11 (pages 212–213), to William Sheldon's *Varieties of Temperament* (87), or Louise B. Ames's *Child Care and Development* (5).

years on his Incomplete Man responses. His response to the Bender Gestalt Perceptual Test was close to his chronological age of nine years, while his response to achievement tests of reading and arithmetic ability was near eight years.

Intelligence was his strong point. His verbal I.Q., as measured on the WISC intelligence test, was 121, his performance I.Q. 111. This gave a full-scale intelligence score of 118, close to the very superior category. In fact, James, with his high I.Q. and his strong interest in science, gives, *at times,* almost a quiz-kid impression. His eyes sparkle and he looks happy and enthusiastic, but this appearance surfaces only occasionally, being covered for the most part with his slow, unhappy, depressed air of noninvolvement and nonsuccess.

Thus, James showed the usual difficulties characteristic of schoolchildren in trouble—he was seriously immature and showed a marked unevenness of function. He also had his own special problems, which made him interesting and unique and at the same time gave clues as to the things that could be done to help him toward more effective ways of responding.

His response to the Rorschach Inkblot Test made it evident that he was an abnormally depressed and unhappy boy, a boy of adequate intelligence but extremely discouraged and upset by the world around him. Though it suggested a potentially normal personality structure, it also showed that James at this time was neither happy nor comfortable with himself or with his surroundings. James, then, according to this test, is an intelligent but rather immature boy who has a potentially rather strong personality structure, who is pretty much at the mercy of his emotional impulses, and who cannot yet use his inner or psychic drive for effective living. He is a boy who views the world as a dangerous, violent, and unsatisfactory place but tries to put up a good front and to mask his rather substantial inner conflict and anxiety. That is, he tries to put a cheerful face on what he apparently considers to be basically a hopeless situation. The need for psychotherapy seems rather definitely indicated.

James also expressed rather serious visual problems. Though his eyes appeared to be healthy and free of disease, he did show some myopia, only partially corrected by his present glasses. His greatest difficulty, however, was in the area of visual performance, which was extremely restricted. He had considerable difficulty with fusion and with depth perception. Thus, a serious visual problem interfered with effective vision. In fact, considering his visual restriction, it is difficult to see how he has been able to do as well as he has in school. It seemed evident that James needed both more effective glasses and a program of vision training before it could be hoped that he use his eyes effectively.

All this involved his personality and functioning. As to his physical person, his problems were even more obvious. James was a very fat boy, even for a child in whom endomorphy prevails; he was considerably overweight regardless of his body type. By temperament we might expect a boy of his physical structure to be unathletic, slow, relatively uninterested in physical activity and exercise, but at the same time extremely interested in food and in eating. Add to this the fact that unhappy children often do eat more than others as a sort of solace for their unhappiness, and what results is a vicious circle. A big, heavy, fat boy likes to eat and doesn't care much about exercise, so he eats more and more and exercises less and less. The more he eats and the fatter he gets, the less he exercises (72).

The extreme lethargy of James's movements, and his excessively overweight condition, raised the possibility that though by nature a boy of his physique will always be expected to be heavy, or, as his parents put it, "well padded," a glandular problem might also be involved.

Putting all these things together, we come up with several serious and specific recommendations for things that must be done for

James, and with James, if we are to have any hope of helping him to a level of comfortable and successful functioning.

First of all, as with many, it did seem obvious that James was overplaced in school. Since most of his functioning is at no better than a third-grade level, it might be best if he could be replaced into third grade. Caution, however, suggests that we wait on this recommendation. Just as some children, if surroundings and conditions are unfavorable, test out to have a lower I.Q. than one thinks may be their "true" I.Q., similarly one suspects that James may, because of many adversities, be expressing less than his true potential of maturity. Unhappiness and poor physical functioning may be causing him to put less than his best foot forward.

The clinic suggested the following further recommendations for James: (1) endocrine coverage, to see if some endocrine help or treatment might help him function more effectively and more comfortably, plus a good diet, which might be able to help him lose some weight; (2) visual training, definitely indicated to help James use his eyes more effectively; (3) the possibility, raised by the degree of unhappiness and possibility of disturbance shown on the Rorschach, that a certain amount of psychotherapy might make things happier and more comfortable for this extremely unhappy boy.

Fortunately, it has been possible to get help along several of these lines. Visual training has been started, with good preliminary results. Perhaps even more important, the parents were able to find one of those all-too-rare endocrinologists who will undertake treatment of boys and girls who exhibit endocrinological problems. This physician has placed James on a high protein diet, hoping to control his weight problem, and has also diagnosed a pituitary gland deficiency for which he has prescribed. He describes James not as hypoactive, as the school psychologist had indicated, but, rather, "hyper-tired."

Psychotherapy, which may eventually be needed, is for the time being held in abeyance till one sees just how much help and change

48

can be obtained from the new diet, medication, visual training, and, if necessary, grade adjustment. The parents report that James now seems highly motivated and very cooperative about the visual training, the medication, and the diet. He is especially pleased that his pants are now too big for him at the waist.

Behavior Outside Normal Limits

Harris, aged eight years and six months and near the end of second grade, was referred by his parents because of his general immaturity, speech difficulty, and rather poor coordination, and because he was not doing too well, not working "up to capacity," in school. There was no indication by his parents, at the time of his referral, that except for his immaturity and poor grades he was anything but that "sweet, quiet, considerate, amiable and generally happy child" they described.

The school's report was less positive. According to them he was reading at only a primer level and had trouble "unlocking" new words, was good at math but poor at spelling. Though he was not considered a behavior problem in school, he "sits in class all day slouched over his desk and either stares around the room or fidgets. Much of the time he appears to be in his own dreamworld. He gets very upset when things go wrong."

A behavior examination for Harris, and a further interview with his parents, revealed that much more was wrong here than simple immaturity and school performance. The parents admitted, on questioning, that they had been aware that Harris was quite different from other children ever since he was six months old. They were especially concerned about his inability to relate to others, about the machinelike noises he made, and by his atypical and often peculiar and inappropriate behavior.

On examination, the boy showed himself to be in serious difficulty. Gross immaturity was one of his greatest handicaps. Though his chronological age was eight years and six months, his behavior level ranged from only five to five and a half years of age. His Copy Forms was no better than five and a half years; his Incomplete Man, near five; his orientation to right and left, from five to five and a half. His response to the Bender Gestalt was at a good six-year-old level, and his response to the Healy II was close to six and a half. Immaturity of this magnitude often becomes more than mere immaturity and must often be classed as atypical behavior.

Unfortunately, the atypical quality of Harris's behavior was made up of more than extreme immaturity. Response to the Rorschach Inkblot Test gave every evidence of schizophrenic qualities. Certainly, Harris did not appear to live in a very real world. His response was highly variable, good form and poor form alternating in typical schizophrenic fashion. The large number of blood and anatomy responses suggested some degree of emotional disturbance. Perhaps most significant were "the big machine which goes up and down" on one card and the "big man that is magic" on another. His accuracy of perception was at rock-bottom level, below that of the usual two-year-old. Harris based his interpretations on vague, poorly comprehended, whole images. The response suggested a very poor grasp of reality.

In his response to the Lowenfeld Mosaic Test, Harris made a vertical lineup of diamond shapes, horizontally oriented, and then described his product as "soldiers, and this is where they go to the bathroom, not in front but in back." When asked to draw a tree, he drew a reasonably good tree but then beside it drew what he called a television set, explaining that the plugs were wired to the tree, that it was a "television tree."

Intelligence was low: verbal I.Q. 82, performance 94, full-scale I.Q. 87. Physically he was like a six-year-old, with a somewhat atypical physical build.

Though Harris stayed with the examination situations surprisingly well, there was considerable silly behavior and much that seemed inappropriate.

The present school situation seemed most inadequate for this boy. Not only was the class too large to give him the individual attention he required, but he was overplaced even in the second grade. It was recommended that his parents try to find a special class for admittedly emotionally disturbed children.

More than that, we recommended psychiatric help and some type of psychopharmacologic help directed at stabilizing his behavior. Hopefully, psychotherapy both for Harris—to help him see himself and the world in more effective relationship to each other—and for his parents—to help them admit and accept the severity of their son's problem—will be sought in the near future.

A report from the parents one year after our examination suggests that they have made considerable progress toward accepting the real seriousness of their son's personality problems. A school that could provide a very small class (only six students) has been found and some academic progress is being made, though Harris still (at nine and a half) has not achieved a breakthrough to "real" reading. He does not relate well to the children in general but *has* found a friend.

Chemotherapy has been tried, and the mother reports that both the tranquilizer and the vitamin therapy "seem to be helping." Home behavior is in general more comfortable than before, though he still acts "odd" at times and still makes machinelike noises. In addition to attending special classes for the emotionally disturbed, Harris will also attend a special summer camp.

Harris is one little boy for whom simple replacement in a lower grade of a regular school was obviously not enough. Like many others, he is not at this time suited for the work of the ordinary classroom. He is not up to either the work or the large size of the usual class. Special class placement is essential, now and for some time to come.

51

Already chemotherapy is helping, but as time goes on it still seems probable that a certain amount of psychotherapy (which has not yet been sought) may be needed, both for Harris and for his parents. It is not easy to live with, or to be, a boy like Harris.

CHAPTER 3

THE CHIEF CAUSES OF SCHOOL FAILURE

We hope that the cases just described speak to you as they do to us. We very much hope that they may serve to make you realize that every child's behavior, strange or unsatisfactory as it may be at times, does make sense. There is a reason, a good reason, behind almost everything that any child does or fails to do. Please believe that, even though your child may be having some trouble in school, chances are he's doing the best he can *under the circumstances*.

And the most important circumstance of all is his own body. Some children are large, some are small. Some are bright, some not so bright. Some have maximal academic drive and ability, some have not. Some are mature as compared to the theoretical average child of their age, some are immature. Some are well coordinated, some are poorly coordinated. Some are able to use their eyes and hands and the rest of their bodies effectively, some suffer from severe visual and perceptual handicaps. Some are healthy, some are not. Some are stimulated by the demands of school, some are swamped by the same demands.

Sometimes in working with handicapped or troubled children we tend to become a little too clinical—to think of the child as a *problem* and to forget that he is also a child. We all need to remember that whatever the developmental level, whatever the level of intelligence, whatever the personality, whatever the problem, each child is a marvelously, in fact a miraculously, growing organism—one who expresses himself clearly at every step of the road *if only we are willing and ready to listen to what he is telling us*. As we work with older children, and with problem children, we sometimes lose sight of the thing that those working with infants and normal preschoolers know almost without verbalizing it. That is that behavior has shape and that it changes in orderly and predictable ways.

Keep in mind Dr. Gesell's statement that environmental factors modulate and inflect but do not *determine* the progressions of development. And remember also, if it suits your beliefs, that behavior is a function of structure. This means simply that teachers and other professionals can do a very great deal to help children express themselves to their fullest, but that they do not determine what these children are or what they can do. We all need to think more about what any child really is and less about what we are trying to do with him.

The children described in the preceding chapter illustrate the more common causes of school failure and the more common types of learning problem. They include:

Children who are immature for the grade they are in.
Children suffering from visual or perceptual problems.
Children who are emotionally disturbed in a large or small way but who, if given psychotherapy or very understanding handling, may make it in the regular classroom.
Children actually not suited to the ordinary kind of public school learning, who need to be placed in some kind of special class— a class for the brain-damaged, emotionally disturbed, or retarded—or perhaps even in a special school.
Children whose intelligence is low but who still can make it in a regular school class specially designed for the not-quite-so-bright child.
Children whose widely scattered abilities present a problem.
Children with highly atypical personalities.
Children with whom there is something physically (medically) wrong, who need drugs or endocrine help or possibly some sort of chemotherapy or other medication. This includes those children currently described as hyperkinetic.

Thus of the children described, typical of those seen by our school clinical service, the majority need either to be replaced in a younger grade, to be placed in a special class or school, to receive

54

some sort of visual help (glasses or perceptual training), to receive some sort of glandular help, or in a rare instance to receive some sort of psychotherapy or at least extremely warm, understanding, and sympathetic treatment at home.

Of these several recommendations, the most frequently made is that the all-too-often overplaced child needs to be put back into a lower grade. Sixty-seven of the last hundred children seen by our clinical service in 1970 needed to be put back into the grade below their present grade.

Next most frequent (61 percent of a typical group of one hundred children seen by our clinical service) is the recommendation that the child needs glasses. There are many children, faltering and failing in our public school classrooms, who can be helped to reasonably effective performance simply by being given the lens help they so sorely need.

There are others suffering from vision problems for whom glasses are not enough. Thirty-four percent of our typical group of children showed themselves to be in need of visual or perceptual training. (This might be with or without the additional prescription of lenses.)

Psychotherapy used to be the most usual recommendation of many clinics and of many psychologists when children were in trouble. This was based on an unfortunate and, we believe, incorrect interpretation of child behavior. For all too long many child specialists, when things went wrong with children, put the blame squarely on parents and on what they called "the emotional atmosphere of the home." And so to cure the child they first "cured" the parents of whatever it was that made them treat their children incorrectly or damagingly.

Psychotherapy for child and/or parents may still be the necessary prescription in a minority of cases. But today it is far less frequently prescribed than in the past. Now people are beginning to look at the child himself and at all of his surroundings, rather than just at his parents, when a child is in trouble. We recommended therapy, in 1970, for 12 percent of children seen, though for none of the parents.

A recommendation frequently given is that many a child seems to need the special facilities and handling offered by the so-called special class or special school. We recognize that in many communities these special classes are not available. The diagnosis is useful, nevertheless, since it means that for such a child, at the very least, lessened academic demand and lessened attendance, or very special attention from regular classroom teacher will be required. That is, the recommendation of "special class" may be more a warning of special vulnerability and special inadequacy than an expectation that a special class will actually be available. Of our hundred typical clinical cases, the recommendation of special school was made for ten children, special class for seven.

The kind of special class will of course depend on both the needs of the child and the flexibility of the community, but there are at least in some communities in this country classes for the brain-damaged, the emotionally disturbed, the perceptually handicapped, the retarded, or those who are not actually retarded but not quite up to the demands of a regular classroom situation.

Uneven endowment—that is, good or mature abilities in some areas of behavior, poor or immature endowment in some other areas—also makes trouble, as demonstrated in some of the cases described in Chapter 2.

One last important possibility of need is that a child in trouble in school may need and might hope to benefit from some type of endocrine help. Of course we can hope to change any child himself only within rather narrow limits. But gradually—if all too slowly— medicine *is* coming to our aid. This is something we can't tell you very much about as yet, but it is one of the most important possibilities that has opened up for both parents and children in the last many years.

There are today a few rare and ahead-of-their-time physicians and endocrinologists who do offer help. The more conservative still deny or doubt the usefulness of such intervention. But effective medication in the form of drugs, thyroid, or other endocrine help, or even attention to the chemical balance of the body, is beginning to be provided, on all-too-rare occasions, for those who need it. The recommendation that the child obtain an endocrine checkup and probably endocrine therapy was made in 9 percent of the cases seen by our clinical service in the past year.

Inevitably, many children have not merely one but several of the problems just listed. But whatever other difficulties they may experience, *the majority of children referred to our clinical service because they were doing poorly in school were overplaced and underendowed for the schoolwork being demanded of them.*

That all but one of the children described in the preceding chapter are boys is no coincidence. It is not too far out of proportion with the number of boys as against girls referred to a typical child behavior clinic. Approximately five times as many boys as girls seem to find themselves in severe enough trouble in school to be taken by their parents for clinic help.

One of the main reasons for this seems to be that, though young boys on the average appear to develop more slowly than do young girls, no account of this fact is taken by most schools. The arbitrary entrance age in most communities is the same for boys as for girls. This means that many more boys than girls start school before they are ready, and subsequently fail or have difficulty.

Note also that the girl described is of a more unusual or more atypical personality structure than are most of the boys. Girls, to be in serious trouble in school, seem to need to be farther off the beaten track than do boys. A girl for whom only a few things are wrong seems able to make it to the satisfaction of others better than does a boy of similar endowment.

Boys in general are considered by both parents and teachers to be more difficult than girls—harder to raise, harder to teach. We don't know all the reasons for this. We do believe that if boys could wait till they are ready before starting school, and if curriculums in the early grades could be adapted to the active bodies and behavior of boys, school would in all probability be a happier place for many presumably unhappy and certainly unsuccessful little boys. A seven-year-old boy of our acquaintance once complained "My teacher teaches me too hard." This complaint could be made by all too many of the children in our schools today.

We have described a variety of children, but you will see that there is much that is similar about them all. Though their problems are multiple, one thing they all share. In every instance the primary failure seems to have been not so much in the child's accomplishment as in the failure of the school to make realistic demands of that particular child. Children are placed in school and subsequently promoted all too casually, even carelessly.

If a boy or girl is reading and otherwise functioning at a beginning second-grade level, it is unrealistic to keep him in third grade, even though he may be eight years old. If his ability to solve arithmetic problems is merely at a first-grade level, second grade may be too much for him, even though he may be fully seven years of age.

If an eight-year-old is behaving in most ways like a seven-year-old, and thus among other things is reading at a seven-year-old level, we cannot correctly say that his reading is below age and needs remediation. It *is,* admittedly, below his chronological age, but it is not below his behavior age and thus should neither concern nor surprise us. The answer for such a child is to place him in a school situation where second- and not third-grade reading will be required of him. The answer is *not* to keep him in third grade and then provide remedial or tutorial help.

If a child's intellectual level is much below a measured I.Q. of 90, he may be expected to have difficulty in an ordinary classroom. If he has visual or perceptual problems, as many do, any school demand that requires interpretation of the printed word is likely to present an obstacle. If endowment is highly uneven—that is, if the child is mature in some things but immature in others, or highly effective in some things but ineffective in others—it will be difficult for the school to find a place that will do justice to both his highs and his lows. Dr. Lendon Smith (93), and others, have found that when endowment is uneven and there is thus a wide scatter between scores on different tests, as between the verbal and performance scores on intelligence tests, it is a possible indication of some hurt to the nervous system. We should at least be aware of this kind of problem when it exists.

And, if a child's personality is highly atypical, merely trying to conform to the usual social demands of a school situation may present a substantial hurdle even in the presence of a high intelligence.

People tend nowadays to behave as if the problems of students (whether they are in primary school, secondary school, or college) are quite different from those faced by students in the past. There is really not that great a difference. For instance, there is a great deal of talk today about the child who experiences so-called learning difficulty. As Dr. Herman Frankel (28) so perceptively advises: "There's nothing specially new about learning disabilities. Children have always had them and we have all known many such children. The children aren't new. It's only the massive professional interest which is new and which makes the whole thing seem perhaps more formidable and different than it actually is."

Any readers concerned with the severe and sometimes seemingly unsolvable problems faced by children living in the so-called inner city may feel that the difficulties we have described in the preceding chapter are bland indeed, in that nearly every child discussed has the advantage of coming from a relatively stable, middle-class home. This is true. The ghetto boy or girl may have the hardship of experiencing any or all of the problems described, plus the fact that his home and neighborhood may not be able to offer the protection and support he needs.

The many problems of educating inner-city boys and girls are a story in themselves and will not be solved in this book. We would, however, like to give a warning:

First of all, we would like to remind readers that as Freeman (29) has pointed out so convincingly, compensatory education so far has not been effective in improving the responses of children who have taken part. As Freeman points out:

Most of the approaches tried so far were based on the assumption that the schools are responsible for the educational deficiencies of their students. This is not true. Could it be that the causative factor is the reverse of what it is widely assumed to be? Could it not be that the educational quality of the school is determined by the characteristics of its students more than vice versa?

In other words, in inner city or suburb, let's look hard at the students we are trying to educate and try to understand their individual needs and abilities, and not merely be content to blame their poor performance (when it is poor performance) on the schools. Keep in mind that, when a child consistently fails in school, the cause of failure may well be in the child and not in the school.

If a bright, somewhat privileged, middle-class boy or girl has the misfortune to be overplaced in school—or to be visually or perceptually handicapped, as so many are—he may still make it in school due to the advantages a stable, enriched home life can give. If a child has the misfortune to be overplaced or perceptually handicapped or not very bright *and* to be from an unstable or impoverished home, he has too many strikes against him. For this reason, though some consider any sort of intelligence or behavior testing to be discriminatory and an invasion of privacy, it is our position that the underprivileged child needs and deserves the protection of both an intelligence and a behavior test so that he may *at least* (whatever his environmental handicaps) be placed in the type and level of class he belongs in and not in one whose unrealistic demands defeat him from the start.

As readers will realize, nearly all of the children described in the preceding chapter as having troubles in school were not having difficulty because of something their parents were doing, or were not doing, at home. They were having trouble because the schools did not appreciate, and apparently were not in the position to appreciate, what the child was really like, what his abilities or disabilities were, what kind of learning situation he would be able to respond to. And, not knowing, they were not providing the necessary situation.

The reasons we have listed are, of course, not the only reasons why children have trouble in school. Though less emphasis is now given to "adverse emotional factors in the home" than in the past, admittedly some school failure does occur because of an unhappy home situation.

If any boy or girl, whether "reasonably" so or not, is unhappy and miserable in his personal life, this unhappiness more often than not is reflected in his school performance. It may be that the way his family treats him, or at least the way it seems to him that they treat him, makes him feel that he is stupid or dumb or just not much good. If so, this feeling of expected failure can keep him from trying in school. It may be that the way his family treats him makes him dislike his parents and wish to hurt them. What better way than by conspicuously failing in school?

Or the trouble at home that disables him academically may not be specifically related to him. If there seems to be great danger that Father will lose his job, if Mother is ill or unhappy, if there is a great deal of quarreling going on between his parents, any of these situations can have a crippling effect on the child's school performance.

Home, of course, is not the only place where things can be unhappy. Though school people, and psychological clinics, very frequently refer to the "adverse factors in the home" that in their opinion lead to school failure, parents are equally quick to point out that sometimes the "factors in the school" are not as favorable as one might wish. The most conspicuously unfavorable factor in school that can and sometimes does lead to school failure is an unfriendly or unfavorable teacher, or one who has an unfavorable personality.

The majority of teachers are reasonably well equipped for the work they do, and by far the majority do have favorable personalities. The possibility that either may not be the case must not be overlooked, though parents should take care not to lean on the possibility, since more often than not the child's teacher will not be the main source of his difficulties.

No case presented in the preceding chapter illustrates either possibility—that is, unfavorable factors in the home or school. Such cases have not been included because as a rule these kinds of problems are not presented at the usual normal child behavior clinic.

One final, and glorious, possibility, which many parents hope for and which does once in a rare while turn up, is the possibility that all of a sudden things may take an unexpected turn for the better. It is unlikely but possible that in a rare but beautiful instance a boy or girl who has been failing in school will, suddenly and as it were spontaneously, improve. It is not safe to coast and merely count on this possibility, but it can and sometimes does so happen. If and when it does, consider yourself blessed.

CHAPTER 4

WHAT YOU CAN DO

Get Help

Let's say you are one of the many parents whose boy or girl is having trouble in school. *Should* you try to do something about it? You most certainly should. *Can* you do something about it? Chances are you can. Can the Establishment (school, psychologist, clinic) help you? Very probably. Can it *guarantee* to solve your child's problem? No. No more than your doctor can guarantee to keep you well.

But certainly your doctor doesn't give up without trying, no matter how serious the malady. And certainly you and the school should not give up without trying, no matter how difficult your child's academic or personality problem may be. The important thing, when there is difficulty, is for you to try to *do* something about it.

People tend to coast all too long with their children's school problems, hoping, presumably, that these problems will go away of their own accord. Few parents, if their child is physically ill, put off going to the doctor year after year. Yet many do just that with school problems.

So, if over any substantial period of time your boy or girl seems to be having substantial trouble in school or even to be doing markedly less well than you think he should be doing, get help. If your child's school problem is real, and not just that he doesn't always get straight As or that he isn't always utterly enthusiastic about school, seek help.

Where to Go for Help

Your first step might simply be to ask for an appointment with your child's teacher and then, if need be, to seek a conference with the principal. Often these people so directly related to your child will know, or feel that they know, what is wrong. Often some simple, practical recommendation—such as that he repeat a grade, get the visual help he needs, be placed in a different kind of class or group—will turn the trick.

Often, however, the school may be as baffled as you. Here's where you call in the specialist. Many schools, or school systems, now have their own school psychologist or guidance counselor. If the teacher and/or principal do not suggest that you consult this individual, it is perfectly in order for you to make the suggestion yourself.

If there is no such person available, or if his or her waiting list is too long, hopefully your community can offer a child behavior clinic or a community mental health clinic staffed to handle school behavior problems. (If your community does *not* have such a clinic, see if you can't get one started. Every community needs one.)

The specialist, if you do obtain his or her services, will give some of the usual behavior and psychological tests we have talked about in describing the case histories presented earlier, and which are described in detail in the appendix. A child behavior clinic will give some of the same tests but will also, hopefully, add the services of a trained vision specialist, possibly of a pediatrician, and hopefully of somebody trained to make an evaluation of the child's glandular picture.

If no clinic is available, then you may need to seek the services of a child psychologist in private practice.

Hopefully, by the time you have gone this far, and often long before, you will have received the diagnosis you seek and will know what the trouble is, what kind of help your boy or girl needs. And, if you are fortunate, at some point in this process you will receive a clear-cut recommendation as to what you can do to solve, or at least begin to solve, your child's problem.

So What Will You Do?

In the case of very benign problems, your child may simply need more help at home, more attention to or supervision of his home-work study habits. Chances are, however, that if you have been seriously worried and if the school has made serious complaints, the problem may lie in one of the directions illustrated by the case studies presented in Chapter 2 and evaluated in Chapter 3. Then the solution may very probably lie in one or more of the following directions, implied or mentioned in these earlier chapters.

Your child may need no more than transfer to another section of his same grade, into the care of a teacher who is more experienced or who has more understanding of his particular personality or problem than does his present teacher.

It may be that your boy or girl would benefit by transferring to a different school, as from parochial to public, or from public to private (or vice versa). Or he may be one who needs the help of some special kind of boarding school. If the change of school is to be merely within your own community, here you will probably do your own exploring. If the answer is to be a boarding school, your own school may be able to give you the name of an educational counselor, a person who makes a profession of finding just the right school for every child. Or you may want to consult either *The*

Porter Sargent Handbook of Private Schools (78), or *Private Independent Schools: The Bunting and Lyon Bluebook* (79) and their related counseling service. Parents needing information as to local community resources available for children with learning disabilities may write to Closer Look, Box 1492, Washington, D.C.

Your child, like some of the children described earlier, may not need so much a special school as a special kind of class: one for the retarded, the 80- to 90-I.Q. child, the brain-damaged, the perceptually handicapped, or the emotionally disturbed. Here again, the school should be able to help you find out where and if such classes exist. If the school can't help you, check with a member of your state legislature. Many states require that such special classes be set up if they do not exist, or that your child be transported at community expense to such a class in some nearby town or city.

If you suspect, or are told, that your boy or girl needs glasses or visual or perceptual training, if the school cannot arrange for this (and it probably cannot), seek the services of a qualified optometrist trained to work with the visual problems of children.

In the rare instance that the child is emotionally disturbed in such a way that psychotherapy may be hoped to help him, this kind of help should be found at a local mental hygiene or community mental health clinic or through your local family service agency. If glandular therapy or chemotherapy or some similar medication is needed, ask your doctor.

One special problem that parents find hard to solve is the problem of the child who doesn't want to go to school. Here again, prior to solution, one needs to make some kind of diagnosis as to just how serious this objection is. There are some shy, reluctant little children hesitant to try anything new, afraid of the unknown, awkward at making any transitions, who at least at the beginning of school make a big fuss each morning. But once they are in school, the teacher reports that everything goes fine. In such cases, a mother is fully justified in putting on a little pressure and maintaining the position that Johnny is going to have to go to school and no more fuss.

The situation is more serious when objection to school is emphasized by nausea and other illness or ailment, extreme anxiety, poor performance in school, and possibly interference with usual good eating, sleeping, or other home behaviors. In such cases one must assume that very likely the school demand is in some way altogether too much for the child. School and home will need to work together to determine what is wrong and what can be done about it. More often than not replacement in a lower grade and/or reduced attendance does solve the problem and bring an end to complaints.

A third level of seriousness occurs when objections to school are so extreme as to amount to what is called *school phobia.* Children who have school phobia for the most part absolutely refuse to go to school. They seem terrified of the whole situation and tend to cling to their mothers, kicking and screaming, when any effort is made to get them to school and into the classroom.

In cases of true school phobia, help from the specialist (psychologist or psychiatrist) is usually required. Most specialists agree that the most important first thing in treating such cases is to get the child back to or into the school *building,* even if not into his classroom. Even if he will only sit in the principal's office, a start has been made.

But getting him to school does not solve the problem. What needs to be done is to find out *why* he is experiencing such excessive fears. The interpretation usually given for this behavior may seem farfetched to some readers. We merely report it as it exists. The assumption is made that many of these school-phobic children, though they usually claim that they don't want to go to school for fear something bad will happen to their mother while they are gone, actually feel hostile to their mother and secretly hope that something bad *will* happen to her. But they are afraid of their fears and don't like to admit them even to themselves, and this need to camouflage real feelings adds to their misery and confusion.

67

There's more to it than that, though. Psychiatrists believe that in many cases of school phobia the mother, though she thinks she wants her child to go to school just like everybody else, harbors an unconscious desire to keep him at home with her. The child senses this unconscious desire and responds to it by insisting on remaining at home.

In every serious case, then, it is thought to be the mother herself who can't separate. Though it first appears that she is trying to persuade her child to go to school and that the child is refusing, it later turns out that the mother is unconsciously preventing the child from going. Thus school phobia may actually be a misnomer, since the problem is not so much a fear of school as a fear of separating from Mother. It has been suggested that these children are more "mother-philes" than "school-phobes."

Whether or not this all sounds sensible to you, this is the way some specialists figure. So, as a rule in solving such problems, they combine an insistence that the child at least get to the school building, with counseling for both mother and child in order to try to straighten out their tangled feelings for each other. The best discussion of this problem, and its treatment, available will be found in Dr. Richard A. Gardner's book, *Therapeutic Communication with Children: Mutual Storytelling Technique in Child Psychotherapy* (31).

Fortunately, school phobias are relatively rare. We mention the problem here because obviously a child is not going to be able to succeed in school unless he goes to school, and thus getting the child to attend his classes is one of the things that must be done if we are to prevent school failure.

Don't Be Afraid to Repeat

We've saved the easiest and often the best thing you can do for last. In perhaps a majority of the cases in which a child is having trouble in school, his basic problem may very well be simply that he started school too soon and thus is in a grade ahead of the one where he can successfully do the work. In this case, a behavior examination can be given to find out if he *is* overplaced. Or perhaps a simple conversation with the teacher will reveal the fact. Or you may already realize it yourself.

And if, as with so many, the problem does turn out to be simply that he is in a grade ahead of the one where he can do the work, *don't be afraid to repeat.*

In days past some parents feared that having a child repeat would be a disgrace to the family and an emotional blow to the child. Psychologists, years ago, argued that repeating a grade did indeed harm a child emotionally and more than that very likely would not improve his school performance. Small wonder, then, that this normal, natural, and commonsense solution to the problem of overplacement came into generally bad repute. Fortunately, as time went on both clinical opinion, practical experience, and new research evidence all combined to put repeating in favor in an increasing number of schools.

This whole subject of repeating has been discussed at length in our earlier book, *Is Your Child in the Wrong Grade?* (3), to which any reader interested in the subject is referred. Suffice it to say here that the weight of our clinical experience affirms that almost without exception those parents who take the step of having a child repeat a grade he has been failing are pleased and satisfied with this solution. What these parents tell us is, "He's a changed child," "He's a different boy," "Except that he's in the same skin I wouldn't know it was my own son, he is so happy and successful now that he has repeated."

Research evidence (19, 85) now also affirms the positive effect of repeating. Once psychologists took pains to refine their research methods, including as research subjects *only* those children whose school failure was considered to be due to sheer immaturity, for which repeating provides a sensible solution, results obtained were overwhelmingly favorable to repeating.

The grades of such children improved significantly after repeating, and both teachers and parents agreed that repeating produced little or no bad emotional effects on the majority of children repeated. In addition, after repeating, the children liked school better, were less fatigued, felt more confident and successful in school than before repeating, were better about finishing their work, were easier to live with, and got on better with their friends. Most differences between behavior before and after repeating were statistically significant.

It is our sincere hope that any parent whose child is failing in school, if it appears that the child's only serious problem is immaturity, will at least give repeating a try. If a boy or girl is overplaced in school, putting him back into the grade that fits his behavior level seems to us a most sensible and reasonable solution to his problem.

Motivation

Let us assume that no outside professional help is indicated, that there appears to be nothing that needs improving about your child's vision, that he appears to be physically healthy, of good intelligence, in the right grade, emotionally stable, and that the school or class he is in is considered by you and the teacher to be right for him, then admittedly it's going to be hard to know what *to* do.

If professional assistance fails, as it sometimes may, then you are once more on your own. And you will probably try all the things parents have tried for so many years in their efforts to help their children do better in school.

There are, of course, many perfectly commonsense things that parents customarily do try when a boy or girl turns out to be doing badly in school. First they talk the whole thing over seriously with the child, impressing upon him the fact that they are less than satisfied with the way he is doing. Then they promise or threaten as

70

the case may be—promise rewards for improved grades, threaten dire results if grades do not improve.

Then chances are the parents will make plans to see to it that the child in question is more conscientious about his homework. They set up a schedule to be sure he does his work. Maybe they decide to help more with it. They hear him recite. They check to see that he has completed any home assignments. Very possibly they arrange for him to cut down on outside activity—play after school, movie attendance, and such—in order that more time will be available for studying.

And then, most difficult of all, a parent will try to *motivate* the child to do better. One of those hopeful fancies which many parents invariably pursue is the notion that a child would do better, in fact that his performance would become perfectly satisfactory, if only somebody could *motivate* him.

People tend to speak as if motivation were something that could be put into a child from outside—something one could add, like a pinch of salt, to make things right when they are wrong. But sometimes it seems to us almost as useless to say, "If only we could motivate him," as it would be to say, "If only we could give him a higher intelligence."

Motivation is a complicated and somewhat mysterious force, not understood any too well even by those who have written books on the subject. It almost seems to result from a mysterious combination of factors within an individual. Some children seem highly motivated, highly driven, highly competitive, highly goal oriented. Others, equally intelligent and from equally favorable environments, just really do not seem to care—and those who have tried often discover that "there just doesn't seem to be any way to motivate that child."

We, no more than others, can provide a magic recipe for motivating the unmotivated boy or girl. The one thing we have found to work in some cases is, first, to remove, change, or do away with as many of the adverse factors in any child's life situation as can be managed and, then, to move him into a situation where he can reasonably hope to succeed. But keep your expectations reasonable. Don't expect a second-grade C student to be doing third-grade work and bringing home Bs.

Personal success, we have found, tends to be one of the very best motivators possible for any human being. So do everything you can to provide your school-age child with a school situation where he can enjoy success and move on to further success. That may be his best motivation.

Self-Confidence

Since one of the best motivators for any activity seems to be success, let's think a bit about ways in which we can help the child toward success. One way toward school success, as we have emphasized, is to try to see that the child is in the right grade and in the right kind of school situation.

Another motivator, and one you *can* work on at home, is a feeling of self-confidence. Sometimes the difference between the child who succeeds and the one who fails is not a difference of intelligence or even in maturity. It sometimes is mostly a difference in self-confidence.

Some children just naturally seem to feel that they *can*. Others seem to feel that they *cannot*. Fortunately, even if your child is one who lacks a basic feeling of self-confidence, there are some things you can do, not to change his personality, but at least to increase his basic feeling of self-confidence or self-esteem.

Some of the best suggestions available about how to do this will be found in an interesting book by Dorothy Corkille Briggs titled *Your Child's Self Esteem* (15). In brief summary, here is what she has to advise. She suggests that strong self-respect is based on two main convictions: "I am lovable" and "I am worthwhile." One way to encourage these feelings is to appreciate that it isn't so much what we say to our children that influences their feelings about themselves as it is the way we treat them. Since each child values himself to the degree that he is valued, the way we ourselves feel about our children actually builds in (or builds out) self-confidence and a sense of self-worth. That is, a child builds his picture of himself from the words, body language, attitudes, and judgment of those around him.

Negative self-attitudes can be changed to high self-esteem by providing a child with a nurturing climate of acceptance and experiences of success. Mrs. Briggs suggests that a good way to make a child feel worthwhile is to help him feel that you are satisfied with him and that he is living up to your expectations. A child rarely questions our expectations. Rather, if he does not meet them he tends to question his own personal adequacy.

In order that your child will be able to live up to your expectations, of course, you will need to take quite a lot of pains to be sure that they are reasonable. One way to do this is to know quite a lot about child behavior, about what ordinary children can and cannot do at different ages.* Your expectations are more likely to be fair if they are based on the facts of child development, on alert observation, and on sensitivity to past and present pressures. Check your expectations frequently. It is easy for them to get out of line.

It may help if you ask yourself the following questions about anything you expect or require of your boy or girl:

> Why do I have this expectation?
> Where did it come from?
> What's in it for me?
> Is it based on my needs or on my child's?
> What purpose does it serve?
> Does it realistically fit this particular child at his age
> and with his temperament and background?

* For detail as to what behavior to expect at different ages the reader is referred to the so-called trilogy: *Infant and Child in the Culture of Today, The Child from Five to Ten,* and *Youth: The Years from Ten to Sixteen,* all authored by Gesell and Ilg and published by Harper & Row.

One further suggestion, and one that agrees with things that psychotherapist Haim Ginott has voiced in his well-known book *Between Parent and Child* (38), is the notion of making a specific statement about the thing that is bothering you or that you don't like about the child's *behavior,* rather than making a generalized criticism *of him as a person.* Thus, "I'm worried about your grades" is better than the criticism, "You're stupid," "You're just plain lazy," or "You really don't try." That is, don't tie personal lack of worth in with undesirable behavior. Don't make the child feel that he is personally worthless just because his schoolwork, or something else about him, doesn't come up to your expectations.

Encouraging Creativity

Parents who are not entirely satisfied with their children's ways of behaving quite naturally look for ways in which to make them brighter, smarter, more scholarly, more creative. Though we have never held that there is too much a parent can do to make her child smarter than Nature intended, it is possible to help and encourage any child to express fully what intelligence he has.

The same is true of creativity. Though some children are by nature highly creative, and others minimally so, regardless of basic endowment there are ways in which any parent can try to encourage maximum use of whatever creativity a child may have or to try to help him use his thinking powers more effectively.

The most specific advice we know of along the lines of encouraging creativity will be found in a book by Milton A. Young titled *Buttons Are to Push: Developing Your Child's Creativity* (111). The anecdote that apparently gave Dr. Young his title seems well worth sharing.

Six-year-old Paul, a beginning first-grader, proudly showed his teacher a drawing he had just finished. His paper was covered entirely with different sized circles.

His teacher was not impressed. "What a mess," she said critically. "Can't you do something neat and nice instead of just messing up your paper?"

Paul was crushed. Tearfully, he asked if he could show his paper to his last year's kindergarten teacher. Permission was given and he left the room. His kindergarten teacher wasn't really quite sure what the circles represented, so she asked Paul to tell her what he had made.

"They're buttons," Paul explained. "All different kinds of buttons. These are for a rocket, this one rings a bell, this one blows a siren. You know. Buttons are to push."

Some of Young's practical and specific suggestions for encouraging creativity in thought and action are as follows: He points out that most children do start out with a rather active imagination and intense curiosity about what goes on around them. A parent can nurture this imagination and curiosity, which are the foundations of effective thinking. In other words, answer the child's "whys" and "what fors," at least as long as your patience lasts.

Parents who give children solutions to problems, rather than helping them think things through themselves, are teaching the youngsters that solutions can be found by using outside resources. Children need to be encouraged to think through and solve their own problems, although they must first understand a problem before they can begin to solve it. Help should be available when needed, but it is usually wiser to wait until a child asks for help before stepping in.

As children get older, they can be taught to analyze situations critically through actual practice. Having children test their solutions by actually trying them out is probably the best way to teach them that it is essential to think a situation through to its conclusion before settling on a solution.

Critical thinking starts at a very early age. You can encourage young children to develop this ability by verbalizing your own critical analysis of things.

Fantasies, wishes, and dreams seem to play an important part in developing imagination and, therefore, in developing the ability to think. When children express these fantasies, they are not intentionally lying. Youngsters think imaginatively in many different ways. You should not try to set a pattern for your child or for other children, since controlling imagination tends to deaden it.

Listening to what children say encourages their creative self-expression, and new situations and new experiences help children to become aware of and sensitive to the stimuli that surround them. Making resources available to children, so that they feel encouraged to use them, leads to their learning how to find needed information. Emphasizing the process rather than the end product encourages imaginative solutions.

Since thinking and working creatively is something best exercised when the child is very young, Young emphasizes materials and activities that will help the four-year-old and the five-year-old to get started early.

For a four-year-old he recommends that you make available materials for making papier-mâché; ask your child to draw a picture of an animal that does not live on this planet, and explain how it lives; ask him to do some classifying, as, for instance, naming things that can fly, parts of a car, things that are red; ask him to describe something without looking at it; ask him (with some help from you) to keep a notebook of things he would like to do and places he would like to visit; have him express his ideas in drawings or with hand puppets; check his understanding of words he uses and ones that you use; ask him to think up new names for such ordinary objects as couch, chair, bed, etc.; ask him what he would have to do to an object to make it run, fly.

For five-year-olds, Young suggests that you ask the child to find new uses for such familiar objects as pencils or paper clips; ask him to imagine a well-known thing functioning as something else (a door as a wagon, for instance); set up frustrating situations, ask the child to deal with them, and test his solutions (what would he do if he lost his milk money, for instance); ask him how he would help a friend with a problem (the problem being, for instance, that nobody likes him); help him to start a collection of rocks, butter-flies, stamps, match covers; help him to ask the right questions and to gather evidence to bring out the whole story of some incident (such as a man being hurt on the street); list a group of objects and ask the child to find a common quality (a tree, a squirrel, an ant, a plant, and a fish are all alive, for instance).

You yourself, with this much of a start, can quite certainly think of other practical ways to encourage creativity of thought and action in your growing child.

The Child's Needs

We have said a lot about the child's body and behavior, and what kind of situation he needs in order to function at his best, but we have said relatively little about his feelings. The Reverend George von Hilsheimer, superintendent of the Green Valley School in Florida, in his current book, *How to Live with Your Special Child: A Handbook for Behavior Change* (96), does discuss feel-ings, and he suggests that every child in trouble in school (or else-where) has the following needs, which we should recognize and respect. Each child needs:

to be able to feel that he is worth something;
to be able to think that he can change himself and some of the cir-cumstances around him;
to be able to feel that change is worth making;
to know some adults who will listen to him and answer him courteously;
to have skills and something to do with them;
to know some adults who behave toward children with the same gravity, respect, attention, and lack of impertinence that they would grant a friend in trouble;
to know some adults who will give them attention most strongly

77

when they are doing worthwhile things and who are obviously not interested in them simply because they are bad or in trouble; to know some adults who are strong enough not to need to make children need them, who can force children to make decisions for themselves and can help them live with and overcome bad decisions and so learn to make good ones.

Now, all of this may seem awfully difficult, and may not be what most readers have in mind. In these days of "how to do it" books it is natural that some parents will have harbored the hope that this book would tell them things they could sit right down and do *at home* to guarantee that their child would do better in school. There's nothing wrong with trying, and, if your child is in only very slight difficulty, chances are that home efforts could be all that are needed. But, if a child is in serious trouble, in most instances it will take more than home-made remedies to set things right.

From what we've told you in this chapter you will see that, when things go wrong in school, though there are many, many different things you can try to do to help, your solutions tend to lie in one of two opposite directions.

One is to seek outside help. Whether you look to the teacher, principal, school psychologist or guidance counselor, psychologist in private practice, clinic, vision specialist, physician, or psychiatrist, try first to get a clear-cut diagnosis from some qualified professional person as to what is wrong with your child. And then try to follow this up by insisting on getting help in carrying out the advice given.

The other extreme is to do what parents have done from time immemorial. Do the best you can at home. It is not likely that even your most sincere efforts are going to make your child substantially more creative, more intelligent, more academically oriented than Nature intended. But they may be enough to help him use those abilities he does have effectively enough to get by.

The situation is not identical with, but in some ways resembles, that which exists with regard to a child's eating behavior. A hungry child normally will eat unless he has an allergy or some other illness such that some foods actually disagree with him. Or unless his mother has pushed to get him to eat more food or more different foods than he wants to eat, or to eat foods that he especially dislikes. Or unless he has learned that he gets more attention by not eating than by eating. Or unless he has learned that he can control his mother by his refusal to eat.

Though mothers usually spend much time in planning and bribing and wheedling and cajoling and scolding or praising, they often, and sadly, discover that, if a real feeding problem has developed, little things they do and try often don't help matters much. It usually takes a specialist (hopefully the pediatrician) to help set them straight.

It is the same with school. If things are seriously wrong, they will require more than just a little conversation and supervision, more than letting your child know that you are taking a serious and determined interest in his schoolwork. If things are right for your child in school—if the work is not way beyond him, and if he is emotionally and physically well enough to do it—chances are he will meet the school's requirements with enthusiasm. The hungry child eats. The reasonably intelligent child learns.

But when your child is having trouble in school and your normal parental efforts fail, accept the fact that some major change in the total situation may be needed and that you may well need professional help in finding out what is wrong and in effecting a solution. Try to find that help! And, whatever you do, don't panic and don't give up. The majority of normally endowed children do get through school.

CHAPTER 5

WHAT YOU CAN EXPECT

Does Every Child Have a "Right" to Academic Success?

We hear a lot nowadays about the child's "right" to read, or his "right" to have a successful school career. Parents often ask, "Don't I have a right to expect the school to find out what's the matter with my son, and can't I insist that they fix it?"

Actually, all this talk of rights is somewhat exaggerated. A right is something that some person or group or body is empowered to give and does give. We *give* people the right to vote, and there are many other rights that society bestows on its members. But there is no sense pretending that you are bestowing a right unless it is in your power to do so. Take, for example, the current "Right to Read" program sponsored by the United States government. The idea is great, and the campaign itself certainly is aimed in the right direction. But as a matter of fact a child does not have a right to read. He has, perhaps, a *right* to expect that somebody will try to teach him. He deserves the *privilege* of being taught effectively. And one has the *hope* that he will learn. No more.

That is, schools are responsible for doing the very best they can for every pupil. But they cannot *guarantee* to solve all his problems any more than a physician can *guarantee* to keep all his patients healthy. (You do not have a "right" to perfect health.)

A good teaching situation can help any boy or girl make the most of such intelligence as he may have, but the very best teaching in the world cannot help the child with an extremely low I.Q. to read. Glasses and visual training can often do wonders for the child with visual or perceptual problems, but some children with severe perceptual difficulties cannot be helped substantially even by very good perceptual training. Therapy can help many children who are emotionally disturbed, but even the very best therapy cannot cure all children with emotional problems.

That a child cannot be helped to total or even substantial success is not always the fault of the school. Many schools are not, in a real world, run as well as one might wish. All school personnel are not ideally well qualified or well trained. But, even if schools were perfect, there is no reason to expect that they could solve every single child's learning and personality problems. So it is meaningless to insist on every child's "right" to a successful school career. All that we—superintendents, principals, school boards, teachers, remedial staff, psychologists, and others—can do is to put forth our very best efforts and do our very best to help.

But *parents and school must work together.* It is not any more useful for parents to blame the school because the school doesn't do better with their children than it would be for the school to blame the parents because not all the children sent to school are prime academic material. We're both stuck—parents and school— with the kinds of children sent to school and the kind of teaching that can be provided. Both, hopefully, are great. Both, sometimes, are less than perfect.

One of the most ineffective things a parent can do is to decide that her child's academic problems are all the teacher's fault. If you think that something is seriously wrong about your child's teacher, you can discuss this with the principal. But don't decide on your own that it is the teacher's fault that your child does not do better in school.

Accountability

An extreme version of blaming the teachers, or blaming the school, is the new concept of "accountability" proposed by some.

81

This notion holds that, if teachers taught as effectively as we can expect them to teach, then all children would or should learn successfully. So if your child does not successfully learn to read, write, and perform other academic activities you can, according to this rather unrealistic notion, hold the school accountable. And can sue the school.

This will, we hope, sound pretty wild to most readers. We mention it here because the concept was brought up in all seriousness at the 1970 White House Conference on Children and Youth. Though it was rejected, the fact that it was proposed at all suggests how far some people are from a realistic approach to learning problems.

This notion of holding the school (or any other outside factor) accountable when any child fails to learn is the opposite extreme of our own finding, over the years. Our finding is that when any child is in academic or other behavior difficulty *the answer more often than not lies in the organism, not in the environment.*

Forewarned is, hopefully, forearmed. We very much hope that all readers of this book will reflect seriously on the dangerous fallacies that underlie this new concept of accountability. We hope, too, that you will reflect on the chaos that any attempt to put such a notion into practice could and would produce.

What You Can Expect

Now, saying that parents don't have a right to expect perfection from the school or to expect it to solve all their problems doesn't mean that they just have to sit back and take whatever the school hands out. There are many reasonable expectations that parents *can* have of schools, just as there are many reasonable expectations that schools can have of parents. Since this book is for parents, we'll talk about what parents can expect of schools.

What things, then, does a parent have a right to *expect* from his child's school? What other things should he merely *hope* for?

Among the most common questions parents ask the specialist are these: "Don't I have a right to expect that they can teach my child to read?" "Don't I have a right to expect them to make him mind?" "Don't they have to provide a suitable class for him even if he isn't too very bright?" "Don't they have to provide a class for the brain-damaged (the perceptually handicapped, the emotionally disturbed)?" "Isn't it their responsibility to find out why he cannot seem to learn?"

These questions are hard to answer. Every one of them represents a real, human, and natural parental wish that each child be given what many people *do* consider a right in this country—a good education for every child. Yet are these things that parents long for actually rights, which each community's educational system can and should guarantee? Or are they more like the pursuit of happiness mentioned by the Declaration of Independence?

Nobody can *guarantee* you happiness. That you should be relatively free to seek happiness is about the most anyone can promise for sure. The same is, we think, true of a good and successful education for all, and what we can and should and frequently do provide is a situation in which parent, child, and school together may *seek* an adequate education for the child. *We can by no means guarantee that every child will end up stable and well educated.* And, since we cannot make this guarantee, to speak of "rights" in this respect is perhaps a trifle unrealistic.

(Of course, in some instances there are laws that define people's supposed rights so far as education is concerned. In a state where the law says there *must* be classes for the retarded, the brain damaged, or the perceptually handicapped, parents presumably do have a right to *expect* such services. But pursuing such rights in communities where the service in question doesn't exist can still be difficult and frustrating.)

Community resources vary. Some are superb. In many others, parents pursue a frustrating course when they try to get the help that children with special problems may need. It doesn't improve the picture if they become angry at the school because their own and their child's supposed rights are being denied.

We can't even solve all the problems of the supposedly normal and well-endowed child. All too often a perfectly nice, bright, generally well-constituted child from an advantaged family just cannot or does not seem to be able to make it in school, and nobody knows why—nobody is able to solve his problem and get him onto the right track. How much more difficult, then, if the failing or unsuccessful child is disadvantaged in one or several of the major ways in which it is possible to be disadvantaged!

To us, it makes more practical sense for parents to think in terms of their reasonable *hopes* for their children's education rather than in terms of their supposed rights.

And so, after this long preamble, let's talk about some of the things that parents can reasonably hope for, for their children, in our American schools.

What You Can Hope For

First and foremost, any parent will hope—though there is no guarantee that this wish will be granted—that his boy or girl will enjoy the great and unequaled blessing of having an effective and dedicated teacher. For all the elaborate and modern refinements that have been introduced into our schools in the past fifty years, none can take the place of a good teacher, and no class can be totally effective without her.

What next? A second reasonable hope that any parent might entertain is that his child's school will provide a good developmental examiner, trained to determine each child's behavior age so that each child will start school, and subsequently be promoted (or "advanced," if he is in a nongraded school), only when he is behaviorally ready.

Third, we would very much hope that every school or community might provide or make available an adequately trained vision specialist who will routinely determine for every child whether or not he needs glasses and/or visual training.

Thus, if a normally endowed child starts school at the right time, has a good teacher, and has no severe visual problem, or if he has such a problem and receives the help he needs for it, the battle for a good education is more than half won.

A fourth hope—and we are still talking about the normally endowed girl or boy—is that there be good enough rapport between parent and school that reasonably frequent parent-teacher conferences will permit easy and comfortable discussion of the problems that do arise in the schooling of even the well endowed.

Parents of especially bright children may have their own special hopes, among which will be, presumably, the hope that their child will be given scope to express his special abilities without being pushed too far ahead of himself gradewise.

But suppose that the child in question is less than well endowed, or has special problems. What can a parent expect or hope for then? (We have already discussed this question, in a different context, in Chapter 4. But since this is a subject of vital importance to the parent of any child in academic difficulty, we'll take the risk of being somewhat repetitious here and summarize what we said earlier.)

If problems arise with such a child, as they most likely will, you can certainly hope that the school will provide a well-trained school psychologist who can examine your child, find out what is wrong, and prescribe for the difficulty. Among the most important things a psychological examination should reveal, if these facts are present and not already known, would be a dangerously low intelligence (say below an I.Q. of 75 or 80), brain damage, perceptual handicap, serious visual or hearing difficulties, unusual inability to read, or marked immaturity.

If the child's problem is so severe or so complicated that the school psychologist cannot solve it or successfully prescribe for it unaided, then hopefully the school will refer you to a public or private local clinic that can provide the detailed diagnosis you require. A diagnosis, obviously, is only a first step toward solving your problems, but it is certainly an essential first step.

Once you have received the diagnosis, and found out what it is that your child seems to need, you must hope that your community facilities will provide it. Not every community, by any means, will provide all the special classes needed, but, increasingly, smaller communities are banding together to furnish such services even when the individual town or city cannot.

These are some of the things that parents can hope for from our schools today. Perhaps the most important thing to keep in mind is that the schools are on your side. If your particular school, as it often may, fails to solve, immediately and completely, whatever academic or emotional or behavior problem your child may be experiencing, it is not because it is not trying.

Schools are, most of them, doing the very best they can and often (though it may be hard for parents to admit this) with less than completely promising material. There are many things a school *can* do. But it cannot, so far as we now know, substantially raise low intelligence. It cannot in every instance cope in the classroom with a seriously brain-damaged or emotionally disturbed boy or girl. It cannot solve *every* learning problem.

We guarantee that in nine out of ten cases the school is doing the best it can. Work with it, not against it, when it makes recommendations about your child. Try not to be defensive or feel insulted if they tell you that your child has problems in certain areas or that he needs some special sort of help.

And, in the unfortunate situation that the school cannot provide the special class or service it knows your child needs, try not to be angry with the school. Our schools in a democracy are only as good as what we can provide or pay for. There is no "they" out there who can promise to solve all your problems. And no guarantee came with your child's birth certificate that he would certainly and inevitably end up, so many years later, a well-educated high school graduate on his way to college.

CHAPTER 6

FATHER'S SPECIAL ROLE

When we talk about what "you" can do to help your child in school, or what "you" can expect, we mean you *fathers* quite as much as you *mothers*.

"His father needs to spend more time with him" is one of the prescriptions commonly given by teachers and psychologists and others when they really don't know what is wrong with a given child. In spite of the fact that it is an overused cliché, there is considerable truth in the statement. Most children could indeed do with more time and attention from Father.

Fathers often, even the most concerned, tend to play a somewhat secondary role so far as their children's schooling is concerned. Proud of success, they tend merely to scold and punish for failure and sometimes seem to feel that rewarding or punishing at report-card time about takes care of their school responsibilities.

We'd like to point out that a concerned and participating father can often make the difference between school success and school failure for his boys and girls. And what he can do is not necessarily time-consuming, since it is more the quality than the quantity of his participation that matters.

Perhaps the biggest thing a father can do to help a school-age son or daughter toward school success is to work *with* his wife in this area. This doesn't mean that Mother decides how things will be done and Father merely agrees. It does mean that they will decide together what their policy and approach shall be.

Any child who can play Father against Mother in any situation whatsoever is likely to do so. So it's essential for Mother and

Father to agree, and for Father to back Mother up, if need be, about the importance of finishing homework, completing outside assignments, working for better grades (if they decide this is needed). Father's role, however, can and should be much more than merely getting together with Mother and then supporting her in joint decisions. There are many situations relating to school where Father can and ideally should play a primary role.

One of the places where he can help most is with homework. Like other educators, we definitely feel that parents should never do their children's homework for them. But this doesn't mean that they don't need to give a lot of help. Often Father, with his more logical mind, his firmer voice, his less vulnerable attitude toward his children, can give more substantial and more effective help than can Mother. This may be especially true in the field of arithmetic, an area in which mothers may be as hopelessly lost as their children.

Father can also help by taking an interest, but a rational interest, in report cards. Too many fathers are either indifferent, or become violently angry when grades are bad. A sincere and serious interest can give a child a good feeling of support. But don't show your interest by shouting and losing your temper. You do care, one hopes, but try also to keep your sense of proportion, even when your oldest and dearest gets a C instead of the A you had in mind.

Another big way that a father can help is to try at least to keep an open mind when his wife comes up with the notion that a boy or girl may need another year in nursery school, or in kindergarten. Try not to carry on about, "No child of mine is going to be considered a dumbbell," or "You're not going to hold *my* son back."

It may be because fathers aren't with their very young children as much of the day as mothers are, it may be because a child's school performance seems to reflect more on his father than on his mother, but fathers are the ones who tend to raise the biggest objections when the question of starting school later, or of repeating a too-demanding grade, comes up. It's bad enough when Mother has to fight the school to obtain what she thinks best for her child. If she has to fight Father, too, chances are she will give up and let the child enter into or continue in a situation she knows full well is over his head.

A further thing that fathers can do, their jobs and schedules permitting, is to go down to school with Mother if and when a serious conference about a child's folly or failure is scheduled. This doesn't mean that fathers should be expected to attend every routine parent-teacher conference. But Mother can use your support, and the school will respect your interest, if when things go seriously wrong and your wife has to go down to school to try to straighten them out, you go with her.

In fact, if you can bring yourself to it, your presence, not only at a scheduled parent-teacher conference, but at regular PTA meetings will be more than appreciated by all concerned. It isn't just that the presence of fathers makes the meetings more fun for the mothers. It delights the school to see that the fathers care. And most children are extremely proud to know that they and their school doings are important enough to Father that he will interrupt his own busy life to go to PTA meetings.

But more than the emotional satisfaction it will give everyone, a good supply of father-members of any PTA strengthens the effectiveness of that organization in bringing about school changes it may consider desirable but despair of achieving. A strong, active PTA can sometimes accomplish a surprising amount *if* the mothers don't have to try to do things alone.

Another thing we'd like to suggest to fathers is that they think twice before they shout out all those shop-worn truisms about their children's schooling, truisms that really are not true at all. How many a father has commented, when his child's schoolwork fell below what was desired: "He's just got to try harder. He could do the work well enough if only he would try." Or, "You've just got to make him study harder. You let him get away with murder."

Or, "There's no reason at all for such dreadful grades." Father—there's always a reason!

And now, one final and general suggestion that some fathers, admittedly, may consider a lot of nonsense. We have never gone along with those school psychologists who so glibly verbalize that most school problems and school failures are a result of unfavorable emotional factors in the home. We have never gone along with those clinics which, whenever a child had trouble, in school or elsewhere, routinely prescribed psychological "help" for Mother and Father.

One must admit, nevertheless, that when things are wrong, seriously wrong, at home, if they are bad enough to upset the children and make them anxious and unhappy, schoolwork very often will suffer, will show the bad effects of the tension and strain felt.

Trying to see to it that you and your wife are reasonably happy together, and that you provide for your children a moderately relaxed and comfortable home atmosphere, may seem a rather roundabout way to go about helping them in school. But it can help—more than you sometimes think.

No child should be made to feel that the whole family's welfare and success rest on his performance in school. It may be as bad to overfeature child and school as it is to underfeature them. Nevertheless, each schoolchild does deserve at least a temporary place in the sun. And, if Father really cares about schoolwork, and expresses his interest in a calm, consistent, and constructive way, it decreases the likelihood of serious and prolonged and unremedied school failure on the part of boy or girl.

CHAPTER 7

EACH CHILD IS AS OLD AS HE ACTS

Behavior Age and Birthday Age

How old *is* your boy or girl?

You may think we're strange to ask. Yet when you have answered this question correctly you're halfway home to seeing that your child has a successful school career.

This is because every child has at least two important ages. One is his chronological or birthday age. The other, and equally important, is his *behavior* age, the age at which he is behaving.

You all know this, and allow for it, when your boy or girl is a mere infant. Say he's nine months old, but you've noticed that he's a little slow for his age. In fact, his behavior may seem more like that of a seven-month-old baby. Most nine-monthers are able to creep, but he has just begun to sit alone, and seems nowhere near ready for creeping. Since he seems bright enough, and your doctor tells you he's really okay, you don't worry. But you do permit him to behave, not like the nine-monther he is by birthday age, but more like the seven-monther he is by behavior age.

This is easy when he's a baby, but it is not as easy when he approaches the usual school age. Custom dictates, and the law in most places allows, that five-year-olds shall start kindergarten and six-year-olds shall start first grade. In fact, in many states a child can begin kindergarten even if he is somewhat less than five years old in September when school begins, and start first grade even if not quite six.

That would all be very fine if we could assume that all children whose birthday age is five, or thereabouts, actually behave like five-year-olds, and all six-year-olds act like six. Unfortunately, this is by no means always the case. A substantial number at any age will be *below* the average expectation.

And just as you did not expect nine-month behavior from your somewhat slowly developing baby who at nine months was behaving only like a seven-monther, so you must not expect five-year-old (kindergarten) behavior of your five-year-old if his behavior age is substantially below five. Or you must not expect full first-grade behavior from your six-year-old if his behavior age is substantially below six.

Determining the behavior age of any boy or girl is called *developmental examining* or *developmental diagnosis*. But even with no help from the teacher or child specialist, many of you probably have a pretty good notion that your child's behavior is immature (assuming that it *is* immature). That is, you know it if his behavior is a little babyish or younger than that expected on the average from a child of his age.

To objectify your judgment we, and others, have provided what are called *developmental* or *behavior tests*.* These tests tell you rather exactly whether or not your child's behavior is up to the average expectation for his age, and, if it is not, at what age he *is* behaving. And this is what you need to know in order to decide whether or not your boy or girl is ready to start school, or, once in school, whether or not at the end of any school year he is ready for promotion to the following grade.

Gesell Developmental Philosophy

Just a word here about the philosophy of development (or, as we call it, the developmental philosophy or developmental point of view) that underlies all the Gesell work with children.

* Readers interested in knowing more about developmental examining are referred to *School Readiness* by Ilg and Ames (56). Workshops that teach professional people how to give a developmental examination are provided at the Gesell Institute in New Haven, or can be arranged for in local communities.

As Dr. Gesell himself used to say, "Behavior is a function of structure." What this means is that people tend to behave as they do largely as a result of the kinds of bodies they have inherited and the stage of development those bodies have reached. Thus men, as a rule, behave differently from women in many respects, babies behave differently from two-year-olds, and teen-agers behave differently from ten-year-olds.

Another rule to remember is that behavior develops, to a large extent, in a patterned, predictable way. Just as it is possible to predict the stages a person's *body* will go through as he grows older, so to a very large extent it is possible to predict the stages that *behavior* will go through. And these stages are only slightly influenced by what you do or do not do to the child.

Contrasting Behavior in Two Five-Year-Old Boys

Let's consider, as an example that not all children of the same age behave at the same level of maturity, two five-year-old boys, Carl and Donald. Though both are just starting kindergarten, as both are legally entitled to do, and both are assumed, in the eyes of the law, to be equally ready to do, in reality these two boys are at very different levels of maturity.

A comparison of their response on the developmental examination (figures 4–7) shows the vast behavioral differences that can and do occur among children legally eligible for the same educational experience because of their chronological age. The law says that each of these two boys is eligible to enter kindergarten because both are five years old. The law assumes that each child will somehow miraculously be *behaving* like a five-year-old, with all the eagerness and compliancy of the five-year-old who so dearly loves the activities of kindergarten. But these two developmental screenings reveal how unrealistic, and even cruel, the law can be to children whose own growth does not necessarily conform to that expected by the law.

Each of these boys is a perfectly normal child and shows good intellectual potential. Each is capable, but capable at his own level of development. Each has good ways of solving problems, and each has excellent ideas about the way things fit together and are related. They each attack the jobs to be done with ingenuity and skill. But there is a vast difference between the age levels of their excellence.

One boy, Carl, is performing at a not much more than four-year-old level (figures 4 and 5). For example, he dashes off the Copy Forms with a sweeping, gross motor stroke. He does not make a good triangle, and the divided rectangle and diamond are way beyond him. Details of precision, such as closure points, good corners, and a strong stable stroke, do not worry him. In fact, he seems completely unaware of them. Nor does he line up his forms. He is perfectly satisfied with his own level of accomplishment and thinks he has done a mighty fine job. His Incomplete Man has the belly button, big eyes, and straight-out arm of the four-year-old.

The second boy, Donald, though the same age as Carl, is performing with excellence at a five-year-old level or somewhat above (figures 6 and 7). For example, he works much more slowly and carefully, needing much more working time than the boy with the four- to four-and-a-half-year-old behavior. He strives to gain control of the pencil, and his movements are no longer whole-arm, gross motor strokes. He is beginning to move with much finer control.

Donald is not only aware of form, but of many of the details of precision. He is quite often aware when he misses a closure point or a corner. And his five-year-old understanding of the job to be done is much more comprehensive than the other boy's understanding. (Satisfaction for Donald lies not only in the completed form but in the approval *you* register in his accomplishment. Carl needed only to please himself to be successful.) Donald makes a

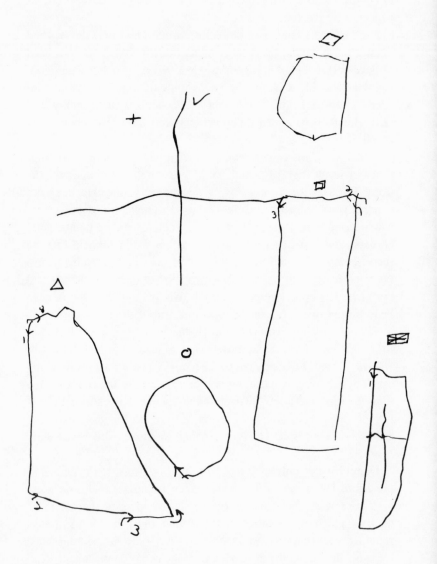

Fig. 4. Carl (5¹): Copy Forms

Fig. 5. Carl (5¹): Incomplete Man

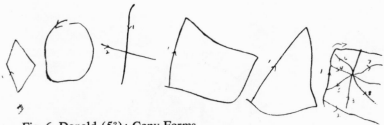

Fig. 6. Donald (5^2): Copy Forms

pretty good diamond, tries the divided rectangle, lines up his forms in good order. His completion of the man shows the nicely balanced eyes, shaped ear, and effort at a tie characteristic of five and a half years or even older.

Each child has his own style, his own speed, his own level of awareness, his own ways of deriving satisfaction. To place both in the same educational experience and to expect both to be able to handle the same kinds of tasks in similar working styles is to violate one child or the other.

For example, if the teacher adjusts the working time of the class to Donald's five-year-old level of performance so that he can take the time he needs for concentration and care, Carl will be at a disadvantage. He may not understand the task at all, he may wander about aimlessly with nothing to do, he may bother others who are working.

And, most likely, with his four-year-old energy he will get himself busy in gross motor play that is noisy, boisterous, and disturbing to those who are trying to work with concentration. He isn't being "bad." His natural energy and enthusiasm just carry him into excess. He can't help but talk loudly, move too quickly, knock things over if they are in his way.

It is entirely possible that Carl will understand the given task, but he will understand it on an entirely different level from that of Donald with his more mature behavior. Because details, complexities, subtleties are not yet a part of his understanding, because he works with speed and doesn't need to pause for approval or to

Fig. 7. Donald (5^2) : Incomplete Man

ask questions to make sure he is proceeding correctly, Carl will be finished in a flash. He will be up and off and running, looking for something else to do.

Chances are he won't enjoy the quiet, sit-down activity that would allow the ordinary five-year-old to continue working without disturbance and distraction. He has too much energy bottled up inside him. He's just got to be on the move. Even if the teacher can convince him to work at a quiet, sit-down activity, it is highly unlikely it will turn out to be quiet, though it may be sit-down. He will begin to release his energy through his mouth. He will talk and talk and talk.

On the other hand, if the teacher adjusts the working pace of the class to Carl's less mature level of performance, Donald, with his five-year-old behavior, will be at a disadvantage. He may not be finished with his tasks when the class moves on, and, because the five-year-old has such a sense of totality and completion, he may feel frustrated.

He will not have had time to take care of all the details, he won't have had time to check with the teacher to find out if he is doing a "good job." He won't be ready to move on to the next thing. The class may move on to a new activity, but it is more than likely that his mind will still be back on the job he didn't finish. As a result, not only will he not have completed the first task to his satisfaction, but he will be missing out on the second task, too, because his attention is still absorbed by what has gone before.

Each child should be allowed the right to perform as a capable child in an experience that is both within his grasp and in part just *one step* beyond his grasp. He should have the right to be himself, to do what he can with ease, confidence, and success. But he should also have the right to experience new and challenging activities that are just one step beyond him—activities so intriguing and so related to his own life that they make him want to move forward into new and untried areas, forward toward the development of new ways of doing things and new ways of thinking about things.

It is frustrating and demoralizing for a boy with a four-year-old level of behavior to have to struggle constantly to work way beyond that level. This overdemand tends to produce a child who begins to think of himself as a child who *can't,* and helps produce a child who begins to act *as if he doesn't want to.*

On the other hand, it is frustrating and demoralizing for a child with five-year-old behavior to have to work constantly on tasks *below* his level, to have to conclude before he is ready because others do not have as long an attention span as he; to have always to do the old, the familiar, the already accomplished because others are not yet able to move into the "next step" areas. Such frustration tends to produce in a child the idea that school is not a very exciting place and that learning is not challenging, exciting, or rewarding.

Two Six-Year-Old Girls

A second example of the tremendous discrepancy possible in the behavior of any two children of the same chronological age is seen in the responses of two six-year-olds: Lisa, exactly six, and Karen, aged six years and three months, both examined in October and both in the same first-grade class.

Lisa's response (figures 8 and 9) is at a good six-and-a-half-year-old level. Karen (figures 10 and 11), though she is slightly the older, is not up to a full five-year-old level. Lisa is well placed in first grade. Karen would be much better off in kindergarten.

Ready for School?

Both sets of children described and pictured here, the two five-year-old boys and the two six-year-old girls, had at least in

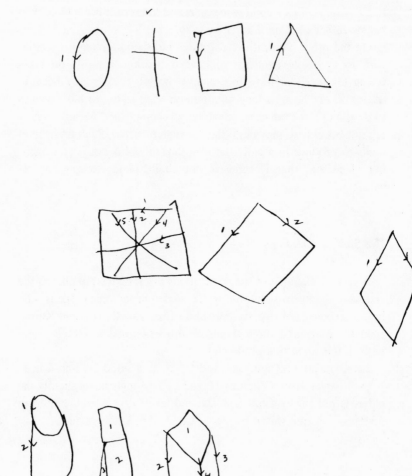

Fig. 8. Lisa (6⁰) : Copy Forms

Fig. 9. Lisa (6⁰) : Incomplete Man

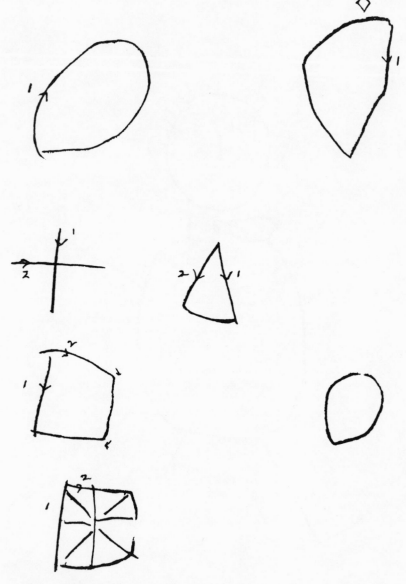

Fig. 10. Karen (6³): Copy Forms

104

Fig. 11. Karen (6³): Incomplete Man

common that the two in each pair were of the same sex and the same age. And yet there was almost a year's difference in the *behavioral* age of the two children in each pair.

Suppose for a minute that we were comparing a girl of say five and a half and a boy of four years nine months—both of whom by our Connecticut law would be eligible to start kindergarten in the same September. Think of the differences here! Consider how much greater the possible discrepancy, especially since girls tend to develop more rapidly than do boys. If, as is possible, the girl should be somewhat mature for her age and the boy somewhat immature for his, there could indeed be close to a two-year difference in their behavior ages.

Clearly something more effective than chronological age *must* be used as a basis for determining the time at which children are permitted to enter our public schools.

How Many Children Are Immature?

Readers may feel that we place undue stress on immaturity. We give this subject as much emphasis as we do partly because being immature for the academic requirements made of him can be so substantially handicapping for a child, partly because immaturity is not only one of the chief causes of school difficulty but one of the easiest to diagnose and to do something about.

How many children are there, immature for their chronological age and thus immature for the demands the school makes upon them? It is difficult to say, and the number certainly varies from school to school. But if our norms for what one should expect, on the average, from a child of any age are correct, then according to usual expectations one quarter of all children might be expected to be seriously immature, as the so-called normal or bell-shaped curve shows (figure 12).

106

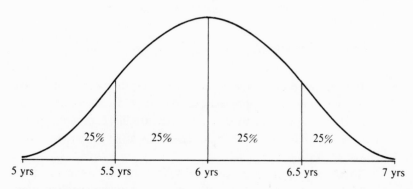

Fig. 12. Normal Curve

The numbers on this curve tell us several things. If the line down the middle represents the mean or average six-year-old expectation, obviously 50 percent of any given population will be expected to fall above the norm, 50 percent below.

But not everybody below this middle line is in trouble. The 25 percent *just* below the mean (or average) are usually considered to be near enough to it that, theoretically, we don't have to worry about them. So, according to the normal curve, only the bottom 25 percent should be seriously immature, or, if we're talking about the six-year-old, immature for the work of first grade, which is the grade in which the law and/or the custom of the community usually places them.

This may seem a small number, numerically speaking, but it represents a good many children. The situation is worsened by the fact that, considering the somewhat formal, fixed, and often fairly demanding schedule of many first grades, not even all children who are fully up to a six-year level of maturity actually can make it in school. So that in real life, regardless of theoretical expectations,

107

often substantially more than the expected 25 percent of children are actually not fully ready for first grade when they begin.

Solution for Immaturity

Parents often ask if there isn't something they can *do* to make their immature child more mature. So far as we now know, there isn't. By giving a child freedom and responsibility you can help him express the fullest of what maturity he has attained, but *you can't speed up his development*.

There are two things parents and schools *can* do for an immature child. First you can, as this book suggests, seriously consider having him start school a little later than the law permits, and thus begin school and proceed through the grades in accordance with his developmental rather than his chronological age. Since at present most schools in this country tend to have a somewhat fixed curriculum, it often seems the best solution to have all or most of the children in any class pretty much ready for the work the school is going to demand.

An alternative suggestion, and one which some people favor, is taking all five-year-olds into kindergarten, all sixes into first grade, and then simply teaching them as much as they are ready and able to learn. Ideal as this alternative may seem to some, and though it may be one the schools will eventually have to adopt, most schools are not run that way today. Standards and requirements seem to be becoming stricter and more rigorous rather than more liberal. Thus, at the present time the best policy for all parents seems to be to make every possible effort to ascertain that every child is developmentally ready for the work customarily expected of a child in his grade.

(A third possibility, the ungraded primary, though it has much to be said for it, has not, in most communities, worked out as well as its originators had anticipated. Though we do not oppose the notion, it does not in our opinion present the ideal solution.)

Age Levels Like Shoe Sizes

There are many parents to whom the notion of age levels comes quite naturally. It is easy for them to see that, if they are but willing to wait six months or so, something they have been unsuccessfully pushing and struggling to get their child to do comes about quite easily and with little effort on their part.

There are others who feel that their child *ought* to do what parents and school desire at the time *they* feel it should be done. So they teach and train and urge and argue, only to discover that in the long run a child cannot and does not perform any given behavior till his brain and body are ready for him to perform that function. As Piaget has commented, "An organism won't respond unless it's sensitive to a stimulus" (77).

And so eventually even those who are not age-minded do come to accept (at least in retrospect) that a child does have to be ready before he can creep, walk, talk, stay dry at night, read, write, tell the truth, take his share of family responsibility. In fact, he really has to be ready no matter what the task or behavior one has in mind.

To us, recognizing age levels and age changes is the heart of understanding child behavior. And to us age differences in behavior are fully as important as differences in shoe sizes. A child can wear, and keep on his feet, a shoe that is the wrong size. True, if it's too small it pinches and may harm his feet. If it's too large it may be hard to keep on, but he *can* stumble along.

The same with small age differences and the fit of the age for the grade you're in. If you're not quite ready, school demands *will* pinch. If you're over-ready and thus are not challenged by the school's demands, school may not be as satisfying as it otherwise could be. Just as even one size off *can* make a difference in shoes, so one age level off can and does make a difference in behavior fit. A child needs to be fitted into his grade in school just as carefully as he should be fitted into his shoes.

How a Parent Can Recognize Unreadiness for Kindergarten

Psychology, as we hope you're coming to recognize from the things we've been telling you, is not necessarily entirely different from common sense. Thus, you by no means always need a psychologist to tell you when your child is not ready to start school. We have often found that a parent's own instinct about this matter can be a very sure guide. But if you don't want to depend entirely on your own judgment, and a psychologist or clinic is not handy, one of the best ways we know of for deciding this important question is to consult a very good checklist called *Ready or Not? The School Readiness Checklist* by John J. Austin and J. Clayton Lafferty (8).

If your child is old enough, legally, to start kindergarten at the beginning of the coming school year, but there is any doubt in your mind as to his actual readiness, you can check the forty-three questions that Austin and Lafferty provide. According to them, if you can answer yes to from forty to forty-three of these questions, your child is surely ready for school, and, if you can say yes to even thirty-five to thirty-nine of them, he is probably ready. If you can manage only thirty-one to thirty-four yeses, there is a question about his readiness; if only twenty-six to thirty, readiness is doubtful. If you can answer yes to only twenty-five or fewer, readiness is unlikely.

We give you here, with the authors' permission, the nine questions from this list that they consider most significant. If your boy or girl is about to start kindergarten, you should be able to answer yes to most of them if he is really ready.

110

1. Will your child be five years and six months or older when he begins kindergarten?
2. Can he tell you the names of three or four colors that you point out?
3. Can he draw or copy a square?
4. Can he name drawings of a cross, square, circle?
5. Can he repeat a series of four numbers without practice?
6. Can he tell his left hand from his right?
7. Can he draw and color beyond a simple scribble?
8. Can he tell what things are made of, as cars, chairs, shoes?
9. Can he travel alone in the neighborhood (two blocks) to store, school, playground, or the homes of friends?

Determining Readiness for First Grade

Determining readiness for first grade is even more important (if possible) than determining readiness for kindergarten. The ordinary kindergarten curriculum is such that even if a child is not fully ready for the "work" involved, failure is neither as stark nor as defeating as failure in first grade. Success or failure in first grade strongly influences any child's attitude toward school and toward the years to follow. *It is vital to determine that every child entering first grade be ready to do so.*

Here are some of the things for a parent to check on* in making this determination, assuming that there is a question in her mind and assuming that it is not possible to get a professional opinion:

1. Does the child's kindergarten teacher recommend that he go on to first grade? (If she does not, be guided by her advice. Kindergarten teachers do not, as some parents suspect, advise that a child stay back just because they are prejudiced against him, or don't like him. They advise that he stay back, when

---

* These are quoted from an earlier book of our own, *Is Your Child in the Wrong Grade?* (3).

they do, because they have good reason to believe that he can't make it in first grade.)

2. Will the child be fully six years old or older before the September date when first grade starts?
3. Does he seem to you as mature as other children of his same age, or as mature as his older siblings were at his age?
4. Has the ordinarily "good" behavior of the typical five-year-old broken up a bit and does your child show some of the signs of being or becoming a rebellious, argumentative *six?*
5. Can he copy a circle, counterclockwise and starting at the top? (This behavior is expected by five and a half years.)
6. Can he copy a triangle?
7. Can he copy a divided rectangle, angled lines crossing center line?
8. Does he hold a pencil in a good two- or three-finger grasp?
9. Can he print at least his first name?
10. Does he know his upper- and lowercase letters, out of context?
11. Can he count to 30?
12. Can he write numbers up to 20?
13. Does he know right from left?
14. Does he know his age and the month of his birthday?
15. Can he stand on one foot while you count to 8?
16. Can he throw a ball overhand?
17. Can he tie his shoelaces?
18. Can he repeat four numbers after hearing them once?
19. Can he calculate (add and subtract) within 20?

Possible Indications of Overplacement

Now, let's say your boy or girl has already started school, and his own behavior or his teacher's complaints make you suspect that he may possibly be overplaced. Let's say there is no psychologist available to examine him and give you an expert opinion. Here are some questions (3) you can ask yourself about your child and his response to school. If you must answer yes to even four or five of these questions, chances are that he may be overplaced.

112

1. Does he dislike school?
2. Does he complain a great deal that "it's too hard"?
3. Does he have great difficulty in completing the written work assigned in class?
4. Does he seem unduly fatigued when he gets home from school?
5. Is he a "different" child in summer when school responsibilities have been removed?
6. Does he have terrible trouble, almost every day, in getting ready for school?
7. Does he complain of stomachaches, or is he actually sick at his stomach before he goes to school in the morning?
8. Has any marked change for the worse in his health taken place since he started school? Does a normally healthy child suddenly begin to have a series of colds, one after another?
9. Have any of his home routines taken a marked turn for the worse since he started school? For instance, does he eat less well, have trouble in sleeping, exhibit a return to bed-wetting after having been dry at night?
10. Has a normally "good" child suddenly become rebellious, difficult, quarrelsome, cranky at home once school has started?
11. Does your child get much less good school marks than you and the teacher think he is capable of getting?
12. Does his teacher assure you that he "could do better" if only he would try harder?
13. Does he have trouble socially, either in class or on the playground?
14. Are most or many of his friends chosen from children in a lower grade?
15. Is his teething considerably behind that of other boys and girls in his class?
16. Does a normally "good" child find it terribly difficult to behave in class? Are there constant complaints from the school that he has had to be reprimanded, was made to sit out in the hall, or had to be sent to the principal's office?
17. Does he do desperate things at school as, for instance, not finishing his paper and then scribbling all over it?
18. Does he find it unduly difficult in class to wait his turn, speak only when he's supposed to, refrain from "bothering" his classmates?

19. Does he daydream in class or fail to pay attention, to an extent which the teacher considers unreasonable?
20. Has the teacher or anyone at school suggested to you that your child really is not up to the work of his present grade and would be better off in a lower grade?
21. Last, and perhaps most important, does he seem to you babyish for his age as compared to other children his same age, or compared to the way his brothers and sisters (if any) behaved when they were his age?

Characteristics of "Learning Disability Children"

We hear so very much nowadays about children with learning disabilities that it may be of interest to readers for us to list here some of the outstanding and most commonly observed characteristics of such children as listed by John H. Meier of Denver, Colorado (74).

In a questionnaire study conducted in 110 second-grade classrooms in eight Rocky Mountain states, Meier screened 2,400 children and identified 361 as having specific learning disabilities. Two hundred eighty-four of these were available for study.

Characteristics observed in half these second-grade learning disability children were: inability to recall oral directions, inability to comprehend spoken words, slowness in finishing work, daydreaming, falling asleep, poor handwriting as compared to peers, reversal or rotation of letters and numbers as he writes, inability to sound out words, inability to carry out written directions, reading level at least three-quarters of a year below most peers, inability to tell time, repetitious behavior.

Two-thirds of these children exhibited the above behaviors plus an unusually short attention span for daily work, high distractibility, slow reading ability, substitution of words in reading so that meaning is distorted.

114

Any one or two of these characteristics or behaviors might appear in almost any second-grader, but any substantial number of them in one child might be a clue to parent or teacher that the child expressing them may have a serious learning problem. However, you will note a slight overlap between this list and our own list of signs of overplacement. This leads us to the warning that, while any of the above behaviors may indeed, if seen in second-graders, be indicators of a true "learning disability," they may just as likely be clues that the child is overplaced. One might hope that if any such second-grader could be replaced into first grade, school adjustment and school performance might then conceivably be entirely satisfactory, and the child might not need any further kind of special help.

We'd like to close this chapter with a poem written by Kay M. Innes of Madison Heights, Michigan, developmental coordinator at the Edmunson Elementary School, a poem we think describes very neatly the plight of the overplaced child.

> I'm a bright November boy,
>   School for me is not a joy!
> How I dread to hear the bell,
>   How I pray for old Gesell.
> Dr. Ilg, please rescue me
>   From this shame and misery.
>
> Teacher thinks I'm rather slow.
>   I just need more time to grow!
> Next to me sits prissy Pearl,
>   Teacher's "good" December girl.
> Pearl just loves her A, B, C's—
>   Wants to learn to make her threes.
> I prefer the trucks and water—
>   Teacher doesn't think I oughter.

Johnny's March—he really shines,
  Colors well within the lines.
April Smith can write her name
  In big round letters, all the same.
Teacher says that I don't try—
  All I do is blink one eye,
She thinks that I am not too bright,
  I still mix my left and right!

Teach says I should listen more
  And spend less time down on the floor.
I can sing and march and play,
  I can paint—but not her way!
I made a person—red and blue
  With lots of hair and buttons, too.
It was good—but what the heck!
  All she said was, "Where's the neck?"

Teacher's getting rather riled,
  Thinks I am a stubborn child.
Hopes that I don't have a brother—
  Says she couldn't stand another.
Warns if I don't pay attention
  She is thinking of retention.
That threat of hers it thrills me so,
  Then I would have more time to grow.

Teacher—young as I may be—
  I do know biology.
Birds and bees aren't celibate,
  And as long as people mate
There will be November boys
  Who look forward to school's joys.
Teacher, hurry to Gesell—
  Don't make all their lives a hell!

CHAPTER 8

WHAT YOU SHOULD KNOW ABOUT YOUR CHILD'S VISION

PART ONE: A CHANGING VIEW OF VISION AND VISION PROBLEMS

"One picture is worth a thousand words." Almost everyone has heard or used this expression, but, in spite of this verbally accepted everyday awareness of the important role that vision plays in understanding and communication, many people fail to recognize the significance of vision as it relates to children. Even the members of the vision care professions are divided in their views about how vision relates to child development and achievement. Though there is actually a wide range of opinions, it is possible to identify two main clusters of beliefs.

The major disagreement among professionals is not so much as to whether or not vision is important but in terms of *how* vision is important. A good deal of this difference focuses around the concept of what vision *is*—a definition of what is *involved* in seeing for humans. The difference in definition can generally be stated as a difference in the extent to which vision is considered to depend on self-involvement.

On the one hand, vision is viewed as something happening *to* a person, with a minimal degree of self-involvement. This view holds that vision has little or no relationship to a child's scholastic and general behavior and achievement. According to this position, the eyes as optical systems are viewed as responding in a relatively automatic, instinctive manner relatively uninfluenced by the individual doing the seeing. The main concern is getting light and light patterns (images) into the eye in a logical, acceptable manner. When this takes place in a satisfactory way, and there is no eye damage or disease, the necessary conditions for seeing are generally satisfied within this definition. This is a sight-oriented approach.

A second and contrasting approach holds that what any person sees is highly dependent upon what the person is doing in the act of seeing. Specialists who hold this second view believe that *vision and visual abilities must be considered as one part of total human functioning. They believe that vision is a very important component in the way a child develops, learns, and achieves in school.* They emphasize the need to evaluate the efficiency of the visual system in relation to the activities the child is normally faced with during the course of his or her day. They believe that the eye and body adjustments that the individual makes to control and monitor his visual system will affect what he sees. Seeing with meaning and understanding is considered to depend as much upon what the seer is doing as upon what kinds of images are presented to his eyes. Vision is considered to be an involved process, not a passive event.

This viewpoint agrees that it is important to get light and light patterns into the eye in a logical, acceptable manner. But the logic and acceptability are contingent upon the viewer's logic and the viewer's acceptability, as well as on the visual presentation itself. Seeing is thought of as an active process involving patterns that, though instinctive, are subject to modification and change. A changing flexible visual system is considered necessary in order to see both similarities and differences. The modifications and changes necessary depend upon how the individual understands, adjusts, and responds in order to coordinate his active participation with the visual presentation.

These two different definitions of vision admittedly do result in different approaches to vision care. Both approaches emphasize the importance of regular eye and vision examinations and of eye health, and both employ lenses as a major vehicle to help people see. But there will be differences in their decisions as to when and how lenses should be used. There will even be disagreements as to whether or not a child's problems involve his vision. Some practitioners do not even consider or believe in programs of care involving vision training and vision remediation.

These different beliefs within the visual care profession must at times be very confusing to the public, especially to a parent who has received two contradictory opinions and diagnoses from two different vision or eye care specialists. Parents often have to make a decision as to what to do about their child's vision without understanding the background and concepts related to the two different approaches.

We hope that the theoretical and background information given in this chapter will provide you, as parents, with knowledge that will help you in your practical decisions about your own child's vision. It is especially important for you to understand the ways in which the different approaches result in different care programs. By more clearly understanding why there are these differences, and what the different approaches are attempting to do, you will be in a better position to choose a specialist whose views are consistent with your own desired goals for vision care.

The viewpoint that vision is a relatively fixed function, predetermined before birth, leads to a more specific care approach. Within this approach, there is little or no attempt to change vision development, growth, and general performance. The goal is to give the person the best *sight* possible, to get the sharpest picture into the eyes.

Within this viewpoint, vision is not only considered to be predetermined, but is also considered to be a passive function. Seeing happens to one. Accordingly, the major consideration is to get the light focused into the eyes by using either spectacle lenses or contact lenses. When the eyes do not work coordinately as a team, the usual decision is to use prisms or to perform surgery to change the muscles that determine where the eyes point.

The use of lenses then is mostly determined in terms of improving acuity. The distance visual acuity is measured at and corrected for is across the room (twenty feet). When a person has healthy eyes, 20/20 acuity* across the room, and can control his eyes so that they generally point together, vision is considered to be normal. Any problem the person has when these favorable conditions are present or can be achieved with lenses is said not to be a vision problem.

In contrast to this view, the second, expanded, and more involved approach (*the approach we ourselves favor*) is much more concerned with ways in which vision, vision abilities, and vision performance can be efficiently developed and utilized. It holds that the person himself is involved with a visual system that operates at birth through a series of definable reflexes. But as the child grows older, what he does, how he understands his own reactions in relation to incoming light patterns, will change and will modify the original reflex patterns. To the degree that this is possible, vision may be said to be learnable or adaptable.

These modifications and changes can work for either the betterment of visual development or can lead to vision and eye problems. According to our view, vision care should be directed, not just to compensate for aberrations of the eyes, but, more important, toward the evaluation of the child's usability of his eyes and vision system while doing tasks that resemble those required in life, and especially in school. (As suggested earlier, studies show that the majority of children with learning difficulties tend to show some degree of difficulty in visual or visual-perceptual skills.)

Under our approach, lenses, guidance, and vision training are

* When the two numbers are the same, as 20/20 or 6/6, then acuity or central seeing sharpness is considered normal. When the first number is smaller than the second, as 20/100, then a person's sharpness of seeing is reduced. When the first number is larger than the second, as 20/15, then sharpness of seeing is above average.

programmed to help the child perform more efficiently and effectively than he may be doing. Visual care is directed toward allowing the child to use vision efficiently to do things, the doing including moving, writing, reading, problem solving, and even thinking. We now know that when a person hold his eyes "still" and thinks of hitting a ball, or when he works an arithmetic problem in his mind, the eyes change focus in order to do the "thinking." The program of care we favor is designed not just for the *now* of seeing, but to help promote better vision and visual development.

This chapter will discuss vision care as well as vision in school. Special emphasis will be given to explaining some of the changes that follow when vision is considered as an involved process rather than as a mere passive happening. It should help you to understand how an acuity test can be misleading, since children can have normal acuity but still not be able to use their eyes for effective performance.

Another factor that might contribute to confusion for parents is that vision and eye care is customarily administered by two different groups of specialists. These two professions are optometry (O.D.) and ophthalmology (M.D.). The expanded and more involved approach described above has been more generally accepted and practiced by optometry than by ophthalmology, though differences of approach do not merely follow professional lines. Some optometrists still hold to the more limited definition of vision, while some ophthalmologists are now accepting the more involved definition.

It is understandable why optometry has found it easier to change more quickly toward this second view, which emphasizes the functioning of vision. Optometry is a profession that specializes in vision and the *function* of the eye. While optometrists are trained to recognize eye disease, they do not themselves treat diseases or do surgery. On the other hand, ophthalmology is a profession that specializes in the treatment of disease and surgery of the eye, though many ophthalmologists do also prescribe glasses.

121

Part Two: Vision Care

Every Child Should Have a Visual Examination

While all children are more or less the same in many ways, in other ways each child is different from every other. Vision is a very personal thing—even more personal than one's own handwriting. Each person has his own way of seeing and understanding what he sees. *A child's vision can be an important key, not only to his success or failure in school and/or on the playground, but also to an understanding of how he can be guided and helped to a more complete and fruitful life.* Because vision is so personal, a child's vision can be fully understood only through an individual examination.

No child should enter school before his or her eyes and vision have been thoroughly examined and evaluated. Though many people think it is impossible to accomplish this until a child can read letters, today there *are* ways to test a child's seeing skills even under one year of age.

Ideally, children should have their first eye and vision examination no later than four years of age. If indications of difficulty are noted earlier, steps should be taken immediately, as soon as the difficulty is first noticed. After the first examination, there should be a minimum of one examination a year, though your doctor will no doubt give you specific recommendations about how long it should be safe to go before seeing him again.

A thorough eye and vision abilities examination of a child should take from forty-five minutes to one and a half hours of testing and conference time. This examination should include (1) an evaluation of the child's eyes and eye health; (2) an evaluation of the flexibility and skills of eye and vision changes; and (3) an evaluation of efficiency in using vision to obtain and utilize information.

EYE HEALTH AND CONDITION OF EYES

The eyes are part of the body and are affected by specific diseases as well as by general body diseases. There should be a thorough examination of the outside of the eye, the lids and related structures, as well as of the inside of the eye. The inside of the eye is examined by special instruments that allow the examiner to look through the pupil—the little black window in the center of the eye—and examine the lens, nerve layer, blood vessels, and the inside wall of the eye. The instrument customarily used for this is an ophthalmoscope, a special flashlight that allows the examiner to look into the eye. The focus of the instrument can be changed by use of a small wheel that changes lenses as the examiner looks into the eye. More elaborate instruments are used when needed. Fortunately, only 1 to 3 percent of children are found to have eye health problems (95).

The eyes and related mechanisms are parts of the body specialized to respond to light. The eye is a complicated piece of equipment with many parts, which usually work in harmony to take in, filter, and bend light so that it focuses properly for the distance we want to look. When parts of the eye do not work in harmony, or when some parts do not work well in conjunction with all the others, the eye may make an error in focusing. It may measure as too strong a focus, too weak a focus, or an unequal focus.

Sometimes our two eyes can measure differently. That is, they can get out of balance in where and how they focus. One can get ahead of the other or behind the other. Then they become an unmatched pair, each going a little bit its own way. To serve us well, our eyes need to work well together as a team.

Among the most common eye problems are the following:

When the focusing power of the eyes is too strong, only things close by or in near range are clear. This condition compares to what happens when a person is *nearsighted, shortsighted,* or *myopic.*

123

When the focus power of the eyes is too weak, then only things far away can be seen clearly and a good deal of effort will be required to overfocus in order to see clearly at near. This condition is analogous to *farsightedness, longsightedness,* or *hyperopia.* When the focusing for one or both eyes is unequal, such as one strength of focusing for things up and down and a stronger or weaker strength for things from right to left, this condition is analogous to *astigmatism.* Another focusing difficulty exists when the range of focusing is diminished or lost. This usually occurs in middle age and is called *presbyopia.*

These various focusing difficulties can also occur in combination. One eye may measure myopia and the other eye may measure hyperopia. Or eyes may measure myopia or hyperopia *along with* astigmatism. When there is a great deal of difference between the two eyes, other complications, such as size differences of images, arise. The focusing difficulties can also occur with difficulties in eye pointing.

The more common difficulties in eye pointing abilities are usually the most obvious to the layman. Gross difficulties in eye pointing or alignment are classified under the general heading of squint, or *strabismus.* There are several different kinds of strabismus. Usually a person with strabismus selects one eye or the other to point more accurately at what he is trying to see. A smaller percentage will switch the eye used as the pointing eye. Still others will only mispoint their eyes at certain distances or for only part of the time.

The two most common kinds of strabismus occur when an eye points in too much, or when an eye does not turn in enough to get to a pointing position. When an eye points too close, closer than the place the person is trying to see, this is called *cross-eyes,* or *esotropia.* When an eye is out too far and does not move toward the nose enough to get alignment, this is called *walleyes,* or *exotropia.* Less common are conditions where one eye points too high or too low. These would be classed as *hypertropia* and *hypotropia.*

Another condition of seeing difficulty, which has been highly publicized recently, is the condition known as *amblyopia,* also referred to as "lazy eye." While the whole eye is involved in seeing over a wide area of space, only one little spot in the eye, the fovea, is capable of seeing really sharp detail. When a child has never developed this part of seeing, or when a child suppresses or filters out the information from this area to reduce the need for fine and accurate pointing, then acuity or sharpness of seeing is reduced. Amblyopia is a dimming of the sharpness of central fine-detail seeing.

All the conditions just described are gross eye disabilities. They are flaws in the eyes or eye system that can generally be described in terms of difficulty in just getting information or "images" into the eye. All members of the visual and eye care professions, regardless of their orientation, agree that these are conditions that deserve attention.

In most cases, the professionals will even agree upon the general kinds of treatment that are appropriate. If the problem is one of focusing, then lenses that let the eye focus over greater ranges with more accuracy should be used. If the problem is amblyopia, efforts should be made to allow and encourage the "lazy eye" to develop more completely. If the problem is one of an inability to point the eyes together, methods should be employed to help the person achieve better coordination of the eyes.

FLEXIBILITY AND SKILLS OF EYE AND VISION CHANGES

If all of our work was at the same distance and of the same nature, our eyes could be set in one position in the way they focus and point. But the human organism is very active. We need to see at close ranges for reading, writing, drawing, eating, and many other skills. We also need to see far distances to look at the moon and stars, down the highway, at a chalkboard or movie screen. We need to change our eye focus from great distances to close-range seeing,

125

and we need to do it in split-second timing. This shift of seeing not only requires a shift in eye focus, but also a shift in how our eyes are pointing. When we look at an object in the distance, our eyes have to diverge, or move apart. When we look at something close by, they must converge, or turn in, so that they both point to the same place.

Not only must we be able to change the focus and eye pointing to see different distances, but these changes must be synchronized to work together. Since all seeing is not straight ahead, we also need to keep this synchronization when we look to the right, left, and up and down. We need to be able to make unequal shifts to keep the eyes balanced.

Today we know that an eye can be focused accurately at a target, but in order to see it must keep making rapid, tiny, tiny sweeps or movements or the "picture" will fade out. Likewise, an eye can be accurately pointing at a target, but it must make rapid, very-small-focus changes or it stops seeing sharply. In order to see, we need an active eye that can keep making rapid intricate changes in alignment and focusing without losing its place in either function.

Our eyes must have the capability of being selective in what they see. Not enough attention has been given to this skill in the past. At one moment we may need to see all of a large scene and the next an exact spot in the larger view. But all this requires changes, changes that should be able to be accomplished without losing the relationships of parts to wholes or wholes to parts. Even when a task is at a relatively constant distance, as when you are reading this print, your eyes are making constant shifts of position and areas of focus. You have to see the words but not lose their relationships to each other, how they are put together.

A child who has difficulty in following a slow-moving visual target at near is pretty certain to have difficulty in moving his eyes along a line of print. A child who has difficulty in shifting focus and pointing—eye posture—from far to near or near to far is at a distinct disadvantage in a classroom working from chalkboard to

126

book or paper. Many children with healthy eyes that focus normally across the room have difficulty in either maintaining focus at near-by areas or in shifting eye posture and focus back and forth. Is it any wonder, then, that even children who have healthy eyes, normal eyes, or equipment still have difficulty in school? Today there are vision specialists in most parts of the country who do not stop short with just an eye examination that merely measures the adequacy of the child's visual equipment. You don't have to allow your child's future to be shortchanged just because his visual *equipment* checks out okay. Maybe he, like many others, does have a legitimate problem in putting his equipment to work!

EFFICIENCY OF USING VISION TO OBTAIN
AND UTILIZE INFORMATION

Seeing is valuable to a person only to the degree to which it allows him to understand, react, and act in accordance with what he sees. We do not see just to see. We see to get information that lets us know and do something. Each child and each adult wants slightly different things from his seeing, depending on his interests, activities, work, and pleasure.

A child's occupations include play, school, and physical activities. The visual examination he receives should include measures of his vision functioning as he is doing these very things. One cannot completely predict how a child is going to use his eyes when he is reading a book from the way he uses them reading the customary letter chart across the room. These are very different kinds of activities. To know how a child's eyes are working while he is reading at school, observations and measures of his vision should be made *while he is reading appropriate reading material that he is holding in his hands.*

A thorough examination of your child's vision abilities should include an evaluation of how effective his vision is when he is doing tasks like the tasks that confront him every day. Too often, the

127

child is examined as if he were a small adult, carrying out adult activities. Probably even more inadequate, all too often his vision is not evaluated at the area he most frequently uses—at arms' reach. No child's vision abilities can adequately be assessed without an examination of visual performance for tasks at near distances and tasks in which his hands are involved.

GENERAL COMMENTS ON EXAMINATIONS

It may be advisable at times, when there is suspicion of disease or serious eye abnormalities, to temporarily paralyze a child's eyes with drops in order to test them. But a child's eye flexibility or vision performance cannot be adequately assessed when his focus is paralyzed. The most critical, intricate, and meaningful tests of children's vision usability and performance can be made only under conditions that approximate those in which he normally uses his eyes and vision.

The working order of a child's eyes, which is of utmost importance, cannot be evaluated when some of the functions are paralyzed. When in the course of an examination it is necessary to further check out the health of the eye, then the use of paralyzing drops can be understood. But when such procedures are deemed necessary, a conscientious and informed practitioner will usually carry out the examination in two separate appointments—one for health and the other for performance.

In summary, a visual examination, which every child should have early in life, should assess how a child is using his or her vision, how vision is serving or not serving the needs of the child. The next step should be to determine if there is anything that can be done to allow vision and vision functions to be more efficient. Different functions and skills are often tested first without lenses, and then retested using various lenses and prisms to ascertain how the youngster and his visual system respond to the changes produced by the lenses. Sometimes these can be dramatic; at other times there may be little or no change.

Different Uses of Lenses

As already mentioned, the use of lenses changes when the view of functioning changes. That is, different specialists will prescribe different lenses for your child depending on their view of vision. The major use of lenses formerly was to make up for an eye deficiency, usually for an error in the way the eye focused. We now know that lenses may also be useful and beneficial in changing visual skills, visual performance, or the efficiency of vision as a director of action as well as a guide to future vision development.

To help you understand the different kinds of lenses we prescribe, we can classify lens prescriptions according to the purposes for which they are prescribed. The main classifications are (1) compensatory lenses, (2) remedial lenses, and (3) developmental lenses.

COMPENSATORY LENSES

The purpose of a compensatory lens is primarily to make up for (compensate for) a lack of ability in, or an error of, the individual's visual mechanism—without a doubt the most commonly thought-of use for a lens prescription. Such lenses allow a person to experience more normal sight by compensating for inaccuracies in the way his eyes focus. Thus they allow the person to function more nearly as if his eyes did not have the inaccuracy.

The conditions that normally require a compensatory lens are: nearsightedness (myopia), excessive farsightedness (hyperopia), differences in meridional focusing power of the eye (astigmatism), two eyes focusing significantly differently (anisometropia) and crossed eyes (strabismus). Most often these lenses are worn most or all the time because the person doesn't see sharply without them, and often the person who needs a compensatory prescription will need it for the rest of his life.

While the most usual form of compensatory lens is spectacles, contact lenses are gaining in popularity. With the rapid advancement in the technology of contact lenses and improved cosmetics, more and more people are wearing this type of compensatory lens. This is especially true for people manifesting nearsightedness.

In addition to their improved cosmetic properties, contact lenses employ some different optical properties from those provided by the usual spectacles. Because they are fitted right on the eye rather than in front of the eye like a spectacle lens, contact lenses do not restrict the field of vision as much. They also do not produce the minification effects (reduce the apparent size of things) nearly as much as do concave spectacle lenses needed to compensate for myopia. Contact lenses are used frequently by people who engage in active sports because the interference of a frame is done away with.

In the past, contact lenses were used mainly for adults and teenagers. The main reason for this limitation was the dexterity required to insert the lens as well as the extra care the lenses require. More recently contact lenses have been successfully used with younger children, especially when there are special problems in which the advantages of this kind of lens prescription outweigh other considerations.

Compensatory lenses are sometimes inaccurately referred to as "corrective" lenses. This can be confusing, for people rightfully expect that, if they are corrective, the condition for which they are prescribed should get better. It is true that these lenses make up for (and in that sense they do "correct") inaccuracies of the focusing of the eye. But, normally, compensatory lenses do not *correct* the conditions for which they are prescribed. They merely *compensate* for them. Often, in fact, the conditions can be expected either to stay the same or, especially in nearsightedness, to continue to get worse.

Most children who become myopic, or nearsighted, continue to progress into more nearsightedness year after year. The younger the child when he first manifests this condition, the more it can be expected to progress. This progression usually slows down or stabilizes after puberty. It sometimes continues to progress, but at a slower rate, until young adulthood.

Because of this pattern of development, it was formerly thought that nearsightedness was almost exclusively caused by the eyes growing too fast. Today we know that young adults, and even people in the middle ages of life, do develop nearsightedness. The one factor that seems to correlate most closely with this development appears to be certain kinds of demands for concentration and for close distance seeing over long periods of time.

There is still much that is not understood about the development of myopia. Some of our work and that of others does show promise in sometimes slowing the progression, and even more promising are steps that can be taken before its onset to *prevent* myopia or nearsightedness.

All the different eye and vision care professions utilize compensatory lenses. The professionals who limit their view of vision more closely to eye functions usually limit the use of lenses to this one goal and purpose. We and others who hold the more encompassing view of vision (see pages 118, 120) recognize the value of additional kinds of lenses—lenses that can be used to change visual performance (remedial) or those which give direction to future development (developmental).

REMEDIAL LENSES

A more recent use of lenses than compensatory lenses, and one that is equally important, is that intended to bring about corrective changes or to allow vision and other performances to work in better coordination. Lenses used for this purpose are called *remedial lenses* and are sometimes referred to as *training lenses*.

Children who most often benefit from remedial lenses are those who have normal or near-normal visual acuity (sharpness of sight) for distances across the room. They may be children who are doing well in school but who suffer from visual symptoms after doing schoolwork. More often, remedial lenses are used with children who show moderate or severe difficulty in some or all school tasks or in physical activities that require fine eye-hand-body teaming. Most often when remedial lenses are used, the children who use them do not have "bad" eyes, but their visual skills may be clumsy; their eye pointing and focusing may be out of time or balance. These children may not have learned some of the refinements needed to sustain visual attention for the work they are required to do.

Remedial lenses are usually not strong-powered lenses. Sometimes, when such a lens is considered beneficial for reading or other close work but would interfere with distance seeing, the lens form prescribed may be bifocal. Such a lens in effect lets the child look at the chalkboard without any additional power, but, every time he looks down at his desk area, gives him the help of the remedial lens for this seeing distance.

This prescription of bifocals is just more dependable and simple than asking children to take their glasses off every time they look across the room and put them on every time they look at things close by.

Because remedial lenses are prescribed to bring about corrective changes, the outlook is that the child will need them for full-time wear for a relatively short period of time. This may be only weeks, or may occasionally be for as long as a year or two. Once the child's visual system has made an adjustment in the desired direction, the lenses are normally used only at certain times—generally for schoolwork, reading, and other concentrated nearby activities.

The decision to prescribe remedial lenses is based upon the child's demonstration that the lenses increase levels of performance in physical activities and reading or writing skills, as well as in visual skills. The child shows better coordination of visual skills and eye-hand skills with than without the lenses. There usually is a measurable increase in the smoothness exhibited between seeing and doing. The child may catch a ball better, be able to follow a moving target more accurately and smoothly, or be able to read faster and more smoothly.

Unfortunately, not all children having school or learning difficulties can be helped with remedial lenses. A child must have attained a certain level of visual and academic skills before remedial lenses can be effective. When basic visual and/or academic skills are not present, it is advisable that the child receive remedial and developmental help. When there is a reading problem, for instance, this help can sometimes be provided by special remedial aid or tutoring. Sometimes help can be provided by vision therapy or vision training programs.

As discussed earlier in this volume, many things besides visual problems can contribute to school and learning difficulties—such things as physical problems, psychological problems, developmental lag, hearing problems, even lack of basic learning potential. But while vision and vision care provide no magic answers to school learning difficulties, they certainly should be one of the first considerations—especially in our schools of today, which are so oriented to "look-hear" learning.

DEVELOPMENTAL LENSES

Vision and vision behavior develop, like other behaviors, through an orderly and predictable pattern. There is a lawful arrangement to the development of visual skills and abilities. But sometimes this development does not proceed as it should, and then lenses are

133

sometimes a help in directing and guiding visual development. When glasses are prescribed to serve this function they are called *developmental lenses.*

One special reason for using developmental lenses is to try to direct or control the development of vision and eyes during the school years. This use is sometimes also referred to as *preventive care,* or the use of *preventive lenses.* These lenses are used as occupational lenses—to aid the child in his tasks, to help protect him and his eyes from the adverse effects often produced by the demands of school.

Later in this chapter we shall discuss the relationship of some common visual problems to school behavior. The fact that school does demand that children keep their visual attention concentrated at close-by areas for relatively long periods of time is theorized as being one of the culprits. When lenses have been used *before* a problem develops, at least some of the potential problems can be avoided.

We all wear shoes to protect our feet, and gloves to protect our hands when it is cold. When we engage in certain activities we even take extra protective steps. When we play baseball, for instance, we wear a glove to protect the hand and to make it easier to catch the ball. Should not our eyes and those of our children receive this same consideration? It is possible to prevent at least some eye problems, to do something about them *before* they occur.

Vision Guidance Training

Lenses do not solve all problems of vision. They can provide a convenient and relatively easy way to effect favorable responses with *some* vision problems. We wish all problems of vision were simple enough that the child could achieve significant improvement with merely a lens prescription. Unfortunately, problems are often more complex. They may, for instance, be problems that involve the lack of development of fundamental vision skills, making it necessary to employ more direct programs of developmental guidance or to use vision training procedures or programs of vision remediation.

Programs of developmental guidance and vision training and remediation require a greater commitment on the part of the patient, the parents of the child, and the doctor. Such programs generally involve continued work over some period of time, and all are designed to help children develop more adequate ranges of vision functioning as well as learn to utilize vision and visual information efficiently.

DEVELOPMENTAL GUIDANCE PROGRAMS

Such programs are often worked out, with the help of his parents, for home guidance of the child. They may include guidance on how to structure a better visual environment, and may also often involve working through some preschool kinds of activities designed to encourage visual development. The activities may be very specific, aimed to develop certain special functions, or they may be more general in nature.

If the child is a young infant, the specialist might suggest bottle-feeding the baby from the right and left sides alternately. This will stimulate more equal development of both eyes. Nature intended this process, and it comes about naturally when a child is breast-fed. Or the suggestion might be made that the mother place the baby's crib in the middle of the room. Further, it is usually considered advantageous to regularly turn the head and foot of the crib in the room, or to turn the baby in the crib. This is important because one side of the room usually has more light than the other and therefore provides more balanced stimulation.

With school-age children, in addition to attention to lighting, the vision specialist may suggest ways of setting up a home study center. Too often desks are placed against a wall, restricting the child's field of vision. Or, worse still, they are placed in front of a window. Since vision first responds to brightness and movement, the child's vision attention then is being pulled away from his working area.

The height of desks or working tables is important. Too often they are too high. When the child sits in his or her chair and leans forward, elbows should just bump the desk top. Ideally, the desk surface should tilt at about a 20-degree angle. As you are reading this book, sitting in your chair, notice that, when you hold it in your hands, your tilting of it is a natural reaction. You automatically raise the top of the book about 20 degrees so that you can look at it more "straight on." In writing, too, this is a more natural posture. Desks used to be made this way until we became overly concerned with storage wells in the desks. A tilt-top board might be used on a desk.

Activities suggested to develop better eye and body coordination can be general or specific. They may include visually oriented gross and fine motor skills as well as specific games or activities. Specific programs are geared to helping develop specific functions, such as eye movement and eye pointing skills. Others may encourage better eye coordination or aim at better eye teaming, or encourage the development of eye focusing and changing of eye focus. For some of these activities one eye may be covered, or occluded. Often such activities are prescribed as gamelike procedures to be carried out at home every day or at frequent intervals.

When it is desirable for a program of developmental guidance, the vision specialist will want to see the child at regular intervals, which may vary from once a week to once every month or two. The purpose of such visits is for the specialist to evaluate progress and update activities prescribed to match the level of the child's current performance.

136

VISION TRAINING AND VISION REMEDIATION

Vision developmental guidance programs are primarily home centered programs directed and structured through office visits. Most of the actual work, however, is done at home. But with vision training, the program of remediation becomes much more an office-centered program. That is, most of the actual work is done in the office, though the office work is usually supplemented by the assignment of home activities.

Because vision training is an office-centered program, office visits are more frequent, the usual schedule varying from one to three office sessions a week and the time for each visit varying from half an hour to one and a half hours. The visits are designed to provide time to work at different activities, tasks, and procedures aimed to help the child learn to use vision, and vision skills, more efficiently and effectively than he has been doing.

The procedures and activities involved will differ depending on the child's particular problem in vision or in seeing skills. Programs also differ somewhat depending on the orientation of a particular practitioner. The majority of procedures employed involve instrumentation or instructional skills that make it impossible or impractical to relegate the program to an out-of-office setting. Vision training programs may require from twenty weeks to more than a year of work, the time needed depending on the problem and on the cooperation of the trainee.

When the child's problem is of such a nature that obvious seeing skills are distorted, as with crossed eyes, the program may be referred to as *orthoptics* (designed to normalize the eyes). Orthoptics is treated more as an exercise to develop skills that are lacking. Such programs are usually concerned with basic eye skills and are normally limited merely to considerations of eye movements and eye "weaknesses."

Vision training, on the other hand, involves a broader concept in

137

its approach. Here vision is considered, not only in terms of grossly distorted seeing patterns such as strabismus, amblyopia, etc., but also as it relates to the efficiency of using vision and visual information. Many youngsters who still can benefit from vision training actually have normal eyes and 20/20 visual acuity. Their problem lies in that they show difficulty in coordinating their visual system with their hand and body movements. They often show an inability to control their eyes and eye movements.

This lack of control may be something as obvious as a child's inability to keep his eyes looking at a moving target. Or even when the child can keep his eyes on the target, he might jerk his head, or his body generally, because of the excessive effort needed to control a movement that should be smooth, effortless, and without conscious control. When a child needs to "work" this hard at just controlling his eyes in order to be able to get them where he wants to see, it interferes with understanding of what he is seeing. Watch a teen-ager learning to drive a car. He is so involved with the mechanics of steering that he just doesn't see what is going on around him.

With other children, the vision difficulties experienced may not be quite as obvious. They may show up as difficulties in timing, in being slightly out of step in eye movements and focus changes. This kind of pattern can many times be attributed to a miscalculation in motor planning or prediction. After each move, a small corrective adjustment may be necessary. In essence, the child then must take extra steps, disturbing the rhythm or ballistics that should take place visually, and possibly interfering with the child's ability to interpret what he is seeing. He may lose his place while trying to read, reverse letters or words, or not recognize small changes that are being presented. The first signs of such difficulty are usually evidenced by loss of timing.

Small, subtle difficulties in coordinating vision movements and vision timing inevitably show up as some kind of inadequacy in dealing with problem-solving concepts. The child will either act as if there is a relationship that isn't necessarily there or he will fail to see a relationship that does exist. He in some ways will show difficulties in seeing how things are alike and how they are different, and will fail to see how bits of information can be not exactly alike and yet fit together in a meaningful way. To do this successfully requires that the person literally shift his seeing "as if" he were viewing the situation from a different vantage point. Such a shift does involve very small changes in eye pointing and coordination of focusing.

Office training sessions are devoted to activities, procedures, and tasks designed to help the child know better *how* he is seeing. They are also directed toward discovering and utilizing both greater ranges in visual movements and more effortless control of these movements, and emphasis is placed on rhythm and timing of visual acts. Many of the procedures used will involve gross body movements as well as problem-solving responses, in order to help coordinate the visual system with actions of the body and with thinking.

In a general way, vision training strives to allow children to find ways to reconcile what they do in the movement of their eyes with what they understand that they see. Visual movement, or the motor system of seeing, should be consistent with what one sees, or with the sensory system of seeing. It is common to find children with vision difficulties who do not know when their eyes move, do not know how their eyes move, or who do not see changes in a stimulus presented to them. When a change of stimulus is presented, such a child may converge his eyes (point them nearer to himself) and yet report that what he is seeing is now farther away. Would it then be any wonder that he might have difficulty in the next movement required of him?

Along with office vision training, the specialist will usually prescribe some home activities. These may sometimes look like mere exercises to get the eyes to move faster and more easily, or like mere game activities to encourage a child to see small differences, patterns, and sequences, but they are really more. Sometimes prescribed activities are carried out with special equipment, lenses, or prisms. At other times they may be more physical activities to allow for better visual control of body movements. Whatever their nature, these activities are an integral part of the training program.

When a child is engaged in a program of vision training, the doctor will usually prescribe training glasses for him. These may be for general wear or for wear only for specific activities. Often it is desirable to change the lens prescription as the child progresses in training. The use of the glasses is important because it can help the child to better transfer what he learns into everyday life situations. Vision training is not carried out simply in order to get rid of the need for glasses. Most successful cases will continue to use glasses for specific activities even when the training is terminated, most often for reading, writing, and other school tasks. The lens then serves to make vision easier and more efficient while these tasks are being performed and to keep vision development on a better course.

A final word on vision training: The vision training that has been done chiefly by optometrists is not accepted or carried out by all members of the eye care professions. This should be understandable in the light of the different ways professionals view and understand vision, as described on pages 117–121. Those who do not accept vision training agree that it works, but often attribute its success to the fact that it is a way of giving attention and tender loving care to children.

We do not agree with this reason for its effectiveness. Often the children we have worked with have had other programs in which they have been given attention and tender loving care, but without much of any result. Changes in behavior and performance that occur in our patients can, in our opinion, be directly related to change in their vision performance and abilities, and often such changes occur after a session in which the child has had to face and deal with an inconsistency in the way he was seeing a situation and using his eyes. This kind of "facing up" session will look, to an observer, like anything *but* tender loving care, since it is not easy for any of us to have to admit an inconsistency we have accepted in the past. Further, there is no reason to believe that people who are doing vision training have better ways of giving attention and tender loving care than do other professionals.

PART THREE: VISION AND SCHOOL

Use of Vision in School

Before going to school, children spend the greater part of their time dealing with a real-life three-dimensional world. They are actively involved in learning by doing. Their vision is not confined, but continually shifts to different places and distances. Space and distance judgments are probably the more important aspects of their seeing. They need to know "Where is it?" and "Where am I?"

When children reach school, the system is suddenly changed. They are asked to attend to representations of things put down on paper rather than to the things themselves. The world flattens out and becomes more two-dimensional, and the area of concern is nearby. The demand changes from *where* to *what* things are. Almost everything in school is merely a code to *stand for* real things. The world changes from a "look-do" world to a "look-say" world.

School demands of children that they see what isn't there, through some representation or code. They now must develop the ability and skill of using their vision to see what is represented in a code of letters, numbers, and pictures, and at the same time to *translate* that code and *see* what it stands for.

To use their vision this way demands that children have the flexibility of eye and visual skills to literally see in two places at one time. This at first may seem confusing, not clear. Try thinking of reading aloud. To do this smoothly, your eyes must be ahead of your voice—and yet you can hold on to these two different places at one time without getting lost. Or, when you are driving a car down the road at a moderate or fast speed, your eyes are looking ahead. In fact, even your movement of steering the car is "ahead" when you drive efficiently. You are driving where you are going to be, yet at the same time you are seeing and reacting to where you are at the moment. At one and the same time you are seeing what is and what might be.

We know from studies that we and others have made that the majority of children who experience school difficulty have healthy, normal eyes and 20/20 acuity. The problem these children show is not a problem of acuity but rather an inability to look at a situation differently from the way in which it is presented, which requires a change of their focus-alignment set. Children in trouble also show a lack of skill in their ability to control their eyes accurately without losing their place. This control is necessary for the visual manipulation of seeing meaningfully on a school-like task.

There are, of course, many other children who show normal, healthy eyes and 20/20 acuity and who do quite well in school. The difference between these two groups—those with normal, healthy eyes and 20/20 acuity who do poorly in school and those who do well—seems to be in the ability of those who do well to better control the more discrete adjustments of eye posturing and focusing balance. The successful group can focus and point their eyes "as if" the situation presented were in a different place, while still maintaining the ability to read or see what is presented. They show an ability to see in two places at one time.

EYE PROBLEMS VS. VISUAL PROBLEMS

For communication purposes it is possible to classify school-children's problems in vision into two general categories: (1) eye problems and (2) visual problems. The *eye problems* include the conventional problems of sight, reduced or lowered visual acuity, and gross problems of eye coordination difficulties. The *visual problems* include problems related to using vision effectively and efficiently and the finer skills of seeing. These problems can be thought of as visual clumsiness, lack of dexterity, and difficulty in teaming or matching vision in coordination with the other senses and movement systems of the body.

Children can have perfectly good eyes, good visual equipment, and still have serious visual problems. The eye condition by itself does not tell whether a child does or does not have a visual problem. On the other hand, many children who do have eye problems —such as nearsightedness or lazy eye—while they have certain limitations in seeing, can still use their vision very effectively, especially for certain kinds of tasks such as reading or studying. In fact, when most of us think of someone whose life is a life of books and intellectual pursuits, we think of someone wearing glasses. However, some children with eye problems do have serious visual problems, too.

EYE PROBLEMS IN SCHOOL

When children first enter school, only a small percentage of them show any significant eye problems. There are some differences, depending on the population and the area, but most investigations show only about one child in every ten having an eye problem at this age, and during the early years of school relatively few children develop eye problems.

From the third grade through the years of puberty there is a considerable rise in the development of eye problems, the most prevalent of which is nearsightedness, or myopia. While only a very small percentage of children have myopia when they enter school, from 20 to 30 percent of children are myopic when they finish sixth grade. And girls seem to develop myopia about six months earlier than boys.

There is a familial characteristic that relates to the development of eye problems. Children whose parents' or grandparents' families have a history of cross-eyedness are more likely to develop cross-eyes, and parents who are myopic are more likely to have children who will develop myopia. Even today, some professionals adhere to the theory that *all* eye problems are hereditary. They believe the eye is programmed completely before birth and that little or nothing can be done to change this course.

It is impossible to reconcile more recent studies with this belief. For some time it has been known that adults do develop myopia under certain special conditions. For example, submarine crew members—especially of nuclear submarines, which stay under water for long periods of time—are likely to develop myopia. College students engaging in intensive scholastic studies develop myopia, too, as records of the military academies will substantiate, and so do graduate students.

Young (109) has shown that monkeys develop myopia when they are kept in a restricted visual environment. Young and Baldwin (110), in a recent study of Eskimo families at Barrow, Alaska, report that up to 58 percent of the children manifested myopia while the grandparents showed virtually no myopia and the parent group, likewise, was mostly nonmyopic. The one most obvious change in the environment has been that Alaska became a state, and, as citizens of a state, the children must go to school. But whatever the cause, one can scarcely ascribe this sudden increase of eye problems in children and grandchildren of nonmyopic individuals to heredity.

Both our clinical and research data lead us to believe that some children develop eye problems in order either to maintain or attain certain kinds of achievement. Those children who are high achievers in school are more likely than others to develop eye problems, especially myopia. This is even more true when the child shows a fear of not achieving well, when his success is guided by an apprehension of the possibility of failure.

Our concern is that these children who develop eye problems

144

apparently find it advantageous or necessary to give up certain kinds of visual functions in order to attain success in the kinds of tasks demanded for school achievement. In some ways, the world of books and school, the abstract world, seems to become the real world for these children. In turn, the world of life, people, and reality becomes the abstract or "as if" world. If the purpose of school is to help people live more completely, it seems self-contradictory that a child should need to give up some of life's potential to achieve at school.

School vision screening and testing programs are usually designed to identify children with eye difficulties. There is general agreement among all professionals in the vision care field that care should be provided to help these children see more sharply. Children with eye difficulties are usually referred for vision care, but too often the school screening tests give parents a false sense of security. When their child passes the school's screening test, parents assume that he has good eyes and vision, and therefore does not need care. Unfortunately, school screenings say very little about how good a child's *vision* is. They are designed mainly to test his acuity or sharpness of seeing.

Even when a child has an eye defect, the methods of treatment recommended by different specialists will be somewhat different, depending on the specialist's belief. When his belief is consistent with the notion of vision as only an *eye* function, lenses will be prescribed to neutralize the optics of the eye. When a more involved concept of vision is considered, quite different lenses may be prescribed, depending on the skills and difficulties of the child. Also, more than likely the doctor will consider other aspects of seeing, such as differences in faraway and nearby seeing demands, study habits, and posture and activities needed to develop or enhance visual skills.

Those professionals who believe the eye is programmed before birth make no attempt to guide development, because to them it is already predetermined. Those like us who believe that what we do affects our seeing and how it develops, attempt to guide the future development in order to minimize the restrictions of any eye problem.

An example of these differences in treatment can be seen in what is done for the child who becomes nearsighted. Rather than just prescribe lenses to improve acuity, we would give some consideration as to whether the lens prescribed should be the same for distance seeing as for reading and close work. Further considerations would be made to checking study and reading habits, the distance the book is customarily held from the child's eyes, posture while reading, and visual skills that might be improved. The goal would not be to *cure* the myopia. The goal would be to try to help the child develop better visual performance.

VISUAL PROBLEMS IN SCHOOL

Our interest is in finding ways of preventing the development of eye defects and at the same time helping the child develop the kinds of visual skills and functioning demanded in his total life. And this, of course, includes school. In spite of having good acuity, some children often have not learned the necessary visual skills and abilities to handle the demands of school and/or other areas of life efficiently, often showing an inability to maintain good focus and eye coordination skills.

Such difficulties may be seen especially when these children try to respond or do something about what they are seeing. They are easily distracted, get lost, reverse letters and numbers, have trouble concentrating, and show difficulty in making purposeful, subtle adjustments of different systems of their bodies. They may show difficulty in matching eye-hand or eye-hearing activities. They may have the tools for seeing—but not the skill needed to use these tools effectively and efficiently.

Many of the skills and controls of seeing are *learned,* developing through the experience of using them. Vision is relatively slow in reaching maturation. Often children are not ready visually to do the things schools demand of them, since some of the muscles inside the eye that play a role in eye focusing are not developed until between six and eight years of age. Time alone can help some children, but more needs to be done to make certain that all children do have the opportunity to develop adequate visual skills.

Activities Involved in Seeing

It might be helpful to look at some of the main ways vision plays a role in what we do. It is possible to identify four categories of activities involved in seeing. These are: (1) adjustment of the body in efficient relationship to what we want or need to manipulate; (2) identifying significant forms, objects, events, or symbols in our surroundings; (3) synthesizing and unifying other sensations and experiences with the immediate visual ones to derive meaning; (4) directing action and recording significant experiences for later use in making performance and problem solving more efficient. While all of this is going on, one must continually make adjustments to hold his place and balance. In all of these activities, what a person is doing to accomplish them is at least as important as what is happening to him.

1. To see something we must be able to look at it. To look at it, not only do we have to be able to direct our body and attention to focus where we want to see, but we need visually to manipulate what we are trying to understand.

While it is obvious that our eyes are involved in this action, the fact that our general body posture and balance are also involved is often ignored. Indeed, 20 percent of the nerves coming out of the eye go directly to muscles of body posturing. You can check yourself on how seeing changes when your muscles are under extra tension by noticing the difference in what you can see when walking across a room and then when trying to balance on a two-by-four in the same room. As your body tenses, you tend to have to be more selective in your looking. You have to look harder to see a smaller area clearly.

2. When we mention identification of significant forms, objects, events, or symbols in our surroundings, most people can understand that this category includes sharpness of seeing or acuity. But it includes more than sharpness. It includes the ability to see relationships and to reorganize or understand different ways of seeing what is presented. Often people get stuck in what they are seeing—they do not see other possibilities of understanding or relating the parts of what is available. To understand something usually requires the ability to look at it in different ways, and to look at things in different ways requires doing something with the fine adjustments of your eyes and visual system.

To help make this more clear we show you a picture (figure 13). As you look at this picture, what do you see? It is an actual

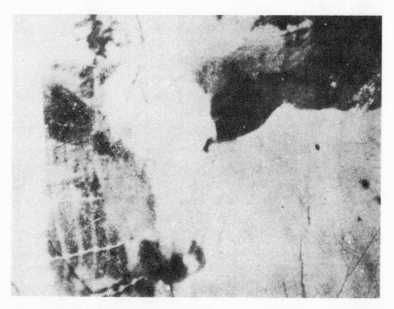

Fig. 13. Photograph of familiar object

photograph of a familiar object. While the photography is not the best, it is possible quite clearly to define what the picture is. And after you once do identify the picture, it will be very difficult *not* to see what it represents.

Certainly, in most cases your *acuity* is going to be the same before seeing the object and after seeing it. But your *identification* has changed, and so has your visual organization. You have been able to form a different figure, to relate parts of the picture in order to make sense, and at the same time to allow other information to recede into the background.

3. Another of the important ways vision plays a role in what we do is in the way we synthesize and unify other sensations and experiences with the immediate visual ones. Each of our different sensorimotor systems is tuned or focused for different kinds of information. They represent our receiving systems, which tell us what is happening around us. The information from different senses is always different—and should not be completely matched. At the same time, there needs to be enough sameness from different systems so we can *unify* them to make sense out of what they are telling us collectively. If we don't pay attention to the differences as well as the likenesses of all this information, we can be fooled into thinking that a total situation is different from what it really is.

An example of this can be shown by a familiar parlor trick. Two people hold a flat board two and a half feet off the floor. Have a child sit on the board. Blindfold him and then tell him that you are going to raise the board and that you want him to jump off when you give the signal. Instead, slowly lower it until it is closer to the floor. Most children can be fooled into thinking that the board was raised, only matching the movement with what they heard, that is, with what you told them. They do not attend to the difference between what you said and the feeling of going down.

4. The fourth thing we must do in seeing is to direct action and to record significant experiences for later use in making performance and problem solving more efficient. Vision is an important director of action. It is our fastest way of getting informa-

tion. Most people immediately think of eye-hand coordination in relation to this area, since this is one of the most critical areas of vision performance.

Many children show difficulties in eye-hand skills when they come to school. Some can do well with eye-hand skills when manipulating real three-dimensional objects but show extreme difficulties in more abstract activities, such as writing and drawing. Other children can direct their actions fairly well but have difficulty in remembering and learning from experience. They have difficulty in seeing how an experience relates to another task. They seem to approach each situation as if it were completely new—as if they had never before done anything that relates to it.

To direct action efficiently requires that we control our movements for coming events. We need to some extent at least to predict what will happen, and to do this we must be able to see ahead of what is going on. It is not uncommon to see children who can tell us what a diamond shape is but who have difficulty directing their hand to move to draw a diamond.

Each of the four kinds of behavior just described requires experience on the part of the child acquiring the skills. To gain skills, some children require more experience than others, and some require more directed development. Fortunately, children who are having difficulty in these areas of vision can usually be helped through care, guidance, and special visual therapy.

Signs of a Vision Problem

Signs of a vision problem can be looked for under three areas: (1) appearance of the eyes; (2) behavior that indicates possible vision difficulty; (3) complaints often expressed when the child is having difficulty. These are sometimes referred to as the ABCs of vision difficulty. The most important of these is the second or the area of behavior which indicates possible vision difficulty.

A. APPEARANCE

Among the more common signs that may indicate difficulty are: excessive blinking of eyes; excessive watering or tearing of the eyes when they are used for concentrated seeing tasks; inflammation of lids or whites of the eyes. Of course, any sign of one eye turning in or wandering out, even for relatively brief periods, should be considered a sign of the need of an immediate eye examination. Frequent sties also suggest possible visual difficulty.

B. BEHAVIOR

The Knox study, carried out at the University of Chicago (64), found certain behaviors particularly significant in relating to vision difficulty. Some of these involve general head and body posture. A child may find it necessary to hold his body rigidly while looking at objects far away. He may thrust his head forward or backward to see clearly across the room. Or, as he works at a desk or table, he may move his head rather than his eyes as he reads. One of the earliest signs of difficulty is holding the head too close to book or writing. Generally, this distance between eyes and object should be approximately the length of the forearm—the distance from the elbow to the knuckles.

There are other behaviors that relate more directly to how well a child can use his eyes. If he loses his place when reading, he is having trouble steering his eyes ahead. Some children may even show difficulty in just getting their eyes to find or move to the area they want to use. They may cover or close an eye while trying to concentrate visually, which usually indicates difficulty in eye teaming or cooperation. Another danger sign to watch for is a tendency to rub the eyes, especially as the child is reading.

In order to use vision efficiently, the eyes should be capable of moving effortlessly. To see something, the first demand is to be able to direct the eyes to point and move to look at whatever one wants to see. Often children have a great deal of difficulty in just following a moving object or looking from one place to another. If they find it necessary to concentrate just to get their eyes to carry out the mechanics of seeing, then it is certainly likely that this restriction will interfere with the work of understanding and learning through seeing. You might like to check your own child's ability to follow a slow-moving pencil or to look from the fingertips on your right hand to those on your left. Watch to see if his movements are smooth and accurate.

We have already mentioned a tendency for reversing numbers, letters or words as a possible sign of a visual problem. Most children normally go through a stage of reversing at about the age of five and a half to six years. When reversals continue beyond age seven, they usually are indicative of difficulty.

Eye-hand coordination is especially important for school tasks. A child who over- or under-reaches for an object is usually in need of help. Watch for signs of unusual awkwardness and of difficulty in getting hands to move closely together. Most children show the need for this eye-hand teaming while learning to read by using their finger to mark their place. We are aware that many schools frown on this practice, but our evidence shows that fingers help the child to keep his place and to read more smoothly more often than they interfere. Of course there should come a time when the finger is not needed. In order to avoid being criticized for looking at just one word at a time, have the child use all the fingers of his hand rather than just one finger to keep his place.

C. COMPLAINTS

We have already mentioned that all too often children do not complain when they are experiencing difficulty. When asked why they didn't mention their difficulties, they frequently reply, "Nobody asked me," or "Doesn't everybody see that way?" Sometimes they may be frightened by their experiences or think they are "bad." This is especially true of seeing double or having print blur out when they are trying to see it. If letters or things change size— look bigger and smaller to a child—it can be a pretty scary experience. Often headaches or nausea following visual tasks go unreported as well. An occasional question can help uncover some of these difficulties.

How Care Is Changing

Because of the changing understanding of what is involved in vision, as described earlier in this chapter, vision care today is likewise changing. It is possible to list three basic principles that give direction and guidance to this current change in visual care.

1. The first principle is a change in the view as to whether or not something can be done to help. When people believed that all of vision and vision development was programmed before birth, implanted entirely in the genes, then there was little or no reason to try to prevent problems of vision, or to guide the development of vision. *One just had to accept his or her (or his child's) lot and make the best of it.* While there still is some question as to how much one can change the visual system, there can be little doubt that environment, experience, and the development of skills *do* play a role in determining how we see. This realization has changed the direction of vision care from a mere patch-up kind of care concerned with the present to one that attempts to guide and direct the acquisition and development of present and future skills.

2. The second principle relates to the way seeing works. When the prevailing belief was that the only thing involved in seeing was to have clear images or pictures on the back of an eye, and the eyes pointing to the same place, then care was mainly thought of in terms of glasses to change the focus, or prisms to change the pointing of the eyes.

As beliefs changed to a recognition that what we do and how we

153

do it is also an important part of seeing, it became necessary to look at other components and behaviors during the act of seeing. This new view requires more extensive examinations, not only of eye focusing, but also of the way the person uses his or her eyes and vision in the kinds of tasks he needs or wants to carry out.

3. The third principle relates to decisions as to how and when to administer or recommend care. Within the conventional eye-camera analogy, prescribing glasses to improve acuity or sharpness of sight was the major consideration. Within the more encompassing concept of vision, even glasses or lenses are used differently. Many times the lens power that gives the best performance is not the same lens power that makes the eye look like a more perfect optical instrument. But when a lens allows a child to read significantly better, to be able to direct his motor movements of drawing or writing or even of catching a ball, it would seem foolish to deny him the use of the lens just because his eye doesn't exactly measure the same optics. Seeing is a function we cherish because it guides our doing and understanding.

Summary

In all considerations of vision care, one question is always foremost in our minds. How well is the person's vision and visual system serving his needs, his pleasures, his desires? The value of vision is to let man take in, manipulate, and understand information so that he can *do things,* so that he can act, so that he can accomplish. Accordingly, programs of care must always emphasize the role of vision and doing skills. The visual care professions are currently shifting their emphasis from vision as something that happens to the person to an understanding that what one does in relation to what is happening is what is important and something that has been a neglected component of evaluation and care. Now we realize that help *can* be obtained to make vision a more effective two-way system—the *motor and doing* aspects of seeing can be better co-ordinated and reconciled with the sensory system of sight.

WHAT PARENTS CAN DO

1. Be more aware of the role of vision.
2. Watch for signs and symptoms of vision difficulties.
3. Talk to your child about seeing. Ask him if he is experiencing difficulties.
4. Provide good lighting, study areas to fit the child, and room arrangements suited for visual tasks.
5. Provide opportunities for children to learn eye-hand and eye-body skills.
6. Have your child's vision and vision skills examined before school and at least once a year while he is in school.
7. When your child's vision is being examined, choose a doctor who will examine vision abilities within arm's reach (where the child uses his or her eyes most of the time). Approximately half the examination should concern itself with near tests.

WHAT SCHOOLS CAN DO

1. Provide desks and chairs that fit the child. In the classrooms we have observed, over 50 percent of the children were using desks that were too high for them.
2. Arrange the room so that children do not have bright window light competing with their work for their attention. Desks can usually be rotated so that no child has to face a window or have glare at one side.
3. Arrange for frequent out-of-desk activities. Young children should not be expected to keep at a concentrated desk seeing task for more than fifteen minutes to half an hour at a time. There should be very frequent opportunities to exercise the muscles of the body, including eye muscles.

155

4. Watch for signs and symptoms of eye or visual difficulty. Talk to the child's parents about your observations. Tell them what you have observed that may cause you concern.

5. Give more attention to sensory-motor skill development in the classroom. See Chapter 12, which is a description of one such program.

CHAPTER 9

DO WE PRODUCE READING FAILURE?

Methods of Teaching Reading

A first question we must ask when we think about reading is, What method of teaching will be most effective for that majority of our children who will be able to learn to read?

Why Johnny Can't Read by Rudolf Flesch was not only a best seller, it was a bombshell that opened many eyes to the fact that American schools in general were trying to teach children to read by a method that for many was proving ineffective. This was the so-called look-say method. Without learning the alphabet and without primary emphasis on phonics (spelling out words by the sounds of the letters), the child started right out reading whole words or sentences for their meaning. He was encouraged to try to recognize whole words on sight with the help of picture or meaning clues. Much of the time he merely guessed. Flesch urged that we abandon this method, and subsequent research, as well as common sense, supported this suggestion.

The best summary of the mass of information available about methods of reading and their relative usefulness is reported by Jeanne Chall in her comprehensive book *Learning to Read: The Great Debate* (18). She tells us:

My analysis of the existing experimental comparisons tends to support the idea that the first step in learning to read one's native language should be essentially the learning of a printed code (the alphabet) for the speech we possess. It does not support the prevailing view that sees the beginning reader as a miniature adult who should from the start engage in reading for meaning.

There is no evidence to show that one or the other leads to a greater love of reading later. There is some evidence that children of below-average intelligence and children of lower socio-economic backgrounds are the ones most in need of a phonic or alphabetic method of learning to read.

She notes that though clinical report suggests that there would be fewer reading failures with a phonic or alphabet method, *not even the very best method will prevent reading failure altogether*. But she emphasizes that those children *do* read best who are taught their letters or at least to pay attention to their letters right from the beginning.

They Weren't Ready

Clinical experience suggests, though as yet we do not have research studies to confirm this, that perhaps the majority of poor readers, or of nonreaders, experience the reading lack or difficulty they have chiefly because they were started in reading too soon, before they were ready.

Thus though some kindergartens and most first grades do attempt to teach children to read, and some people even try to teach preschoolers to read, clinical and practical experience show that, while perhaps the majority of six-year-olds are ready to learn to read, there are many other children who may not attain this readiness till they are seven, eight, or even older. As cases in Chapter 2 show clearly, many children in our schools are being taught reading long before they are ready for such teaching, and as a result fail miserably.

Hans Furth, in his book *Piaget for Teachers* (30), takes the position that in the early grades a strong emphasis on the teaching of reading is harmful. It gets in the way of the child's serious intellectual work: his exploration of the world and the exercise of thought. If allowed to do these things, the child will—almost as a by-product—show spontaneous interest in books and with minimal help will learn to read.

A preliminary report (75) from 216 California school districts that operate reading programs under the Miller-Unruh Basic Reading Act showed that most of the reading difficulties experienced by pupils in the first grade are related to maturation. That is, the children failed because they were not ready.

The result of premature instruction tends to be that the child who is started too soon either is put off reading entirely—it's just too hard, and his efforts give him no satisfaction or success—or he persists with it, tries hard, and becomes hopelessly confused.

Arthur Jensen (61) puts this well when he explains:

> Recent animal research on readiness factors in learning, and some of my own observations of certain classes in which many children appear not to be learning much of anything at all despite heroic efforts of teachers, lead me to hypothesize that ignoring readiness can have adverse psychological effects beyond merely not learning what is being taught at the time it is being taught.
>
> These adverse effects seem to take two main forms: The child may learn the subject matter or skill by means of the cognitive structures he already possesses; but because these structures are less optimal than more advanced structures in the sequence of cognitive development, the learning is much less efficient than it otherwise might be.
>
> The second adverse effect of ignoring readiness by persisting in instruction beyond the child's present capability is to cause the phenomenon of "turning off." I believe this can be so extreme that it may eventually prevent the child from learning even those things for which he is not lacking in readiness.

Nature seems to have planned very wisely for human development. As noted earlier, the child's behavior as well as his body does develop in a patterned, predictable way. We can and do know the usual stages children go through as they learn to read, and the approximate time when each of these stages appears.

But regardless of a child's age, *if* he has not yet spontaneously reached the earliest stages of interest in reading—looking on when read to, picking out initial capitals, spelling out such simple words as *hot, cold, stop, go* (or at least asking what these letters stand for)—there is little use in trying to teach him to read, no matter how eager you may be for him to attain this accomplishment.

A next and quite normal stage in learning to read takes place when the child is somewhere around five and a half to six years of age. Many perfectly normally developing children go through a (usually) brief stage when they tend to *reverse* letters and words.

If they have, of their own accord, already started successful reading before they come to this stage, most get through it with only a little awkwardness, and no real or lasting difficulty. (It is important for teachers and parents of any child who is going through this stage of reversal not to make too much fuss about it. You say, when the child makes a reversal error, "That's your way now. Pretty soon you'll do it this other way.") But if school or parent pushes a child who is in this reversal stage, but has not yet started reading of his own accord, into starting to learn to read, considerable confusion may result.

In fact, when any child is pushed into reading before he is ready to start it spontaneously and of his own accord, trouble and confusion may well be the outcome.

It is the opinion of remedial reading teachers of note that *if all children were permitted to wait to start reading until they showed spontaneous readiness and were thus permitted to proceed at their own rate, we would have very few reading problem children.* If you wait till your child shows a wish and readiness to start learning to read, chances are he will not become a problem reader.

Unpublished research by Norman Heimgartner of Colorado (49) reports a correlation of developmental age and reading level of 0.91, and a correlation of chronological age and reading level of only 0.70. Expressed in a different way, he found that, when the developmental age of a child is known, the prediction for reading success is 0.84; when the developmental age is not known, the prediction for reading success is only 0.51.

Research in progress at the Gesell Institute suggests that many children who are considered reading failures or remedial readers actually are reading at their true developmental level and thus are reading as well as one might reasonably expect. The problem may lie in the fact that they are overplaced in school and thus that the school is expecting too much.

In connection with this, we recently saw an eight-year-old second-grader who was considered by the school to be failing in reading. Careful examination showed that he was reading at a pre-first-grade (five-and-a-half-year-old) level, and that his developmental level—that is, his general level of behaving—was also five and a half. Thus reading matched or went along with his level of development. School, and not boy, was in error. He was reading as well as anyone could reasonably expect. He was merely in the wrong grade.

Whether or not a child will become a good and avid reader will depend largely on his basic endowment. We can't guarantee that, if you wait long enough and place your child correctly in school, he will become a good and eager reader. Some never do. Much research needs to be carried out before we can tell you for sure why some children cannot read, or what you must do to help them. But your chances of having a problem reader on your hands will be much less if you wait till the child shows readiness before trying to teach him.

How long in general should you wait? It may be hard for you to believe, but there are some slow-developing boys who may not be ready to start reading till they are fully eight years of age. It's a long time to wait, but better to wait than start before they are ready, confuse them (often hopelessly), and then subject them to remedial reading instruction that may help temporarily but that may not be of lasting value.

We repeat: *If you start teaching a child to read before he is ready, confusion and failure may very well result.*

More than this, it is important in our thinking about any given child not to separate his unsatisfactory reading out from the rest of his unsatisfactory behavior. If a child is dull, immature, perceptually handicapped (or all three), the fact that he is failing to read at grade level is in no way remarkable. His problem is not just reading. The solution of his problem will not be reached simply by teaching him to read.

How Effective Is Remedial Reading?

Now, what can we do for those many who either because they are taught too soon, are taught by ineffective or inadequate methods, have substantial visual problems that need to be solved before they can be expected to read effectively, or who because of their own special endowment or lack of endowment, will unfortunately fail to learn to read? What can we best do to and for them?

Over the past several decades, remedial reading has been offered as the answer for most. In light of recent findings we must ask, Is it the best possible answer? Is it even a very good answer? It may not be. Yet all over the country thousands of remedial reading teachers work diligently to help those children whose reading is either nonexistent or was potentially present but has been botched up by our educational system. Some school systems even boast, "We have an unusually large remedial staff," or, "We've just added ten people to our remedial staff."

The theory behind this is that if a child has not learned to read, that failure must be remedied. And who more appropriate to remedy it than the remedial teacher? Having pushed the children into failure, the schools quite naturally find it necessary to try to correct that failure. Apparently nobody thinks to question either whether all of this is a good idea or even whether or not it works.

Now, finally, both questions *are* being explored and the answer, some believe, is no to both. Remedial reading may indeed *not* be a very good idea. And it may not even work.

Recent research reported by Drs. Norman and Margaret Silberberg reports the startling and rather shocking fact that though much remedial reading does seem temporarily to improve reading skill, *"follow-up studies almost invariably demonstrate that the beneficial effect of the remediation washes out in a relatively short time after the termination of the remedial help"* (90).* And, more than that, we have evidence that schools do push many children into a need for remedial services by the mere fact that they permit, or require, many children to start reading and other academic work before they are ready for it.

On the other hand, in one elementary school in Visalia, California, we have the report that the number of children requiring remedial help was cut from fifty-eight to eight by the simple expedient of placing all the children developmentally—that is, starting them in school only when developmental tests showed that they were fully ready.

In addition, recent research by George von Hilsheimer (98) reporting results of a study of a resident population of 527 adolescents in a school for children with severe learning disabilities, school failures, social maladjustment, and other problems, found that attempts to accelerate cortical maturity by psychic energizing drugs proved not only safe but, in a triple blind study, significantly superior to placebo or no treatment. Reading ability was significantly enhanced by this type of treatment. Von Hilsheimer suggests that research be directed to regulation of the dynamic homeostasis of the entire biological system as a means of correcting specific learning disabilities. He notes that his study "tends to confirm the findings of other researchers that instruction is not the intervention of choice for specific learning dysfunction, but that biological regulation, and maturation, may be sufficient as well as necessary."

* Italics ours.

All of this does not mean that all remedial reading teachers should suddenly resign. Nor does it mean that if your child is currently getting remedial reading help, he should give it up. Remedial reading will continue to be given in our schools for quite some time. And though the ultimate value of remedial instruction is now being questioned, at the moment it may be the best help available for your nonreader.

The Possibility of a Bookless Curriculum

Waiting till the child is really ready before you start teaching him to read is thus one good way to prevent failure. Another way would be, perhaps, to attempt to provide something different from the usual curriculum for those who need something different.

As the Silberbergs have suggested (91), could not the money, time and brain power currently being spent in remedial reading better be focused on less painful ways of presenting a curriculum to a child? Or could it not be used to look at ways to expand the curriculum to meet the needs of more children, *rather than attempting to find new ways of altering the children's behavior to meet the needs of a rigid curriculum?* We agree that "what is needed is to stop and look at our curriculum in the light of its relationship to problems of the real world. Cannot educators renovate the classical eighteenth century curriculum *designed for the talented few, and foisted on the unwary many?*"*

The Silberbergs suggest, for the many who are not going to be able to read or at least are not going to be able to read well, what they call a "bookless curriculum." They point out that our standard requirement that a child must be able to read in order effectively to pursue education as it is offered today in our schools deprives many of comfortable avenues of learning.

For the nonreader, education then becomes, not a matter of re-

* Italics ours.

ceiving knowledge, but rather an experience of being drilled toward being able to learn to read (something he often never really learns to do) while delaying his education until this elusive skill may have been attained. Historically, it made sense to base learning on the ability to read. It used to be appropriate for the type of student being educated. But now there are many children in our schools who probably will never learn to read very well.

We currently place all our eggs in the reading basket. Could we not and should we not consider other methods for nonreaders? Certainly every effort should be made to teach all children to read. But if and when we fail, could we not try tape recordings, books on records, films, projectors, art, music, role playing, field trips, discussion, guest lectures?

In what is called a bookless curriculum, any means of conveying knowledge without requiring literacy is acceptable. Some efforts at remedying the nonreading will be continued, and any child who is suited should be moved into a reading curriculum. But for those not suited, learning should not be delayed until they perfect what for many may turn out to be a nonexistent skill. How about it?

For some children, the different kind of material or presentation needed may not be as extreme as the institution of a bookless curriculum. Concerned book publishers for some time now have been extremely active in attempting to produce more interesting and more stimulating and more "relevant" reading books. But there is still much criticism of the books available. As Professor Sol Gordon, Syracuse University psychologist, recently commented, "Dick and Jane are now black, urban, relevant, *and as boring as ever.* Kids are interested in fantasy, excitement, new things, not just in something that's relevant. Dr. Seuss is completely irrelevant and everybody loves him" (43).

Dyslexia

Now, at the risk of confusing some of you (and ourselves) we'd like just to mention a strange condition called *dyslexia,** a condition in which a presumably normal girl or boy, of adequate intelligence and with no marked or special visual problems, simply cannot learn to read. This condition in many appears to be congenital, that is, it runs in the family. If your boy or girl does seem to be truly dyslexic, then you will, indeed, require the help of a child specialist. Treatment at present is difficult and often unsatisfactory, but, hopefully, research and improved teaching methods may soon unlock this special problem.

However, before you go to great lengths and/or great expense in this direction, be sure you're not like the group of mothers from a Boston suburb who complained to a visiting psychologist about their dyslexic children. After the mothers had gone, the psychologist asked the school principal how it happened that there were so *many* cases of dyslexia in this one school. "Because dyslexia is very big up here right now," the principal replied with some cynicism.

Be sure you don't rush out to get help for your child's "dyslexia" just because it is very big in your own neighborhood right now. And at least heed the warning of one of the editors of the *Journal of Learning Disabilities,* Dr. Richard L. Carner of the University of Miami, who notes that there is "more than one reading 'expert' in this country who apparently spells out the problem as DY$LEXIA" (17).

It's fair to say that only rarely have we ourselves ever run into the case of a child whose inability to read could not be explained on some purely reasonable, understandable, and usually treatable

* It is interesting to note that no mention of this term was made in the official report of the Right to Read Forum of the 1970 White House Conference on Children and Youth or in the forum discussions that preceded the report.

166

basis. Mostly it seems to result from too-early introduction to the requirement of reading, low intelligence, some (often correctable) visual or perceptual problem, or a need on the part of some individual child for a different and special method of being taught.

Thus, consider the case of Dwight, an eleven-year-old boy who was repeating fourth grade and who was referred to us because of his "dyslexia" and his generally poor school performance.

An examination showed that Dwight was intelligent, but extremely immature (his developmental level no better than nine years at best), of a highly scattered endowment (range from six through nine and a half years), suffering from rather marked visual difficulties (farsightedness, amblyopia, disorganization). His personality as reflected in his Rorschach response was restricted, passive, and showed very low motivation or inner drive and very low or poor sense of self.

But Dwight *could* read. His reading level, like his arithmetic performance, was at an eight-year-old level. This was admittedly not up to either chronological or behavior age, but he *could* read. Labeling him dyslexic and giving him remedial help wasn't really helping very much with his problem, which was a total problem, not simply that his reading was rather inadequate.

Fortunately, he had already been replaced into fourth grade when we saw him, and, hopefully, a correct lens prescription, visual training, and some sort of glandular help (if an endocrine checkup, which was prescribed, indicates as we suspect it will that this is needed) will get Dwight on the road toward a more adequate school, and life, performance.

If, as is sometimes the case, a perfectly normal and bright fourth-grader is reading well at a second- or third-grade level and is thus not up to fourth-grade standards, the path of wisdom may be to permit him to read at a second- or third-grade level. It is not particularly useful to label a child with reading difficulties as dyslexic, or as anything else, *unless* this labeling is used as a first step toward

167

taking action of some kind. Action, as in Dwight's case, may consist of putting him in a lower grade, or at least of having him read at a lower grade level, giving him special individual help with reading (though this did not help with Dwight), giving him the usually needed visual or perceptual help, or even possibly considering some degree of endocrine help or drug therapy.

Positive reports are now coming in from reputable reading clinics and reading specialists as to the extremely favorable effects from the use of Ritalin, a powerful stimulant whose effects are like those of the amphetamines, in those cases where the special problem of hyperkinesis (overactivity) seems to lie at the basis of poor reading ability. However, extreme caution must be exercised in any use of such medication, as emphasized in Chapter 11.

One particular remedy for reading disability that parents should approach with even more caution is the type of neurophysiological training provided by the Institute for the Achievement of Human Potential in Philadelphia. An excellent report on this type of training is given by O'Donnell and Eisenson in the highly reputable *Journal of Learning Disabilities* (76). They point out that

according to the Delacato theory, the frequently observed characteristic of crossed or uncertain lateral expression in children with reading problems is an indication of the lack of hemispheric dominance, a final step in the process of neurological organization. Delacato further asserts that adequate reading skills can develop only after adequate neurological organization has been achieved. Therefore he urges that disabled readers with anomalies of lateral expression be given training, following his methods.

O'Donnell and Eisenson conducted careful research to determine whether or not the much publicized Delacato-recommended training would result in any substantial improvement in reading ability as measured by the Gray Oral Reading Test, or by any subtests of the Stanford Diagnostic Reading Test, or whether it would make any substantial differences in children's visual-motor integration as measured by the Developmental Test of Visual-Motor Integration.

Their careful research indicated that no statistically significant improvement was brought about by the Delacato methods of training.

Vision and Other Related Factors

Current research at our Institute is investigating the relationship of visual performance to reading ability. It is our strong belief that vision does relate specifically to academic performance. Preliminary data support our notion that children with reading problems have difficulty with visual scan, especially in the lateral orientation.

Among first-grade teachers whom we have interviewed, one common observation was made in relation to children having difficulty in reading, namely that such children could not sequence eye movements and voice. That is, the teachers reported unanimously that this group of children looked at the word, said it, then looked at the next word and said that word. Children who scored well in reading could be visually scanning *ahead of* the words they were verbalizing.

When we have covered one eye, and alternately oscillated a prism before the uncovered eye of a child while he looked at a target, there seemed to be a significant difference between many of the children who read in the word-by-word look-say way and those who read with a good flow. This research is in a preliminary state at present, but if this and other proposed relationships between visual performance and reading can be established, it should mean that at least some if not many poor or ineffective readers can be helped, visually, to a better reading performance.

Research of other investigators supports our own belief that visual problems of one sort or another may lie at the root of a substantial proportion of reading disabilities. Thus Stanley Krippner, in an intensive study of 146 poor readers with WISC I.Q.s between 87 and 112 referred to a reading clinic, found that, in the opinion of clinicians making judgments, poor visual-perceptual skills were the most common causative factor in cases of reading disability (67). The table which follows lists the difficulties most often experienced by his 146 poor readers. Though immaturity did not show up in this study as often as in our clinical practice, in a general way these findings agree with our own.

CAUSATIVE FACTORS IN THE READING DISABILITIES
OF 146 PUPILS OF AVERAGE INTELLIGENCE
REFERRED TO A READING CLINIC

PROBLEM	PERCENT OF CHILDREN SHOWING
Poor visual-perceptual skills	62
Unfavorable educational experiences	57
Poor auditory-perceptual skills	36
Neurotic tendencies	34
Impaired acuity of sight	28
Directional confusion (left and right)	26
Brain injury	21
Disturbed neurological organization	21
Defective speech	19
Social immaturity	17
Endocrinal malfunctioning	12
Impaired acuity of hearing	9
Cultural deprivation	6
Sociopathic tendencies	6

Summary

In short, many children who fail at learning to read might be successful if they were not required to start till they were developmentally ready and if they could be taught by a phonic or phonetic method. It is much better to wait for readiness than to start too soon, push the child into frustration and failure, and then try to pick up the pieces by means of remedial reading, which, even if seemingly successful at the time, may have no long-lasting positive results.

Also, since visual-perceptual problems appear to be involved in a substantial number of cases of reading disability, there is also a good possibility that visual research may turn up effective methods of improving reading ability through efforts at improving a child's visual performance.

Waiting, effective methods of teaching, and possibly specific vision help may be the answer for those many children who do, if all factors are favorable, have within themselves the potential ability to learn to read. For the many who because of low intelligence, serious perceptual problems, or possibly some sort of undefined learning disability, which makes reading come very hard indeed, it is just possible that we might and should devise some different type of curriculum that does not base all learning on the ability to read.

CHAPTER 10

DON'T BELIEVE ALL YOU HEAR

So very much is written about child behavior these days that it's no wonder many parents are confused about what *to* believe. Our advice is not to believe everything that *anybody* says. Don't even believe all that *we* tell you if it doesn't make sense from the point of view of your own experience.

We must admit that the main emphasis of this book—that children should ideally be started in school and subsequently promoted on the basis of their behavior age rather than their age in years, and thus should be homogeneously grouped on the basis of behavior level—goes very much against much that is being practiced and recommended in the schools today.

Not only is the importance of readiness questioned nowadays, but even the more basic notion that behavior is a function of structure and that children behave as they do to a large extent because of the way their bodies are built and because of the behavior level they have reached.

Rather than attempt to place every child in the grade for which his behavior readiness suits him, there are those who would do away with grade levels altogether. There are many others who believe that inadequate performance results, not from unreadiness or immaturity, but merely from an unsupportive environment. And, rather than evaluate a child's maturity and level of ability and then suiting the school situation to it, there are many who hold out the hope that maturity can be speeded up, as well as intelligence increased, by intervention programs both in school and at home.

There are some who would go even farther. Not only would they do away with evaluative measures of readiness, and with demarcations between one school grade and another, they would do away with curriculums, examinations, report cards, and even with the schools themselves, as we now know them. There is much talk today about "alternative, optional forms of public education, massively funded by the federal government."

Certainly we must all be alert to the possibility of improving any given child's effective functioning in any way we can. Certainly we must be on guard against stereotyped curriculums, tradition-bound ways of teaching and treating the children in our schools. Certainly we must be open and receptive, not only to different ways of teaching, but to the possibility of establishing different types of schools. But, as George von Hilsheimer has put it, "the whole hate-the-schools cabal has very thin soup to offer. It is easy to criticize. The patient building of effective schools and the patient toil of scholarship seems sometimes to be just too much for the progressive mentality" (97).

This chapter will discuss some currently held notions about school behavior that do not fit in with our own findings. We cannot warn you against everything false that will come your way. But we can discuss a few of what we consider the more widely available bits of misinformation.

There are, of course, great differences of opinion among those who seek to advise you. We cannot guarantee that our own point of view is always the right, true one. But if this book has made sense to you so far, perhaps you will at least like to know what we think about some of the more controversial issues of our time as they relate to you and to your child's education.

"He Could Do Better If He Would"

Of all the sad words of tongue or pen, these may be the saddest. They are uttered, day in, day out, year in, year out, by parents and teachers all over the country—and possibly all over the world.

What they mean is that here is this child, well endowed and perfectly capable of a "satisfactory" performance, who just plain isn't *trying*. And if he would only try he could do whatever it is that is expected of him.

Clinical experience shows that the words in the phrase should be reversed. We should correctly say, not "He could do better if he would," but, rather, "He would do better if he could," for, so far as one can determine, most children do as well as they are able. The notion that they could do better if they would tends to be based on a false conception of ability.

Sometimes people feel that if a child is bright—that is, if he has a high I.Q.—he should be able to succeed in school. This presumes that the intelligence alone goes to school and that mere brightness is enough. Or the child may have done well on some ability test, giving the teacher or parent the notion that, therefore, he should be able to do well in class. Sheer ability as tested on some test or other may not guarantee a total, good school performance. At any rate, in our clinical experience it has seemed that there are few exceptions to the rule that most children do as well as they are able. Ineffective or inadequate as performance may be, most *are* trying.

A corollary of the (untrue) rule that most children could do better if only they would try is the notion that if you could just *motivate* them they would succeed. It is true that some outside force can sometimes set up short-term goals that can cause certain children to work harder or more effectively than they have been doing, at least in short-term gusts and spurts. To be permanently effective, however, it would almost seem that motivation must come from within. And it has seemed to us, as mentioned earlier, that perhaps the most effective motivator is success.

That child who is correctly placed in school, at the right grade level, in the right kind of class, and given tasks he has a reasonable likelihood of accomplishing—that is, the child for whom school is a successful situation—for the most part seems to be the one who shows the greatest motivation.

Don't Believe All You Hear

A word of warning: Some children, whether for health reasons or simply by reason of their basic personality makeup, do seem to have much more energy and drive than do others and thus, quite naturally, give the impression of being more highly motivated than others. So far, in our schools, we do a rather poor job of measuring energy. Thus many children may be faulted for not being motivated, or not trying, or not doing as well as they should, simply because they are, at the moment or permanently, low-energy children.

We need to know much more than most of us now do about children's basic physical endowment and function before we shall be in a position to help all children, as we would so much like to do.

Don't Worry About Immaturity—The Immature Child Will Catch Up, Given Time

This notion is very widely held, and it represents a quite natural error. It seems reasonable to assume that, if a child is immature, given time he will become more mature, and so he will.

Let's say a five-year-old is behaving only like a four-and-a-half-year-old. Give him six months more and he will, in all likelihood, be behaving like five. But, alas, time hasn't been standing still for him, and so, now that he's behaving like a five-year-old, by birthday age he will be five and a half. For him to "catch up," there would need to be a *relative* gain in the rate of growth. His behavior would need to grow more than six months in six months of time—it would need to grow, say, twelve months.

This could happen. An immature child could suddenly put on a spurt of growth and his behavior *could* catch up to his age. If your own child is developing a little slowly you can always hope for such a spurt. But it happens rarely enough so that you should not count on it.

You Can, and Should, Help Your Child to Mature

Along with the hope that a child may just catch up on his own, many parents are hopeful that if they but do the right things they can help him mature. For instance, if told that their child is immature and needs to repeat a grade, parents often ask psychologist or school what they can do, over the summer, to help him mature.

Certainly most parents want to give their child freedom, experience, opportunity, support, so that he will have a chance to express what maturity he has attained. They will try to avoid pampering and overprotecting or encouraging him to act in a babyish way. But maturity level depends for the most part on actual development of the body, especially of the nervous system, and so far we have no recipe for speeding it up.

Dr. Arnold Gesell, as long ago as 1912 (34), phrased it succinctly when he advised that "it is time to have a reckoning and to realize before it is too late the futility of pushing nature."

"He's Babyish Because You Baby Him!"

One of the most aggravating things teachers, and others, often say to mothers is that some certain child "is babyish because you're babying him."

There is sometimes a grain of truth in this accusation. It is possible for a mother to permit her boy or girl to cling to her and behave in a babyish, dependent way because she likes it. Some little birds, do, indeed, need to be given a slight shove out of the nest.

More often, though, when a mother protects her child, when she permits him to behave in a manner characteristic of an individual younger than his chronological age, it is because he actually is im-

176

mature. *Mothers tend to have an instinct as to the kind of behavior it is and is not reasonable to expect from their own children.*

Thus if, on examination, we find that a certain five-year-old is responding in most ways like a four- or four-and-a-half-year-old, it seems fair to consider that he is in almost every such instance expressing a genuine biological immaturity and not merely responding to some degree of overprotection on the part of his mother. That is, a mother might by overprotection cause a child to cling to her and depend on her and fail to venture out into the world as fully as one might expect. But it would be most difficult and most unusual for a mother to baby a child to the extent that he as a total physical organism—hands and eyes and brain—would respond in a manner less mature than that for which he was ready and able.

Prematurity Does Not Present Any Real Danger

In an effort to make parents of premature children feel secure, child specialists have perhaps gone a little bit overboard.

Everyone recognizes, of course, that serious physical danger threatens the prematurely born child. The smaller the baby, the greater the danger. But many parents have been led to believe that, once the baby is strong enough to come home from the hospital, or, if he has been at home right along, once he seems surely to be thriving physically, one's troubles are over.

We ourselves used to say, years ago, that, *if* the premature infant or child appeared to be physically healthy, chances were that no special consideration need be given him other than subtracting the amount of his prematurity from his official age. Thus, say he were four weeks premature, twelve weeks after he had been born he would in reality be only eight weeks old. So you would expect of him only the behavior of an eight-week-old, and this would indeed be serious consideration. But later on, when he was, say, twenty-four *months* of age, and thus should be expected to behave like a twenty-three-months-old child, this discrepancy would not be so great and no special thought perhaps need be given.

Time and newer knowledge have changed this. Now that we know more about child behavior than we did and are more aware of the big difference that small discrepancies can cause, more serious care is given to the premature boy or girl. Certainly you don't want to borrow trouble, and, if your premature child is managing nicely, don't start worrying.

On the other hand, if such a child is having any sort of difficulty, either physically or academically, it may help you in your planning for him to keep in mind that, in general, premature children do seem to have more trouble growing up than those who were carried to full term. It is almost as if the baby had very much needed those final weeks inside his mother in order to mature properly.

Lula Lubchenco (70) in 1963 commented on the high incidence of academic failure and specific learning deficits among premature children, and Katrina DeHirsch and colleagues (20) in 1966 indicated that, in a study of theirs, maturational patterns of prematurely born children seemed much more erratic than those of children born at full term. They also note that the literature tends to report more reading-problem children among those prematurely born.

These investigators found that, on kindergarten tests they administered, the prematures made an almost uniformly poorer showing than those born at full term, reading and spelling difficulties continuing as late as age eight in many of the children. DeHirsch reports these findings with some reservations, since one does not wish to cause anxiety in the minds of parents of premature children. She does note, sensibly, that to ask whether the premature's inferior performance is related to actual neurological damage, or to a severe and pervasive maturational lag, would fail to do justice to the complexity of the problem.

True, indeed. We would like to point out that some of the reportedly poor academic performance of many premature children

178

may be due simply to the fact that when these children are entered in school on the basis of their chronological age, correction is often not made for prematurity. Thus, a one-month premature child who just barely made a school deadline of six in September for first grade would not have been eligible to begin first grade if his true expected birthday (October) were considered.

The I.Q. Is Not a Fair Measure

One of the less rational arguments that some people advance, in this time when many irrational arguments are being proposed with regard to our children in school, is the argument that the I.Q. is not a fair test and should be abandoned.

The excuse is given that, since some children score low on I.Q. tests, these tests are not fair. This notion is based on the idea that intelligence is determined or at least strongly influenced by home conditions and thus that testing is not fair to children from poor homes. For this reason, what are called *culture fair* or *culture free tests* were set up and used with some inner-city children. In most instances, children did not rate differently on the culture fair tests than they did on the traditional intelligence tests.

Since this solution did not work, some cities, like New York, have abandoned intelligence testing altogether. But as somebody has pointed out, abandoning (or prohibiting) the tests because you do not like the results is like throwing away the thermometer because you do not like the fever it measures.

Intelligence, operationally defined, is the aggregate capacity of the individual to act purposefully, to think rationally, and to deal effectively with his environment. (Since one obtains almost the total range of I.Q. scores from children in the same environment, or even in the same family, it seems to many unreasonable to assume that it is the environment that determines intelligence.) An I.Q. is merely a measure of brightness. It merely asserts that, compared with persons of his own age group, an individual has attained a certain relative rank on a particular intelligence test. David Wechsler points out (100), and rightly, that if intelligence tests *are* unfair, they are merely recording the unfairness of life.

As Freeman (29) comments very sensibly:

I.Q. tests are an extremely useful instrument to identify the relative ranking and prospects of any individual. All human traits such as height, weight, physical strength, etc., are distributed on a curve of some shape. There is no reason to assume that intelligence—even if it consists of several components—is not so distributed. Supposing we had no I.Q.'s or other yardsticks by which to measure individuals. There would still be 10% of all people whose intelligence is below that of the other 90%, whether you had test scores to identify these individuals or not.

The whole question of the value and proper use of intelligence tests is a complex one and need not be labored here. Suffice it to say that, intelligence tests or no intelligence tests, some children do definitely seem to be better endowed intellectually than others, regardless of their race or home background.

The more we know about any child's level of intelligence, as about any other aspect of his endowment or behavior, the better job we can do in planning for him academically. It is to be hoped that the measuring of intelligence will soon be restored in the New York City schools and elsewhere.

You Can Increase Your Child's I.Q.

Chances are you can't, substantially. An I.Q. figure may quite normally vary, from time to time, in any one child by as much as ten points or even more. This doesn't mean that the child is actually brighter or basically more intelligent at one time than another. It does mean that it is difficult to obtain an exact measure of anything as complicated as intellectual level.

When special efforts are made to give academic help to low I.Q.

children, and these children are tested before and after such help has been given, they often do better on a second than on a first test. This does not necessarily mean that the child has become brighter or more intelligent. It may merely mean that he has learned to do a better job at expressing the intelligence he has. And often the apparent increase in I.Q. does not hold up in subsequent testing.

Vast governmental efforts at increasing the intelligence of low-I.Q., underprivileged children through such massive ventures as Headstart are generally admitted not to have turned out as brilliantly or successfully as was initially hoped.

Any child's basic intellectual potential is probably given, by heredity, over a fairly broad range. If we do our very best for any child, chances are he will be able to express his highest or best potential, but it seems very doubtful that even by the most studious effort we actually raise basic intelligence. As the *Saturday Review* once commented of Joan Beck's *How to Raise a Brighter Child* (11), "This book reminds us of How to Raise a Bigger Begonia." Perhaps that says it as well as anything.

"Early Entrance" Is Desirable for the Truly Bright Child

"Early entrance" is a sort of will-o'-the-wisp that has danced before the eyes of parents of bright children for far too long. It leads, all too often, into a bog of school failure that nobody can understand. How could Johnny be failing in school when he is so bright?

The way early entrance works is this. Johnny, with a November birthday, misses the school's October cutoff date by a month, and so, being only four years and ten months old in September, is not eligible for starting kindergarten. *"But he is so bright!"* you wail. "Not only does he have a high I.Q., but he's already showing marked interest in letters and numbers."

"Oh, well, in that case," says the school, "we'll give him an in-

181

telligence test, and, if he's as bright as you say he is, he will qualify for early entrance."

When early entrance is invoked, that means that children not old enough to meet the usual age requirement for starting school are made a special exception if they are highly intelligent. This would work out splendidly if we could guarantee that the unusually bright boy or girl would also be unusually mature. Unfortunately, quite the opposite is often the case. A surprisingly large number of unusually bright children (though of course not all) are also markedly immature—to the extent that we use the term *superior immature,* which merely means that the child is bright but immature for his age.

Since far more than the intelligence goes to school, if the special exception that early entrance provides for is made, and this bright but immature child does start school before the law normally permits (and before his actual behavior warrants), he often as not then has trouble with school in spite of his high intelligence.

Early entrance is for most children a special privilege that later on boomerangs to the sorrow and confusion of all concerned. As Paul Mawhinney (71) points out in explaining why the schools in Grosse Pointe, Michigan, gave up on early entrance after trying it for eleven years, nearly one-third of the 777 children (out of 1,378 tested) who were approved for early entrance turned out to be poorly adjusted in school, and one in four had, later, to repeat a grade.

In addition to the failure of this kind of program so far as the children were concerned, it was found that the overwhelming majority of parents whose children were denied early entrance under the program reacted negatively. All were disappointed, most were surprised, a few were riotously angry. Some spoke bitterly, others insultingly. Some wrote vicious letters. The program produced an extremely emotional situation and in addition was excessively expensive.

Even among those who recommend early entrance programs, it is admitted that the underage children who take part, though they do get by, often do not do as well academically as they might have done had they started school a little older.

It's Harmful to the Child with a Low I.Q. to Be Put in a Special Class

Now that so many of us are becoming franker than we used to be about both facts and feelings, we fortunately hear less than we used to about how *unkind* it is to put the child with a very low intelligence quotient in a special class. The argument used to be that if all the low-I.Q. children are grouped together, the other children will call them "dummy" and they will feel embarrassed and out of things.

They *are* out of many things from a practical point of view, whether you group them together or not. Any child with an I.Q. much below 75 (assuming that this is a true measure of his intelligence) is in all likelihood not going to be able to learn in the regular way.

Better to face the fact of a low intelligence, better to be called a name now and then than to face, hourly and daily, the frustration, failure, and despair that may be his lot if he is grouped with children of normal potential and is constantly faced with academic tasks he has no way of performing. Better success in his own suitable group, better the pleasure and even thrill of school success that can come to almost any child if he is suitably taught, than the dubious privilege of sitting in a class the work of which is way over his head.

The dull child needs a special kind of teaching. This can seldom be offered to best advantage so long as he remains in the regular classroom.

Intelligence, Personality, and Behavior Tests Aren't Fair Because Some People Teach Their Children to Pass the Tests

It would be the rather rare, and certainly the misguided, parent who would try to teach his or her child the "answers" to such tests. Tests like these are given to help us find out all we can about a child so that we can fit the teaching situation to his true needs. If you could—and you mostly can't—help him to give the impression of being brighter or more mature than he actually is, the result would simply be that he would be placed in a group or grade in which the work would actually be too hard for him. So you would be doing him no favor.

But actually, and perhaps fortunately, it is most difficult for a parent, unless a highly trained psychologist himself, to teach his child how to "cheat" on a test. Especially in a behavior test, the child's performance is made up of many different parts, all of which we note. It's true that with great effort a parent might teach a child who is not ready to do so on his own to draw a circle from the top down and counterclockwise, to copy a triangle, to omit the belly button from the Incomplete Man.

Even this would not deceive a trained examiner, since there are so many parts to any performance that a parent would not be likely to have covered them all. Say he taught the child to omit the belly button, it is unlikely that he could without much study be able to tell him just how to make the arm, the leg, the eyes, the hair of the man. Nor would he, in all likelihood, be able to tell the child how to hold his pencil, how to sit, what to say, in order to appear more mature than he actually is. In fact the child who has been coached will as a rule give himself away by saying, "Every night I practice to make the triangle," or, "I mustn't put in the belly button."

Or say a parent might with much effort teach his child to make a "good" triangle or divided rectangle, he might still forget to teach the child to line up the various individual forms in a manner that would "match" the maturity of the way he draws these forms. It's very hard to cheat on or beat most tests.

Tests Given Early in Life Don't Predict

There is a large group of overoptimistic, environmentally oriented individuals who believe that testing children when they are young is useless because, they say, early tests do not predict later behavior. Any child may, according to them, get better or worse (they usually seem to think he is going to improve) as time goes on.

The most exaggerated version of this point of view is expressed by a respectable psychologist, J. McV. Hunt, who makes the flat statement, "Attempting to predict what an I.Q. will be at age 18 from tests given at ages birth to 4 years, before the schools have provided at least some standardization of circumstances, is like trying to predict how fast a feather will fall in a hurricane" (54).

There is a wealth of opinion on both sides of this argument, some specialists believing that early tests *are* predictive, some believing that they are not. Many people like to believe that they are not, because this gives them more hope for children who, early in life, give evidence of no very great potential. They like to believe that they can improve these children later on. Others, perhaps more realistic, do appreciate that though one can always hope for a miracle, it seldom occurs.

At any rate, our own research shows great stability in test scores from the very earliest ages on. A recent study by one of the authors (1) compared test scores of thirty-three children examined in infancy on Gesell Infant Behavior tests and forty-four children examined in the preschool years on the Gesell Preschool Scale, with the scores of these same children when tested at ten years of age on a standard intelligence test (the WISC). A substantial percentage of those examined in infancy (63.6 percent) had infant scores that

185

fell within ten points of the ten-year I.Q. score. In 91 percent of the cases of those first examined in the preschool years the preschool and the ten-year scores fell within ten points of each other.

This group of cases confirms our experience of fifty years that in the majority of cases early test scores *are* highly predictive of later performance.

You Should Teach Your Baby (Preschooler) to Read

You hear a lot about this kind of thing nowadays, but it's very poor advice. Babies, as a rule, are not ready to read, nor are most two-, three- or even four-year-olds.

It's always a good idea to read to your children. And, as time goes on, many of them will want to look on as you read, will pick out initial letters of words and ask what they are. They will ask what *hot, stop,* and other short words mean. Then and only then should you respond to their evident interest and readiness by giving them the initial reading experiences they appear to be suited for.

Major efforts to teach babies and very young preschoolers to read do not, as a rule, of themselves do very much harm because nothing much comes of them. But the attitude behind such efforts can be harmful if it means that you as a parent believe it's all up to you and that you can make any child do anything if only you start soon enough and try hard enough.

Shakespeare may not have been entirely correct when he said that "Ripeness is all," but he had a point. Jeanne Chall, a recognized authority on the teaching of reading, tells us (18) that the consensus of concerned and informed reading specialists, regardless of which method of teaching reading they favor, is that six years of age, or five at the earliest, is for most children plenty of time to start.

Sheila Greenwald (45) tells her own story of what it was like to

186

be an early-tutored Omar Khayyám Moore New Haven pre-schooler:

The Life Story of a Modern Four Year Old
My Life Story by Sheila Greenwald

From the day I was born, my parents have seen to it that I am a winner. When I was two years old, I was taken to a cubicle in New Haven where they taught me to type. Two year olds can learn such things and if they don't, they merely waste their time.

When two year olds who don't know how to type meet two year olds who do know how to type, they are overwhelmed and fall behind and are losers from then on.

At two and one half, I was sent to school, where I play with learning equipment. I excel in carrot grating. My play time is not frivolous or wasted. I learn about textures and colors and relationships. At three my mother taught me to read. Children of three can learn to read and if they don't, they waste their time. They fall behind in school from the start and they are losers.

My parents never neglected the social side of my development. I have been exposed to children constantly. After school I attend play group. Relationships with one's contemporaries cannot start soon enough and are vital in the child's development. If these exposures to one's contemporaries don't begin soon enough, the child cannot cope with them when he starts grade school. He falls behind. He is a Loser.

I began to attend rhythm classes at three and one half. I play drums and run like a pony, which strikes me as somewhat frivolous, but it instills something in me they say and I'll be a winner, rhythmically speaking.

Now that I'm four, I feel sure of my ground. When I enter the kindergarten of my choice in the fall, it will be with a sense of purpose and readiness to cope with all situations. I will be on my way as a winner.

When I grow up I would like to be a garbage man.

This Child Can't Read Because He Has Mixed Dominance

All too many parents, and teachers as well, find themselves anxious when a child expresses what is called mixed dominance. (This means that, though his right eye may be dominant, he prefers to use his left hand or foot or some other combination of sides. That is, dominance is considered mixed except when a child prefers left eye, left hand, left foot—or right eye, right hand, right foot.)

Here, as often, the balance of informed opinion does not go along with the popular notion. As Professor Malcolm P. Douglass of Claremont, California, correctly explains (22), it is *confused* dominance, not merely mixed dominance, that makes trouble in reading and otherwise. That is, so far as anybody knows, it does a child no harm to prefer his right eye, left hand, and right foot (or whatever). It is only when he has not established any strong dominance, and thus is confused in deciding *which* hand (or eye) to use, that he's apt to be in trouble.

The Extent to Which Schools Encourage Competition Is Damaging to Children

It's hard to know just why competition came to be in such bad repute. Many people speak as though competition is an evil thing, and as if it would never occur to children to be competitive if the schools didn't encourage it.

Our guess is that many people think badly of competition because many schoolchildren, in groups or grades for which their maturity or basic intellectual level does not suit them, or competing with children from very different backgrounds, find it hard to keep up with the rest of the class. Parents of such children blame the competition, rather than the unsuitable placement or situation, for their children's failure and unhappiness.

Invidious competition should never be encouraged. Most certainly schools should not encourage totally unmatched children to compete, and then make a big fuss over the winners and a big fuss about the losers. Those children in a class who do less well than the others should not be criticized and should of course never be ridiculed.

But competing is a perfectly natural and normal human drive, and is for many a basic life style or pattern. The sturdily built, well-muscled kind of child whom we describe as a mesomorph competes as naturally as he breathes. He loves to win, and even when he doesn't win he enjoys the mere act of competing. He does not compete because the school encourages him to. He would wish to compete even if the school discouraged him from so doing. If report cards and other measures of effectiveness are not permitted, he will compete with his own impression of his own past performance.

There are other children, the round, well-padded children whom we call endomorphs, who as a rule do not like competition. They do not behave competitively even when the school or situation encourages them to do so. They often do not want to win, because this would make them conspicuous.

Cooperation in the classroom is quite as important as competition, perhaps more so. And individual excellence—working for the sake of the work to be done—is also important. But there's nothing wrong with competition as such if it is not encouraged excessively and doesn't take the place of other ways of working. Though certainly it should never be allowed to become what it's all about.

Nongraded Primary Will Solve All Our Problems

One special kind of grouping that all of you are likely to hear much praised (in fact, your own community may be trying it right now) is the ungraded primary. Nongraded primary is by no means a real "no-no" with us, but it still is no better than a "maybe."

The nongraded concept attempts to deal rationally with the problem of individualized instruction. It points out, quite sensibly, that since each child develops at his own pace, it is difficult and in fact

189

impractical to expect that all children of any given age will be ready for exactly the same type of experience.

The theory behind nongraded primary is excellent, since it assumes, correctly, that not all six-year-olds behave at the same level and thus are not all ready for the same kind of learning situation. In fact, it assumes that, even if they all were the same in the fall, during the year some would grow faster than others in academic readiness. This being the case, it realizes that teaching must be individualized—each child must be taught things suitable for his behavior age rather than for his age in years.

The practical assumption is, therefore, that if we took the names off the grades, just taught every child in every subject at the exact place he was ready for, and then let him sort of flow along rather than skip upwards by jumps and grades, everybody would be happy and successful all of the time.

The theory is fine. The actual practice has not always worked out as well as advocates had hoped. It isn't always practical for a teacher to keep clearly in mind twenty or thirty different levels of reading ability, of spelling achievement, of arithmetic accomplishment. Some grouping is needed. In fact, if school is to be anything more than individual tutoring, if the group activity is to stand for anything, quite a few children all at more or less the same level of maturity and readiness will need to be grouped together.

A year or two ago, the most ardent exponents of ungraded primary went so far as to admit that "nobody is doing it right, yet." We don't say it will never work out. (With an exceptionally good principal and good teachers it might, indeed.) We do say that it has presented more difficulties than were anticipated.

In other words, we agree with author Brenton (14), who comments that

despite the force of logic behind the notion of nongraded primary, it has not demonstrated its effectiveness as a superior way of engendering pupil achievement in such skill areas as reading, language arts, and math. What few formal tests have been run fail to show any

190

improved student outlook on the part of the youngsters who are in nongraded classes.

According to its sponsor, Dr. John Goodlad, this "much heralded revolution in American education is being in large part blunted on the classroom door." Others say that in order to be truly effective, non-grading must be integrated with team teaching, flexible space, individualized curricula, electronic instructional systems and hierarchies of teaching personnel. In short, it needs a total transformation of school and personnel.

Because of the wide range of achievement levels in nongraded classes, teachers have to be superior, exceptionally well prepared and sustained at every step. To teach a nongraded class one must be young in spirit, creative in devising new ways to meet new situations and eager to meet new challenges. Does this description fit the typical teacher on the average staff?

The trouble with most innovative schools is that typically they are developed and tested in "clean" laboratory schools, often located on university grounds or close by, where highly competent teachers under expert supervision work with students of above-average ability.

By the time an innovation reaches the "dirty" classroom of an ordinary school for general implementation, it has passed before a number of people—the subject-matter supervisor, the principal, and many others who may alter the original conception. The classroom teacher —who may be poorly trained in the new approach—and who must fit into the realities of classroom routine, will almost certainly alter it.

Unfortunately, the human element always and unexpectedly comes into play. Thus programs conceived with an ideal teacher and ideal teaching conditions are bound to fail. . . . In some form or other both team teaching and nongrading have been around *since the late 1800's*. Yet by 1967 less than 15 percent of the nation's school systems had adopted team teaching, and barely over 12 percent provided non-graded schools.

Charles Silberman (92) reports further criticism of nongraded primaries as they currently exist in the United States. He quotes further comments from Goodlad and Anderson, who note, "While we are heartened by the lively interest that has been shown, we confess to deep concern over the superficiality and inadequacy of much that is being done in the name of nongrading. Many of the so-called nongraded programs are little different from the graded plans they replaced, and except for a 'levels' scheme in reading there are few changes of real significance to children."

As time went on, Goodlad became even more discouraged. "I should have known . . . that teachers and administrators would reach eagerly for the catchy, innovative label and that nongrading soon would be used to describe pitifully old practices of interclass achievement grouping" (41).

Silberman concludes (92) that "most of the schools claiming to have adopted nongraded programs have not done so at all. What they *call* nongrading is nothing more than conventional homogeneous grouping of students by ability *within* the same grade; the vertical grade organization is left unchanged, along with curriculum, teaching methods, and everything else."

In other words, don't be too hopeful that nongraded primary, excellent as it may be in its aims and ambitions, will necessarily solve all or even many school problems.

Schools Without Walls, Schools Without Windows, Schools Without Desks

SCHOOLS WITHOUT WALLS

This term seems to have two meanings. In some communities it appears to mean that learning should not go on for the most part within the school building, but in the entire community. More commonly it refers to the school building itself and means not that the school building has no *outside* walls, but merely that it is not divided into the usual several self-contained classrooms. Rather, for instance, instead of there being three or four separate kindergarten or first-grade rooms, all kindergarten or first-grade students (perhaps one hundred in a batch) are all taught together in one single large area without partitioning walls.

Part of the time this large bunch of children all group together for lessons or activities. Part of the time they are divided, perhaps into four groups of twenty-five each, in separate sections of the room, though still not divided by any walls or screens. Inevitably, with so many children all together, some degree of team teaching is involved, since it will take several teachers to work with so large a group.

This notion of schools without walls seems to be spreading like wildfire. Schools are being built to this design. It seems reasonable to suppose that some children and some teachers will enjoy and even thrive on this new concept in education. We have seen it working out splendidly in one primary school in Lakewood, Ohio.

On the other hand, it seems probable that there are some perfectly good teachers who would not feel comfortable in this kind of setting, and many children who may still function best in a more conventional classroom. It might be the better part of wisdom for those contructing new elementary schools to keep in mind that many new notions such as this do come and go. They might at least make some provision for the partitioning off of those wide empty spaces just in case the notion of schools without walls does not work out as well as its proponents expect.

SCHOOLS WITHOUT WINDOWS

Schools without windows is an architectural notion presumably introduced to solve heating and lighting problems. This it may do, but one may hazard the guess that it does not solve human problems. In fact, it may well produce them.

Experience is showing that neither adults in offices nor children in classrooms seem to thrive in windowless surroundings. Hopefully, except where windowless buildings are required because of problems of vandalism, schools of the future will go back to the old-fashioned notion of having windows in classrooms.

SCHOOLS WITHOUT DESKS

Another "without" that is becoming popular is schoolrooms without desks. This kind of classroom setup is often called the *open school* (an open school could be one without walls between the rooms, or could be merely an open, or deskless, arrangement of a single classroom).

The open arrangement is usually used along with some kind of special modification of the usual type of classroom teaching. Sometimes it is used in some variation of the so-called English primary school described in Chapter 11. In other cases it is used in a "contract" type of functioning, in which individual children "contract" with the teacher as to what kind of and how much work they will do during any given school session.

It is customary to use a definitely open or deskless setup in the usual nursery school or kindergarten, and, for those schools which provide a connecting class or pre-first grade, in this grade as well. We would like to see it used also in regular first grade. Beyond that level, it's hard to say. Most typical second-grade "workers" do seem to like and to be ready for the formality introduced by the availability of desks.

It is too early to say whether or not the open classroom concept will spread and whether or not it will succeed. Chances are, not every child is fully suited for the open classroom. As one fifth-grader, attending an open school, is reported to have commented, "I don't want to do this. I've got to get ready for sixth grade. All we do here is run around and fool."

We are reminded of a New England rabbi who had just managed to finish the building of a school in his local community. At the 1970 White House Conference for Children and Youth held in Washington, D.C., he had attended a session run by Dwight Allen, a rather innovative young educator. The rabbi was upset and appalled by what he heard. "How about my carpets? How about my desks?" he asked anxiously. Our reply would be, "Enjoy your desks. Enjoy your carpets. The whole educational world is not going to change overnight."

There's a Perfect Gadget Somewhere That Can Take the Place of Teachers

Though certainly gadgets, or what is called the "hardware" of education, must be tried, don't be too optimistic that such innovations as educational television, language laboratories, or teaching machines are going to solve all educational problems or take the place of Teacher.

Myron Brenton in his effective book *What Happened to Teacher?* (14) gives a concise summary of the noneffectiveness of all three of these much-talked-about innovations: "Every comparison of results (of these new methods of teaching) shows that though students seldom do worse when using them, they seldom do better. Findings are that differences in student learning (which they produce) are at best only slight and usually only for a small percentage of students."

Brenton describes educational television as "an innovation glorified when it was first mass-introduced in the early 1960's, but one which turned out to be perhaps the most expensive and disastrous single failure in the history of educational technology. As a National Education Association leader summed it up, 'It doesn't hurt anything but it hasn't produced many gains in learning either and it generally costs more.' "

As to the much-advertised language laboratories, in Brenton's opinion these "provided another example of a panacea that hasn't worked out. Comparisons between conventional and innovative curriculum approaches in math, chemistry and biology show no significant differences in the achievement level of most students."

Teaching machines, too, according to Brenton, "have had a dismal history in the nation's schools. By 1967 only 16 percent of the comprehensive high schools were using these programmed instruction devices and many districts, including Newton, Massachusetts, were phasing them out. Materials were poor, students found them boring, teachers were misusing them, school principals were finding that on the whole they produced no significant differences in achievement."

But, as Brenton warns, just because these particular efforts have not turned out too well doesn't mean that we should stop experimenting. It does mean that you should not believe all you hear about some wonderful new gadget or device or method that is going to revolutionize learning in your local school.

The School Is No Place for Sex Education—THAT Belongs in the Home

We hesitate to open up *that* can of worms, but perhaps a brief comment is in order.

We, like the majority of concerned educators, definitely believe that school is a good place, though certainly not the only place, for sex education. Probably the majority of parents, too, go along with this idea. In fact, until just recently the cause of sex education in the school was prospering.

It seemed as if those parents who were doing the best job of giving sex education at home were glad to have help. It almost seemed as if it was the parents who were falling down on the job and whose children thus most needed to have information given at school who objected to the schools' giving this information. At any rate, things *were* going along well, with the battle lines quite cleanly drawn between relatively liberal parents who favored sex education in school and the somewhat reactionary who did not. So that regardless of which position you took, you at least knew who you were lined up with.

Then, just recently, came a new group that calls itself SIECUS (Sex Information and Education Commission of the United States). Its purpose was to promote and increase sex education in our schools. The purpose was admirable. Its philosophy, unfortunately, is one that is not acceptable to many parents. As the SIECUS people themselves explain, sex education before them tended to be informative and prohibitive. That is, teachers taught children about the mechanics of sex and reproduction (the plumbing approach, as some call it) and then encouraged continence. Moral values were presented, strongly.

SIECUS has largely refused to take the moral stand. They consider that conventional sex education is wrong in attempting to subdue and repress manifestations of sexuality in children, or in adults who are not married to each other. Rather than repressing and subduing, they prefer to explore and perhaps change sexual standards and sexual behavior of young people.

According to Lester Kirkendall, one of the leaders of SIECUS, sex education should be concerned with responsible decision making. As he notes (63), "Young people even as early as junior high are faced with situations which require them to decide for or against entering into some kind of sexual relation. . . . So, sex education has to be concerned with the development of an ethical-moral framework which will fit a society radically changed from the society of a generation ago."

Many parents don't like this. They don't want their junior high school children or even their high school children to attend classes in which they discuss, freely, whether or not they should indulge in sexual activity.

And so the whole situation has become extremely confused. Today it isn't just the relatively liberal parents who favor sex education in the schools and the conservative or reactionary parents who object. Now many of the formerly liberal parents who have

197

always favored the idea of sex education in school—shocked and frightened by the SIECUS materials (whether rightly so or not)—have joined forces with those who were against it.

Thus, ironically, the very group that had dedicated itself to promote sex education in school has, unwittingly, introduced one of the greatest stumbling blocks yet encountered by those educators who believe, as we do, that sex education should be included in the public and private school curriculum. It is to be hoped that as SIECUS matures it may cooperate more effectively with those advocates of sex education in the classroom who believe that at least a slight moral slant should be given to what is taught.

School Failure Is for the Most Part a Result of Adverse Emotional Factors in the Home

Though many mental hygiene clinics in this country, for many years, believed this to be the case, let your own common sense advise you here. Many of you know children from extremely happy homes who still have trouble in school, and children from troubled homes who make out very nicely in school.

The cases of Tim and Tex on pages 19 and 29 are excellent examples of the fact that all too often clinics have blamed parents for school failure that is clearly rooted in some aspect of the child's own personality or function. Most parents will do the very best they can to provide a happy home atmosphere. But, if their children have trouble in school, hopefully they will not jump to the conclusion that they themselves are necessarily at fault.

Teachers Make Up Their Minds Beforehand Whether a Child Is Smart or Not

The so-called self-fulfilling prophecy is an interesting, though unfortunate, example of what happens when research still at a

198

laboratory stage becomes popularized too soon and then, if it tells people what some of them wanted to hear, becomes accepted as a scientifically proven fact.

Dr. Robert Rosenthal of Harvard, a responsible investigator, did a piece of research (81) in which teachers were told, incorrectly, that in the psychologist's opinion, certain children in their classes were "late bloomers." They might not be doing too well to start with but they would later "bloom." Rosenthal felt that many of these teachers, not on the basis of the child's actual performance but simply because they had expected him to bloom, gave him credit for blooming. The reverse was also said to be true—that if the teachers thought a child didn't have it, they failed him.

Scientific criticisms of this study are sharp and justified, but, alas, the popular press got hold of the results and ignored the justified criticisms of technique. They found a willing audience. There are many parents who quite naturally feel better about their own child's failure if they believe that he failed because the teacher was prejudiced and had made up her mind in advance.

We can assure you that the majority of teachers base their decisions about pass or fail on something more than "false" data that some psychologist may have fancifully fed them, and on more than their own personal prejudices about that child's schoolwork.

CHAPTER 11

SCHOOLS OF THE FUTURE

Change in the System

And now comes the hard part. It's easy enough for the psychologist or child behavior specialist to advise you on how to help your children. And it's easy enough for *anybody* to criticize the schools.

It's not even too hard to think of things that might make education more effective in an *ideal* society, or if one had complete freedom to revamp the educational system. What is difficult is to make suggestions that might be expected to work in the system as it exists today, with overcrowded classrooms, not enough money, rising costs, and in the face of our almost impossible democratic ideal of universal education. Everybody must be educated, we insist, whether a good candidate or not. Added to this tremendous load is the demand many make that the schools be the place where difficult or impossible social problems are solved.

In spite of the staggering complexity and difficulty of it all, there are plenty of brave souls who do suggest solutions. Most of these solutions seem weak, impractical or just highly fanciful. Though John Holt's ideas to some extent go along with our own, and his amusing "Big Bird, Meet Dick and Jane: a Critique of Sesame Street" (53) goes directly to the point, admittedly his *How Children Learn* (51) and his *What Do I Do Monday?* (52) are much weaker books than his *How Children Fail* (50). Dr. William Glasser's *Schools Without Failure* (40) contains excellent suggestions for improving the mental and emotional well-being of children in school, but it does not pretend to provide a practical educational program to cover all the tasks any school faces. George Leonard's suggestion (69) that we do away with schools entirely, simply having children learn at home by means of educational tapes, seems fanciful. There are many other critical books that generously express their dissatisfaction but that do not have very much to offer when it comes to solving our many and grievous educational problems.

There are, of course, many *different* ways of stopping school failure. This book so far has for the most part concerned itself with ways in which child and school can be better matched. It has pointed out that if any child's abilities and basic endowment do not fit the demands of the school situation in which he finds himself, trouble and often failure result. A different approach to the problem of preventing school failure would be to change the schools, as so many suggest. In addition to the critics just mentioned, there are those like Peter Drucker, who, in his extremely thoughtful and well-written book, *The Age of Discontinuity* (23), expresses the opinion that needed changes in education as in other areas of living will be so great that we will have what amounts to discontinuity between present and future schools. And W. R. Wees (101) and many others are currently suggesting that, instead of encouraging children merely to remember and report what they have been taught, schools should try to encourage the child to think.

Charles E. Silberman, in his almost encyclopedic *Crisis in the Classroom* (92), voices vast dissatisfaction with everything about our schools, from the way in which teachers are trained to the way in which all teaching is carried on. Among his more positive suggestions for ways in which children should be taught is the suggestion that we in America have much to learn from the English primary schools that are gaining such acceptance in that country. In these schools much less attention is given than in our own to the formal teaching of reading, writing, arithmetic, and other academic subjects. Schoolrooms with many different areas of interest are set up by the teachers, and there children pursue their own individual ways of finding out about things.

A basic notion behind these schools is that learning is likely to be more effective if it grows out of what interests the learner rather than what interests the teacher. Thus children to a large extent are encouraged to work things out for themselves, though, as Silberman emphasizes, the teachers *are* there to teach, the children do not merely "discover." That is, the children are not, as some recommend, more or less turned loose to do their own thing. The teacher is very much there and very much in charge.

For a good description of the English "informal" primary schools, which admittedly are making some inroads in the United States, the reader is referred to Silberman's description.

Though there is much enthusiasm for the introduction of this system into our schools, as Fred Hechinger, education editor of the *New York Times,* correctly points out (48), these programs are not easy to establish. Hechinger notes, also correctly, that many teachers and administrators are suspicious of their very informality. The size of American schools, of close to a thousand pupils up to sixth grade—compared with the British Infant Schools' average of two hundred, and up to second grade only—creates problems. So does the more rigid American curriculum control by authorities outside the school. British principals are not only virtually autonomous, they have funds to spend for their schools.

Another difficulty, as Hechinger admits, is that unless teachers are deeply committed and adequately trained and have the help of administrators sympathetic to the whole notion, the outcome can be chaotic.

Others have pointed out correctly that there are several basic reasons why it might be difficult for us in this country to duplicate the success that infant schools have enjoyed in England. In England, not only are the headmistresses of such schools thoroughly trained in the administration of this kind of classroom, but they are fully capable of passing this training on to the teachers. In this country, few principals have this kind of training or are able to pass it on.

More than this, in England the headmistress enjoys an autonomy that is not granted to most of our school principals. She is pretty much of an authority in her own right, subject to neither the school board nor the parental pressure that all too often make our school heads less than sovereign. As a result: (a) she knows what she is doing and (b) she is free to do it.

Informed observers comment that whereas the informal classroom works very well in England, in this country all too often it amounts to no more than chaos. There is further danger. In fact, it seems to us that in spite of many exciting possibilities it offers, the English system may not be *our* answer. Alan Gartner (32) of New York University phrases it effectively when he points out that

There is a danger that just at the time when broad forces in the society are recognizing the failure of the schools for all children, black and white, rich and poor, they will be diverted from working out new forms and the means toward them *by an infatuation with informalization.*

For unless substance is added to process, discipline to creativity, role for the teacher to role for the student, we will lose this moment pursuing the chimera of informalization only to find it a passing fad, incapable of carrying the burden of change so desperately needed in our schools.

Joyless the schools may be, but it is not joy alone which is either the purpose of schools nor the sole means toward its purpose. It is to the purposes of the schools and the means of achieving them that we must give our attention, not to romance with informalization.

And finally, though it may seem to readers that we are devoting too much space to a system that in all likelihood will never predominate in American schools, there is the objection that some teachers and some children are best suited to and most comfortable in a fairly formal, scheduled situation. One cannot say arbitrarily or for certain that informality as such is better than formality.

One admittedly very excellent thing about the so-called English system is that it is more action oriented than are many of our own schools. In this connection, Silberman (92) quotes an ancient Chinese proverb, which says:

> I hear and I forget
> I see and I remember
> I do and I understand.

An action-oriented approach of our own will be described in the following chapter. Interestingly enough, some of the elements of this program are now being used in an experimental approach to teacher training that has been introduced at the University of North Dakota's two-year-old New School for Behavior Studies in Education, which "strives to educate students to acquire the qualities of mind and behavior which will assist them in nurturing the creative tendencies in the young and in introducing a more individualized mode of instruction in the schools" (92).

In this approach, teachers-to-be are taught, by their instructors, as we too suggest, in the same way that they, hopefully, will in turn teach their own students. The emphasis is on "student-oriented activities." More, much more, action, flexibility, and creativity on the part of both teacher and student are devoutly to be hoped for.

Another common proposal for improved teacher training is that any teacher training curriculum must contain much more information than most now do about how children grow and learn and what they are like as individuals.

At any rate, we, more modestly or perhaps just less ambitiously than other writers today, must admit that we do not have all the answers. In fact, if things in this book make it seem that we are critical of the educational Establishment as it exists today, we must say here that the Establishment has our profound admiration.

Considering the magnitude of the tasks imposed on all its members, from the kindergarten teacher right up to the superintendent of schools in the largest city, we compliment the courage and fortitude with which all of these people face the often virtually impossible tasks demanded of them. *It is not easy.* If as a parent you sometimes find yourself highly critical of the way things are going, down at school, just stop and ask yourself how well you would manage, faced with the same tasks, the same hazards, the same inequalities, the same lack of almost everything needed.

So, since we really don't know the answers, this chapter will not be too comprehensive. We shall merely suggest some of the practices we would like to see carried out, some of the things made available, some of the opportunities offered in the schools more or less as they exist today. These are suggestions only. They do not pretend to propose a total structure or overall plan of procedure.

Our suggestions include chiefly more attention to individual differences in children, more attention to the body as such, a few specific suggestions grouped under the label "schedules and services updated," and some generalized comment on good teachers and better-defined goals of teaching. And even in suggesting these changes we must all keep in mind the very true comment of some unremembered educator, who remarked that anyone trying to bring about changes in education must have the time sense of a geologist. In other words, nothing comes quickly or easily in education.

More Attention to Individual Differences

DEVELOPMENTAL TESTING AND GROUPING

If you have read this far, you will be well aware of our basic bias, that all children should be entered in school and subsequently promoted on the basis of their behavior rather than their birthday age.

Our vision of the schools of tomorrow is that all children before starting school be given a simple behavior test, our own or some other, and then grouped accordingly. If this test (which could be brief but still effective) were given, say, in May or June to all children who were candidates for kindergarten for the coming fall, test results would separate children into three groups: those ready for a full kindergarten experience and hopefully to be ready for first grade the following year; those ready only for a pre-kindergarten experience, who thus probably will spend two years in kindergarten; and those few not ready even for a pre-kindergarten experience and whose parents would be encouraged to keep them at home or in nursery school for one more year.

At the end of the kindergarten year, this third group would presumably then be entered in kindergarten. The rest would be re-examined and either retained in pre-kindergarten (not too likely); moved up to or kept in full kindergarten; moved into first grade; or, if this seemed indicated and such a class is available, moved on to a pre-first grade for one further year of school experience before being started in first grade.

The majority of children would in all likelihood need no more than one or two years in kindergarten before starting first grade. But if a child were especially slow in his development, it might indeed be advisable for him to spend two years in kindergarten and one in pre-first before entering a full first grade.

This could make him as much as eight years old or nearly eight before he reached first grade. This will seem to some undue delay. Our position is that failure in first grade can be so emotionally and academically disturbing that we should go more than out of our way to prevent it. Much as we favor and recommend repeating a grade when repeating is needed, far better not to overplace and thus make repeating necessary.

INTELLIGENCE QUOTIENT

Admittedly, some schools have in the past placed too much emphasis on intelligence differences among students. Thus, all too often children of high I.Q. have been allowed to start kindergarten or first grade even though they were too young to meet the legal age deadline. More than that, homogeneous grouping arrangements often placed in top groups children with high I.Q.s who still, for other reasons, found it most difficult to keep up with top group demands.

Other schools seem to have looked on I.Q. figures as immutable, overlooking the fact that some do change a bit with age, and ignoring the fact that some children at some given time may express on a given test less than their full intellectual potential.

The fact that I.Q. scores have in the past sometimes been overused or misused does not require that we should go to the opposite extreme and give up intelligence testing altogether. In planning for any child's school experience, one of the most useful measures we have is that child's intelligence quotient.

We should not place too much stress on it, true. We should certainly make reasonable allowance for poor home background and general environmental handicap. But even when a plausible reason can be offered for a poor performance on an intelligence test, if a boy or girl does rate below an I.Q. of 85–90, some special kind of learning situation will need to be provided for him. Intelligence does make a difference. And why guess at brightness and probable school performance when a simple intelligence test can give you much needed information?

It is not only intelligence testing which currently is in somewhat poor repute. There are those forces that would do away with all testing within our schools. Those who favor such drastic change should be reminded that *diagnostic tests* are perhaps the primary tool of the psychologist. He uses this tool on behalf of children. Without diagnosis, prescription is informal, often uninformed. If we are to help your children we must be allowed to test them. Current agitation to the effect that parents should be allowed to *sue* any individual who tests their children is sheer nonsense, and should not be encouraged. We test children not to keep them *out* of suitable situations. We test them in order to get them *into* those kinds of learning situations that will most greatly benefit them.

SEX DIFFERENCES

Though we by no means seek to make invidious comparisons, we suggest strongly that all primary school teachers, and parents as well, should pay more attention than most do to the differences in the rate of development that exist, *on the average,* between young girls and young boys.

Though there is much insistence today that commonly recognized differences between the behavior of boys and of girls are created by the environment, it is pretty much taken for granted by experienced teachers and parents, and confirmatory research evidence has long been available, that boys on the average do develop more slowly than girls. It seems safe to say that at the usual time of school entrance, girls in their behavior are on the average about six months ahead of boys of the same age. The difference appears to be biologically based.

Some have suggested that in order to adjust for this difference we set up segregated primary school classes of all girls or all boys. We tend to prefer keeping boys and girls together and allowing for maturity differences by grouping all children according to behavior age rather than by their chronological age.

SPECIAL CLASSES FOR THE SLOW LEARNER

Though many educators, notably Dr. Ernest Siegel (89), and many parents, do prefer that the slow-learning boy or girl be taught right along with others in the regular classroom, our own preference is for special and separate classes for any children whose intelligence level is much below 90, certainly much below 85.

Such grouping runs into all the old arguments: it isn't fair, it will hurt the children's feelings to think they are in the "dumb" class; if grouped heterogeneously the duller children would learn from the more intelligent and thus would benefit. But to us the fairest thing one can do for any child, educationally, is to place him in the sort of learning situation where he can succeed. As to his feelings, it is not just being in a certain class that makes a child feel dumb. It is not being able to do the schoolwork required of him.

In our experience, children benefit enough from being placed in a learning situation that fits them to balance anything they may suffer emotionally from being in a special and separate class. And so far as the final argument that, if a dull child is allowed to sit in the same classroom with brighter children, some of their brightness will rub off on him, the likelihood seems slight.

We go along with the mother of a slow-learning boy who once explained to us, "Normal children can learn fast and they can learn something new every day. Boys like my son have to be taught the same thing over and over again until they have mastered it. They could learn enough to allow them to take their own place in the adult world when the time comes, but they require very special teaching."

BOOKLESS CURRICULUM

The possibility of trying what might be described as a "bookless curriculum" has been discussed at some length in Chapter 9 and thus need not be developed here.

BETTER AT LIVING THAN AT LEARNING

Almost any clinician who sees or treats children referred because they are having trouble in school has met some, or many, of those children whom we describe, in nontechnical terminology, as being better at living than at learning. This phrase, though homey, describes some children very well.

Our customs, and in fact our laws, require that children attend school until they reach a certain age. This requirement holds even though a substantial number of children demonstrably are not well suited to formal learning, at least as it is insisted on in most schools today. Many of these same children, nevertheless, give the impression that they will one day, when school is finally behind them, be perfectly solid, useful, contributing citizens of the adult world. We could wish that more special allowance be made for these children along the way.

Trade and technical schools at the high school level go a long way to meet the needs of such boys and girls, but much more should be done than is. Such children should be identified earlier and provided for more effectively than they are at present.

DIFFERENT KINDS OF THINKING

We, as well as others, have long been aware of the child who thinks only in concrete terms, who seems to have no capacity for abstraction. We have termed this child *reality bound,* since he seems to live in complete reality. This is the kind of child who has to count on his fingers and, in extreme cases, such as the one cited on page 39, can count only to ten because he has only ten fingers.

Gradually schools are coming to accept the fact that some children may need to be taught "in reality," or in concrete terms. As Arthur Jensen (60) puts it, many children now failing in school do best at what we call *associative* (or Level I) *learning* rather than at so-called *abstract* or *cognitive* (Level II) *learning.* And yet most school curriculums are based on the notion that everyone must learn the same way, that is, at Level II. Thus, if a child cannot show that he "understands" the meaning of 1 plus 1 equals 2 in some abstract, verbal, cognitive sense, he is in effect not allowed to go on to 2 plus 2 equals 4.

Says Jensen:

I am convinced that all the basic scholastic skills can be learned by children with normal Level I learning ability, provided the instructional techniques do not make Level II the basic requirement of being able to learn. Educational researchers must discover and devise teaching methods which capitalize on existing abilities for the acquisition of these basic skills which students will need in order to get good jobs when they leave school.

A somewhat similar conclusion but one with even starker implications is voiced by Daniel P. Hallahan (46) who reports that

studies have indicated that many economically disadvantaged inner city children tend to have an impulsive rather than a reflective, cognitive style. This impulsivity is similar to the behavior of the hyperkinetic, brain-injured child. Preschool programs for the disadvantaged have not taken account of the impulsivity of these children. . . . It is suggested that further research be done to determine whether methods of teaching hyper-active, brain-injured children may be of value in teaching the disadvantaged.

If it is true, and we believe it is, that different children express often extremely different kinds of thinking and responding, it would indeed be most valuable for schools to identify these two (or more) quite different kinds of thinking and to group and teach children accordingly.

There are, indeed, many ways in which children differ in their thinking and their ways of responding. Not only are some children better at living than at learning, and others better at concrete than at abstract thinking, but still others are much better at original and creative activities than at carrying out prescribed tasks.

One particular area in which individuals, both children and teachers, perhaps vary most is in their response to formalized versus creative teaching and learning. Silberman (92), though he strongly favors the flexible and highly creative English primary school system and methods, does point out, correctly, that not all teachers can teach creatively and not all students are best suited to learn in creative situations. No matter how flexible and imaginative new methods become, some formal teaching and some con-

211

ventional learning will in all likelihood be necessary at least for part of those concerned for part of the time.

A parent must not be too quick to excuse inadequate schoolwork on the grounds that his child is "so creative." But it is admittedly true that many of our schools today give too much credit to the quick, smart child who learns, memorizes, and reproduces well, and not enough credit and opportunity to the truly creative individual.

More Attention to the Body as Such

SOMATOTYPE DIFFERENCES

A special kind of individual difference that we wish to discuss depends so obviously on the body that we classify it here instead of under individual differences. Much of the answer to why children behave as they do, have the successes and failures they do, lies right before our eyes and is often overlooked because it is so obvious. People look different. And that is because they *are* different.

Many of us have been taught, in Sunday school and elsewhere, that "looks don't count." It is true in a sense. People with extremely even, beautiful features are not necessarily more intelligent or more moral or otherwise more deserving or desirable than people with uneven features. But, in a more important sense, looks *do* count. The child with the soft, rounded, well-padded body (we call such children *endomorphs*) may be expected to behave quite differently from the stocky, well-muscled child whom we class as a *mesomorph,* or from the lanky, angular, skinny person whom we call an *ectomorph.*

Constitutional psychology (5, 87), a theory of behavior to which we subscribe, maintains that behavior is a function of structure and that we behave as we do to a large extent because of the way our bodies are built. Psychologists who follow this theory, and we

212

among them, believe that we can tell a great deal about an individual's capacities, aptitudes, and handicaps simply by looking at his body.

Most individuals do not fall entirely in one category or another. Most have some characteristics of each. But in most people one or the other tends to predominate. Thus, for practical purposes and in this nontechnical presentation we may speak roughly as if each individual were of one type or another.

According to Sheldon (87), the endomorphic individual is one who attends and exercises in order to eat. The mesomorph attends and eats in order to exercise. The ectomorph exercises and eats in order to attend. Response to school and studying probably also varies with the somatotype. The endomorph, though often bright enough, frequently lacks competitive drive. The mesomorph, though again often bright enough, requires considerable physical activity; long engagement at completely sedentary tasks is hard for him. The ectomorph, though perhaps no brighter than the others, tends to be intellectually highly aware and active. Often he is an early reader, often he is less mature than others of his same age. This sometimes leads to too-early school entrance and too rapid promotion based on his reading and writing ability and intellectual enthusiasm and does not take into account his physical and general behavior.

The ectomorph is also a worrier. Even when things go well he is inclined to fret and worry, to be apprehensive about what *might* take place, to be extremely resistant to change. Thus the ectomorphic child, in addition to being frequently overplaced in school, is also apt to worry about school and school activities. Parents should of course try as hard as they can to see to it that all their children are happy and comfortable in school, but one must accept the fact that the ectomorphic child tends to have a hard time of it even when he is correctly placed. Life is often hard for the child of an ectomorphic physique, no matter what parents and teachers manage to do for him. We must as parents give up that impossible idea that if only we (or someone) did all the right things, everyone would be happy. We must accept the fact that some children are by nature of a happy and placid temperament—and that others, alas, are not.

One day, hopefully, schools will pay more attention to children's physical builds, and psychologists will be able to tell you more than we can today about the way children of the different physical types respond to school, and how to help them.

THE BIOLOGIC BASIS OF BEHAVIOR

The chief source of the individual differences that we and others consider so important is, inevitably, the child's own body. As biochemist Roger J. Williams points out (105):

Biologically each member of the human family possesses inborn differences based on his brain structure and on his vast mosaic of endocrine glands, in fact in every aspect of his physical being. Each of us has a distinctive set of drives. Unfortunately the opinion makers of two generations have literally excommunicated heredity from the behavioral sciences.

Also unfortunately, serious attention to the body, as inherited or genetically determined and as the basis of behavior, has been largely prevented—in fact rather scorned, at least in many quarters—by the so-called behavioral sciences. Williams points out that the expression *behavioral sciences* came into being as a result of the formulation of Ford Foundation-supported programs. They unfortunately invited the biological sciences to stay out of the precinct of human behavior. But as we have often pointed out, if we are to understand human behavior we must understand and respect the body behind the behavior. We must appreciate the contribution that heredity makes to our behavior. Environment cannot be blamed for all our differences.

And we all *are* different. Even identical twins differ from each

214

other. But many scientists today, certainly many molders of public opinion and even the lawmakers themselves refuse to recognize individual, inherited differences.

Professor Williams goes on to point out that, not only is every individual different from every other (we are *not* all the same), but

the idea that it is all a matter of education and training cannot possibly be squared with the biological facts of inborn individuality. This perversion of education [the idea that it is up to the schools to make everybody the same, to make everybody as capable in all ways as everybody else] perpetuates the banishment of heredity—an ever present biological fact—from our thinking.

Racial relations would ease tremendously if we faced squarely the biological facts of individuality. If we were all educated to KNOW that all whites are not the same, that all Negroes do not fit in the same pattern, that all Latins are not identical . . . it would help us to treat every member of the human race as an individual.

THE ROOT OF DIFFICULTY MAY LIE IN THE BODY

As knowledge about psychology and psychiatry developed in this country, for a while it became rather the "in" thing to say that physical difficulties (headaches, allergies, and other difficulties that school-age children experienced) were *really* caused by psychological or emotional factors and not by *real* physical errors or aberrations.

Now, as Freud fades, we are becoming calmer about all this, and some feel that just the opposite is true. Canadian scientist Hans Selye (86) offers the theory, now rather widely accepted, that much actual physical illness is caused by tension. Along with this goes the increasing feeling that much unacceptable behavior on the part of children is caused by *real* physical illness, which can be treated medically.

We know, or at least we have observed, that six-year-olds tend to have much more illness than do fives or sevens. Some have inter-

215

preted this as merely that sixes were starting school and thus "picked up" communicable diseases. Now some pediatricians are suggesting—and we agree—that it may not be so much reaching the age of six, or picking up illnesses, as it is the strain of first grade, in those cases where it is too much for the child, that causes this excess of illness. This is an instance where school difficulty may actually be the cause of physical illness, but more frequent and more basic are those many instances in which physical illness, or physical inadequacy, lies at the root of poor school performance.

Dr. Ray Wunderlich, a Florida pediatrician and author of *Kids, Brains and Learning,* reports (108) that, in his experience, the child who suffers from a learning disorder

commonly has a history of physical disease of one sort or another. This physical illness has often been unrecognized entirely, or it has been unrecognized as being connected with subsequent learning disability. Such physical disease may be recurrent tonsillitis and/or adenoiditis; recurrent middle ear infection; failure to absorb oral nutriment; recurrent high fevers; recurrent sinus infection; chronic or recurrent allergic states.

Learning disability children also, according to Dr. Wunderlich, often exhibit

a collection of deviations from normal which seem to accompany or be produced by a poorly organized, poorly functioning human body under chronic stress. These include: poor binocular teaming of the eyes, poor depth perception, significantly embedded astigmatism, excessive farsightedness, hyperactivity, sleep disturbances, poor resistance to infection, allergic states, irritability, frequent colds, muscular weakness, poor appetite or excessive appetite, chronic fatigue. It may not be easy to tell when a health item is the primary cause of poor learning or when it is the manifestation of a more basic underlying problem and merely coexistent with learning disorder.

Wunderlich finds that physical or health deviation tends to begin very early in the child's life, even, in some, in the prenatal period. In others, the birth history shows excessively short labor, induced

216

labor, or perhaps breech delivery. The postnatal history may show respiratory distress, low blood sugar, jaundice, or an unsatisfactory feeding experience. Learning disability children may also exhibit an inability to alter their approach to problems, and are often stuck with an inadequate approach to learning. They may exhibit a high frequency of movement disorders, and may suffer from visual and auditory problems.

Keeping in mind the unsatisfactory health history and the history of inadequate function that characterizes many children who do experience difficulty in school, Dr. Wunderlich advises (108) that such children can be worked with and helped in the following ways:

By remediation of the physical disorders that often exist and have existed for years past. I include here the carefully supervised administration of medicine such as brain "stimulants," anticonvulsants, tranquilizers, antihistamines, vitamins and other drugs which improve nutrition and growth. I have found the Cortisone group of drugs to be of inestimable value in the treatment of many learning disabled children. Such treatment should not be undertaken lightly, however, and must always be under extremely careful medical supervision.

By altering the self-defeating habits (fixed attitudes and acts) which limit a child's exploratory strivings and prevent him from trying.

By correcting disorders of movement and coordination and visual and auditory imperceptions through appropriate training programs such as sensory-motor-perceptual training, developmental visual training and the like.

By an appropriate program of academic teaching which captures the interest of the individual child, does not demand too much at any one time, builds gradually on the child's successes, rewards the child for doing (trying) rather than for right answers, diagnoses accurately the gaps in a child's academic education and eventually corrects and closes these gaps.

But always a calm, careful, studied analysis of all factors is desirable. Medical, educational, psychological, sensory, motor, perceptual, behavioral and cognitive areas must be evaluated. . . . Multidimensional diagnosis is vitally important but means nothing unless followed by programs of therapeutic action which *change* existing situations.

THE FORGOTTEN FLESH

The Reverend George von Hilsheimer (96), author of *How to Live with Your Special Child* and superintendent of Green Valley, a Florida school for highly disturbed boys and girls, agrees with Dr. Wunderlich that "almost any troubling child will have a disabling or uncomfortable medical disorder." In a chapter titled, rather poignantly, "The Forgotten Flesh," he reports that out of 272 adolescents treated at his school during a recent five-year period, 191 were clinically diagnosed as allergic with behavioral implications. Twenty-one of these had laboratory workups and *all* twenty-one improved both behaviorally and academically.

This writer gives support to our own feeling about immaturity when he emphasizes that, in his opinion, "Most children in trouble need time to catch up to their growth." He also makes an extremely important point, especially for those who tend to go overboard in explaining away delinquent and other inadequate behavior of some inner-city children on the grounds that they come from a poor environment. He notes that most children in trouble (academic or otherwise) live in neighborhoods and come from homes and go to schools where many other children do *not* get into trouble. That is, he emphasizes that it is not enough simply to blame inadequate behavior on poor environment.

MEDICAL AND DRUG RESEARCH TO THE RESCUE

Always ahead of the crowd are those researchers who give us glimpses of what we may know about children, and of things we may be able to do for them, one day in the future. We tell you about some of the ideas of Dr. A. O. Rossi of New York, not because most of you will be able to get the kind of help he describes, but rather to give you a glimpse of the future.

Dr. Rossi's approach is biochemical and his work is highly com-

218

plex from a layman's point of view. He maintains (83) that "child-hood learning disabilities are related to steroid insufficiency and subsequent impairment of protein synthesis at the level of DNA transcription. The steroid level factor is genetically ordained. The only pathway to protein remedial therapy in all areas of learning disability rests on a chemotherapeutic foundation."

The somewhat technical Rossi hypothesis (1972):

The primary causative factors in learning disabilities are hereditary blocks in the decarboxylation of glutamic acid with pyridoxine defi-ciency or dependency playing a role, and glutamine inhibition due to an inherited deficiency of adenosive triphosphate in the central nervous system.

Dr. Rossi goes so far as to suggest that "only after arranging for chemical balancing is one justified in performing psychologic test-ing. Too often we have subjected children with serotinin imbalance to testings that by their very scatter can result in misleading labels."

He also emphasizes the hereditary basis of much (though not all) unsatisfactory school and other behavior. He tells us that "edu-cationally handicapped parents produce slow learner children. The dyslexic father has a dyslexic son. The mother with a history of psychoneurological impairment may have such a daughter."

He notes that when proper medication was given to 205 Orange County, New York, psychoneurologically impaired children, mod-erate to marked improvement was recorded by teacher reports in 80 percent of the cases. The younger the child, the more prompt and dramatic the change in performance and behavior.

In summary, Dr. Rossi tells us (82) that "a child inherits the nexus of his personality structure and his biochemical idiosyn-crasies." He adds, even as Dr. Gesell assured us so many years ago, "Early experience may modulate the child's personality, but only to a minor degree." And he comments, poetically, "What our labora-tories are discovering in rat brains today, our educators will be applying to your grandchildren tomorrow."

Dr. Lendon H. Smith, in his extremely useful book, *The Chil-*

dren's Doctor (93), agrees that parents should not be afraid, if their doctor so advises, to use drugs to quiet down the overactive (hyperkinetic) child. He believes that pharmacological research will soon have answers and that drugs will eventually become more specific in their application. Dr. Smith admits that "most parents are reluctant to use medication for behavior control, but when the case is severe, I feel drugs are as appropriate as penicillin for strep throat or insulin for diabetes."

Obviously, you will not undertake *any* medication for your own child without careful consultation with your own physician. But we'd at least like you to know that substantial help from medicine *is* on the way for many children who find it hard to learn.

Admittedly, there is much anxiety about the overuse or misuse of drugs with school-age children, and rightly so. It is not reasonable to suppose that all, or even a majority of, children in an ordinary school class will need drugs to make learning possible. The recent disclosure in Omaha that many hyperkinetic (overactive) children were taking amphetamines touched off a furious debate among parents, educators, and physicians as to whether this kind of medication was permissible.*

However, Dr. Thomas C. Points, Deputy Assistant Secretary for Health and Scientific Affairs of HEW in Washington, is reported to have concluded (24) that "when diagnosed by a competent physician or medical team, hyperkinesis lends itself to safe and effective drug treatment."

Even more conclusive,

a panel named by the U.S. Department of Health, Education and Welfare to consider the use of behavior modification drugs on school children has found not only an absence of danger but also a distinct benefit when drugs (such as amphetamines) are properly used in the treatment of behavior disorders. This committee was convened by the

* For a calm, rational and highly informative discussion of the present status of the use of drugs in the treatment of learning disabilities, readers are referred to the November, 1971, issue of the *Journal of Learning Disabilities* (62).

220

federal government because of growing public concern over the increasing use of stimulants to treat the behavior disorder known as hyperkinesis. (62)

This HEW panel, consisting of psychiatrists, psychopharmacologists, pediatricians, and educators, helped in their report to lay the public's fears to rest. Dr. Irving Schulman, chairman of pediatrics at the University of Illinois medical school and a member of the blue-ribbon panel, summed it up:

What we are saying is that there exists a definite entity called hyperkinesis. To handle the problem there is a medication that is effective. Amphetamine happens to be a drug which when used under other circumstances and in other age groups is detrimental. But those misuses should not deter one from using it for the right purposes. It is equally reprehensible to deny a hyperkinetic child the benefit of amphetamine as it is to give it to a teenager to hop him up.

Another panel member said that "clinical experience has shown that the properly diagnosed child is not pepped up under amphetamines or put out of touch with his environment. Instead, his abilities are mobilized and focused on meaningful stimuli. His bodily movements are organized more purposefully."

"How the amphetamines improve the behavior of the hyperactive child with learning problems isn't clear," says Dr. Leon Ottinger, Jr., a noted San Marino, California, pediatrician who specializes in childhood learning problems. "These drugs don't simply slow the patient down like a tranquilizer," he notes. "Nor do they speed up or accentuate excessive activity, as might be expected of a pep pill. Instead, in some manner which is still in dispute, they make the brain function better" (24).

Typically, doctors say, hyperkinesis disappears by adolescence whether or not drugs are given. But the danger of withholding treatment, they add, is that the hyperactive child will lag in school, causing emotional problems that can linger to scar the rest of his life.

And finally, and perhaps most surprising, a very recent study by Dr. James L. McGaugh titled "Biological Bases of Memory" (73) goes so far as to suggest, as a result of his own drug research on animals, that there are a number of drugs that appear to enhance performance when injected after training and, by implication, seem to be acting upon the mysterious processes of memory. From this research Dr. McGaugh generalizes to comment, "The day of the memory pill is not quite here, but it is coming soon. In the future it may be just as common to give Johnny his pill when he leaves the house as it is to remind him to brush his teeth, and to put on his glasses." Well, could be!

MORE EFFECTIVE USE OF THE BODY

We've been talking so far about the child's body and its physical structure. We shall speak briefly here about the body in action. Some psychologists feel that we should spend more school time than we now do to help children come to good terms with their emotional responses. Similarly, some medical men, those concerned with physical education, and we ourselves, would like to see more school time spent in trying to help each child use his or her body more effectively.

As Dr. Wunderlich suggests (106), our children need to know more than many of them do about their own bodies and how they can move them effectively. He notes that

A thorough assured knowledge of what one's body can do and cannot do, under varied situations, is necessary for confident involvement in life's situations, from infancy onward. By movement practice in varied patterns, early in life, one becomes smart and sure about himself in the surrounding world.

The child who can move effectively and who can trust his own movements will be able to function better than the child who is not comfortable with his own body and effective in his ability to move.

The coordinated child, moving in a well-oiled, automatic smooth

222

pattern, accomplishes his tasks without particular attention to the individual movements involved. *Thus his whole energies may be directed to the task, rather than to the movement with which the task is accomplished.*

Movement deprived children fail to grow up in a way. They stay unsure of themselves. They stay reticent to explore and reach out for the new. They get further and further behind. They are often so totally involved with themselves and their own behavior or their worrying about new, unknown, future situations that they have nothing left to invest in the task at hand—whether it be reading, math or geography.

It is only when a child is sure of himself physically in a sensori-perceptual motor world, when he is sure of himself emotionally, and when he is certain of his own self-worth to others that he can disengage himself from self and interact with the rest of the world. It is only when he is sure of himself physically that he can manipulate symbols and abstract values to his own learning advantage.

Schedules and Services, Updated

PRE-KINDERGARTEN, PRE-FIRST GRADE

An assumption basic to the way most of our schools are run today, but not always proved true in actual practice, is the notion that every child's behavior will grow a full year in any given twelve months' time. If any given child does not develop at this prescribed rate, and thus by the end of kindergarten is not ready for a full first grade, little alternative is provided but that he go back and repeat his kindergarten year.

Many children manage to struggle through kindergarten without being ready, come June, for promotion to a full first grade, and, although as a rule all the opportunity the schools provide for them is that they shall repeat kindergarten, many of these chidren not really ready for full first grade work have admittedly gone somewhat beyond the demands of beginning kindergarten.

The solution we would like to see offered is one already in prac-

223

tice in many forward-looking primary schools. It is the provision of an in-between class, call it what you will (pre-first grade, connecting class, reading readiness class), to give the extra year's experience needed for those many boys and girls who in their readiness are somewhat beyond kindergarten but are not yet ready for full first grade. Similarly, but for younger children, we have recommended that every school system provide a pre-kindergarten class for those ready to profit by some school experience but not yet ready for full kindergarten.

HALF-DAY FIRST GRADE, A SHORTER SCHOOL DAY, OR A DAY OFF DURING THE WEEK

A further change in scheduling we highly recommend is the scheduling of first-graders for merely half a day, at least till Christmas, hopefully till Easter, and preferably throughout the entire school year. Since we have discussed this matter in an earlier publication (3), we need not develop this theme at any length here. Suffice it to say that perceptive teachers over these many years have observed the extreme fatigue exhibited by many first-graders in the classroom during the afternoon sessions. As one such teacher remarked, "In the afternoon the good kids wilt and the bad ones act up."

Mothers, perhaps even more than teachers, are all too aware that many first-graders are overly tired when they come home from school either at noon or at the end of the afternoon session. It is our firm belief that the average first-grader would be much better off if he could have a dramatically shortened first-grade day. An increasing number of schools now offer this possibility, in fact to such an extent that we hope it may soon be a universal practice. (After a recent trial in first grades of Woodbridge, Connecticut, Principal John C. Mulrain reports that the shortened school day was even more successful than anticipated. The entire administration and faculty, and sixty-seven out of eighty-one sets of parents involved, hope to have the program continued.)

For those who refuse to move in this direction, one of the major hurdles seems to be the expense of sending home an extra early bus (or buses)—a small price, it would seem, for salvaging the school experience of those many first-graders who come to school in September eager and earnest, only to wilt as the year goes on and school makes the overtaxing demand of all-day attendance.

Along these same lines, some principals, kinder than others, sometimes make the same kind of reduced attendance adjustment but on a more individual basis. Observing that some kindergarten pupils do tire, even with the relatively short kindergarten school day, by arrangement with the parents they permit those boys and girls who do overfatigue to leave school early on those days when it seems needed.

And, though an earlier and more disciplinary approach required that every child attend school for every session, some parents and some schools today are willing to recognize that some boys and girls do find every day all day just a little too much. There are young or specially vulnerable children who still can hold up if they are permitted a day or a half day off in the middle of each week. Others may need even less respite. For them an *occasional* day or half-day holiday, at their mother's discretion, serves.

A MORE REALISTIC CUTOFF DATE

We recognize that it may not be till some time in the future (if ever) that all communities will provide what we call a developmental placement program, that is, a plan by which every child before starting school or before being promoted will be given a behavior examination and then subsequently placed on the basis of his behavior rather than his birthday age.

We must anticipate that for many years to come perhaps the

majority of our children will be started in school on the basis of local custom or state law, which sets some arbitrary calendar time as the time for starting school.

Happily, many states now go so far as to require that children be at least five by September first before they are allowed to start kindergarten. Other states permit a child to start kindergarten before he has had his fifth birthday and some, like Connecticut, go so far as to permit kindergarten entrance in the fall if a child is going to be five the following January. This means that a boy or girl only four and a half years of age (and quite possibly immature for that age) can start kindergarten with the likelihood that, unless something intervenes, he may be starting first grade the following fall when he is only five and a half.

If an arbitrary calendar date or age *must* be the criterion for starting school, we urge all legislators and administrators to require that girls be at least five for kindergarten and six for first grade, and boys be at least five and a half for kindergarten and six and a half for first grade.

Teachers join us in urging that what they call "fall babies"— those boys and girls now permitted by law in some communities to start kindergarten before they have had their fifth birthday—be given the protection they so sorely need and not be permitted to start school till some time *after* their fifth birthday.

REPEATING

Please let them repeat if they need to. Waiting to start till a child is ready is the best prescription we know of for school success. But for any child who is failing because he did start too soon and thus is too immature for the work of the grade he is in, repeating can be an easy and effective, if not ideal, solution.

226

MORE PRACTICAL COURSES

We have mentioned earlier that there are many boys and girls in our schools who are not academically oriented, who will not in all probability go on to college and for whom even four years of the conventional high school may pose an academic challenge too difficult to meet.

Though some state superintendents maintain that trade schools abound, there are many who would like to see such schools multiplied. We would also like to see more frankly noncollege preparatory courses offered in the ordinary high school. We ourselves are naturally very much in favor of the relatively new courses in child care and child development that are being offered to those boys and girls who may have only this much practical chance to learn about babies before they have some of their own.

We think it especially unfortunate that some schools, in an effort to avoid anything that looks like an admission that some people are born brighter than others, try completely to obliterate the distinction between college prep and what used to be called "commercial" courses.

Let's go back to an admission that not everyone is suited to go to college and that not everyone *needs* to go to college in order to become a good citizen, lead a good life, and make an adequate contribution to society. And then let's try to provide good and effective schools for those many who will *not* go to college.

MORE EFFECTIVE USE OF THE SCHOOL PSYCHOLOGIST

One thing we would definitely like to see would be for all schools to have available the services of a school psychologist. But in order for this to work out to the advantage of all students, some school psychologists will need to be better trained than they now are in ways to be really helpful to children who are having academic or other difficulties.

School psychologists in general are today receiving much better training than in the past. Many are required to have had actual teaching experience before they receive their certificates. Hopefully, fewer than in the past will remain satisfied to give diagnoses that are meaningless to everybody but another psychologist.

We maintain that it is not much help to a parent or teacher to be told by the psychologist such things as that "the projectives suggest poor role definition and egocentric approach, child asserts infantile and dependent attitudes very impulsively. He attempts to repress these characteristics by an excessively rigid method. He shows repressive impulses and inferior ego strength." This, alas, is a typical psychologist's report of the past. We are convinced that the future has more to offer.

DIAGNOSIS

If schools are to make the best possible use of school psychologists and psychological clinics, they are going to have to insist that, before treatment is planned for any child whose problems give serious concern, a careful diagnosis of that child's problems must be given by a qualified professional or group of professionals.

Objection to testing and diagnosis has always been with us. It may always exist. To us it stands to reason that, just as diagnosis must precede treatment in the case of medical problems, so diagnosis should also precede treatment when a child has behavior problems.

Always with us, unfortunately, are those who believe that all or nearly all school, and other, problems are caused by factors in the environment. Thus, when children are in trouble, their effort is to change or improve the faulty environment rather than to find out (diagnose) what is wrong with the child himself.

A second reason why some do not diagnose is that diagnosis requires a detailed and specific knowledge of the stages and structure of human behavior change, knowledge not possessed by everyone.

228

It takes much skill and knowledge, but a different kind of skill and knowledge, to do therapy than to make a diagnosis. Many lack this second kind of skill.

Thirdly, some of the objection to diagnosis goes along with the objection that some people have nowadays to any sort of testing. Some people appear to believe that any kind of testing is an invasion of privacy. Our position on that is that a psychological or behavior test is no more an invasion of privacy than is a physical examination. Both are necessary prior to treatment. More than that, if one believes as we do that behavior is a function of structure and that we behave as we do largely because of the way our bodies are built, just looking at a child's body reveals to the initiated so very much about him that it seems rather ridiculous to object to having somebody find out the lesser amounts that formal testing can tell.

Others object to any sort of psychological testing because they feel that it is discriminatory. It should be pointed out that we test not to screen children *out,* but in order to place them *in* the kind of situation that will fit them best.

In short, it is our firm contention that, unless a child specialist is unusually intuitive or a remarkably good guesser, until he has made a careful and thorough diagnosis and really knows what a child is like, he is not in a position to advise as to how that child can be helped.

EFFECTIVE PSYCHOTHERAPY WHEN IT IS NEEDED

There was a time when Freud rode high, and most mental hygiene clinics in this country—and all too many school psychologists as well—based their efforts to help children on the theory that personality is a result of emotional factors in the home. Thus they figured that, if a boy or girl was having difficulty in school, it was probably the result of something his mother and father were doing or had done wrong.

This notion was carried much too far. All too many official mental hygiene clinics ignored diagnosis altogether (since they figured they already knew what was wrong with their patients) and were quite content merely to give psychotherapeutic help to all children in trouble and to the parents of such children as well.

Just because some certain type of treatment may have been exaggerated and overdone, however, does not mean that it should be thrown out the window altogether. Many gifted, effective and dedicated psychotherapists in this country and abroad are every day carrying out marvels of therapy with troubled children and troubled parents alike. Any parent wishing to know more about this kind of treatment will be well repaid for reading Virginia Axline's *Dibs in Search of Self* (9).

Our recommendation is merely that psychotherapy be considered as a last rather than a first possible solution for the difficulties any child may be having in school. This difficult, expensive, and often long-drawn-out solution of your child's school difficulties may very likely not be necessary.

A MORE FLEXIBLE CURRICULUM

Dissatisfaction with school curriculums as they now exist is widespread. The major push seems to be toward greater flexibility and more adaptation to the child's own interests. There is great emphasis on the importance of getting away from fixed, rigid curriculums that require the teacher (and the pupils) to have reached a certain page of a certain book by some certain date.

It may be a bit discouraging to realize that the same criticisms of curriculum were being made as early as 1912 by Dr. Arnold Gesell, in his book *The Normal Child and Primary Education* (34). We quote from this book at some length to show that way back at the beginning of this century the same complaints that many of us are making today were being uttered.

The overzealous parent at the door, and the relentless timepiece on the wall, conspire to keep an artificially precocious atmosphere in the primary school. Order, system, detail and prescription have replaced spontaneity, grace, initiative, and investigation. The spirit of childhood languishes and in its place stalk the stern figures of propriety and formalism. How often the most promising child in the room is thwarted in his growth by the incessant inhibition and prescription of the early grades. The eager, questioning, imaginative child cannot endure the dull tedium of perfunctory instruction. He wants to express rather than to be always impressed. Life is new and invites exploration. He is not willing to memorize and visualize the symbols while the warm, living things which they represent are touching his elbow.

We cannot force our motives and our standards on children without arresting a natural process of growth. Why shut the children up in the prisons which we have made for ourselves out of inhibitions and conventional standards?

Even if an utter revolution of program is necessary, it would be justified if we could, by such a change, preserve emotion, eagerness, and enthusiastic persistence in work. *Programs are too inflexible.* Periods should run over and run into one another. There are days when a protracted session, emphasizing and illuminating one idea, should wipe out all divisions into reading, writing, spelling, etc. These things are not ends in themselves.

Take the programs down from the doors and seize upon the psychological moments when writing, reading and spelling really express thought and make permanent ideas upon some central topic. They should be the means of objectifying, preserving and enforcing ideas. The child's personality cannot emerge and develop unless his emotions are stirred in vital accompaniment to his intellectual work.

It is the boast of some schools that everything goes like clockwork. Such formalistic uniformity and concerted action are foreign to the grace, spontaneity and individuality of childhood. Children who grow up under such systematized direction are denied the very essence of mental growth, which depends upon original constructive effort.

What does the six year old care for print? His fingers are itching for contact with things, and his legs are set for chasing butterflies. Too much formalism in childhood kills spontaneity and interest. Education cannot, by formalizing courses of study, force intellectual functions. The laws which govern the growth of mind are as immediate and

231

irresistible in their operation as those which govern the growth of the body. If we force either the one or the other, personality is foiled. Let us, by putting faith in instinctive impulses, conserve more of childhood to the race.

Dr. Gesell's long-ago suggestions are not, after all, too different from the things that modern-day educators are suggesting, that schools, schedules, and curriculums should be freer, more flexible, less formal, more fun than they sometimes are.

Good Teachers, Better-Defined Goals of Teaching

Any or all of these things described above might, in our opinion, help schools to serve children more effectively. More important than any of them, however, is that so far as is humanly possible our schools should be staffed with dedicated and effective teachers.

We really don't care whether the schoolrooms are round or square, whether the school is graded or nongraded. Even the somewhat new notion of big, barnlike areas that serve one hundred or more children in a bunch, complete with team teaching, can sometimes be made to work *if* the teachers involved are skilled enough. We would even settle in a pinch for that architect's delight, the school without windows, if the teachers were very superior.

Though a really good teacher is probably born and not made, we might, as mentioned earlier, at least look to a time when state colleges of education would do a better job than many now do in the training of teachers. Even students not entirely gifted as potential teachers would be more effective than otherwise if strong courses in child behavior could help them to know a little something about what children are like ahead of the time when they will actually start teaching.

One thing we would especially like to see is for teachers to be considerably less curriculum bound than many now are, and more fully free to teach the things they would *like* to teach.

232

In talking with public school teachers who took part in his perceptual workshops (see Chapter 12) during the past years, one of the authors (JWS) found that most teachers really do have a very good idea of what the goal of school should be. But somehow, somewhere, in between their good ideas and what goes on in the classroom, something comes up that interferes. And what it is that interferes sometimes seems to be the mere mechanics of getting the job done.

When teachers were asked why they thought it was important for children to come to school and what it was they wanted to accomplish with their children, their answers were imaginative, creative, lively. These are some of the goals they expressed:

1. To encourage and help develop the child's potentials as a human being.
2. To help children appreciate their individual uniqueness as well as that of others—in terms of the positive value of differences.
3. To help children learn and develop methods of problem solving. And to help them formalize their thoughts and problems.
4. To help children get along with other people. To help them communicate in terms of words, actions, representations, and symbols.
5. To develop in children the ability to work independently as well as with others.
6. To stimulate children to appreciate the enjoyment of learning for the sake of learning.
7. To stimulate and encourage creativity in thinking and in doing.
8. To help children develop the ability to work within a structured situation as well as to learn the discipline of a situation without becoming a slave to the structure of the discipline.
9. To help children learn to read, write, and do arithmetic as well as to master other academic subjects.

These are all splendid goals. Teachers, born and true teachers, have very high goals for their profession and for what they should accomplish with children. It would be our wish that administrators might find it possible to further these goals rather than to give in to the usual demands of a school routine that all too often stifles any attempt at creativity on the part of the teacher.

Teachers, at least many of them, tell us that they would appreciate some sort of reevaluation of the goals of teaching along these lines. But it's not the teachers alone who would like things to be different. We are all too aware that many college students are more than dissatisfied with the way courses are being taught in college. And it isn't just the college students who complain. A ninth-grader explained to us recently, "I used to be a good student and I used to enjoy school. Now I'm completely bored with it. For nearly all this year all I have had a chance to do is to memorize and learn facts that won't do me any good, just because my teachers told me to."

Certainly there are two sides to all this. We don't hold that the students should run the schools. But when their complaints seem reasonable, when they complain that there is much too much memorizing and too little thinking required, maybe it's time we paid more attention. It's reasonable that a poor student might not like school. But when even the good ones are bored, we think their complaints are telling us something important.

Conclusion

These may seem like all too many suggestions of things we would like to see in education, but what we have to suggest can be summarized very briefly.

We can't do all that we must for the boys and girls in our schools today with gadgets or new buildings or new plans such as non-graded primary, team teaching, or the new open classroom system alone. As we see it, if all children are to be taught successfully, all must be identified and grouped according to their behavior rather than their birthday age. Attention must be paid to the fact that not all children are equally gifted academically or intellectually and not all are up to their age in the way they behave.

Rather than putting all the blame for inadequate function on something that the environment has or has not done for the child, we must accept the fact that, though environment most certainly does matter a very great deal, bodies differ and thus behavior differs. We can hope that before too long corrective medicine may have its own part to play in helping schoolchildren in trouble, but till that time we must deal with the bodies as we find them.

It seems certain that improved schedules and services, more effective routines, more flexible curriculums, a freer and more flexible notion of what it is that children come to school to do, as well as better textbooks and better equipment, will all play their part in helping the schools offer children of the future more than we have been able to offer in the past.

Above all, we must rely most for the help that all children need and deserve on good teachers—teachers not bound down too much by the routine demands of teaching and by formal fixed curriculums, but left free to work toward their own highest ideals and finest goals.

CHAPTER 12

A NEW KIND OF PROGRAM: PERCEPTUAL
TRAINING AND PROBLEM SOLVING

Introduction

It has become extremely popular these days to find fault with our schools and school programs. While this has always been true to some extent, the past ten years have fostered an eruption of articles, books, and even movements, that speak *against* what is being done in education. All too often these criticisms are leveled from outside of education, by those with little or no classroom experience. These critiques often stop after they list and moralize about all the faults of education. Few positive suggestions are offered, and seldom do those making criticisms become involved in classroom situations to field-test any new programs or ideas.

For the past six years we at the Gesell Institute have been involved in the classroom. We do not have *the* answer to education or to the total educational program. We *have* had the experience of introducing and working with *a classroom approach* that is more child oriented and less content oriented than many. This program has made some real changes in children, in teachers, and in what is going on in some classrooms. The kinds of changes we have effected are relatively easy to describe, to feel and to see, though difficult to translate into cold statistical proof of success at this time. This chapter will present some of the ideas, thinking, and experiences of these years of our own personal experience in the classroom.

In January, 1966, Mrs. Gwynette Caruthers, the school psychologist for the Cheshire Public Schools, Cheshire, Connecticut, visited us at the Gesell Institute. Mrs. Caruthers, who had had extensive classroom experience before becoming a psychologist, was disturbed about what was happening to children in the schools. She noted that many behavior problems first appeared, or were intensified, after children enter school. She was also concerned that what was going on in the classrooms, or when the children were referred for special help, often failed to meet their needs.

Mrs. Caruthers had been aware that we were having success in solving some of the kinds of problems about which she was concerned. Most often the children experiencing these problems were classified by others under the general category of "perceptual dysfunction." We had been working with some of these children in our own clinic, mainly through programs of optometric visual training. Mrs. Caruthers' questions were: Could some of the ideas and principles used in optometric visual training be translated into a classroom approach to teaching? Could such an approach incorporate our basic ideas about child development and the development of learning skills? Could these ideas and concepts be translated into an educational program directed toward the customary goals of education, and would such an approach have value?

It was never our intent merely to carry on optometric vision training in the schools. We wished, rather, to use our background and experience in the area of vision in an academically oriented program, an intriguing idea. It seemed a possible way of offering a service to a larger group of children than could be reached in a clinical service. While such an approach would not replace the need for individualized work with children, such as we were ministering to at our visual clinic, it could provide a more economical approach for the children involved. It seemed a possible way to offer a large number of children some of the benefits of this kind of work.

How could such an idea be put into practice? Our joint decision was to structure a program based on general ideas of perceptual development. *One half hour a day would be set aside to involve*

237

children in activities that encouraged movement, communication among themselves, group interaction, and figuring things out. We started with the hypothesis that perception and emotions can be developed and disciplined best in the experience of performance. The activities offered, in addition to involving problem-solving, should be directed toward the goal of using theory and information as the basis for skills of practical application. The problem-solving situations provided should be as "real" as possible, since learning of this kind suffers when the experience is "simulated," and we felt a need for real-life experiences for the children. The program planned was an attempt to integrate school experiences as effectively as possible with actual life experiences.

The question that remained unanswered at this preliminary stage in planning was, Will the teachers find enough intriguing reward and understanding of our goals, as well as a new understanding of children, during this daily half hour, that they will come to use the approach provided not only in the special half hour but throughout the rest of the day? To the degree that this might occur, we believed that the classroom could change.

Now we can answer this question. Yes, a program like this *can* change things in the classroom, *but it depends on the teacher.* As a result of the program some teachers (about one-third) have dramatically changed their teaching style. Another third have made significant changes in style and approach. The remaining third have made from "some" change to only "slight" change.

The in-service training program for teachers, provided by the specialist to communicate the approach to be made to the children, must also be a program of doing. It would be inconsistent to use a verbal approach to teachers and then ask *them* to use an action-doing approach with their students.

To accomplish our aim, workshops were set up for the teachers. Each workshop included a session of working through activities with a class of children, or with the teachers themselves as a class. The discussion that followed each action session centered around what had just taken place. From fifteen to eighteen workshops for any one set of teachers were scheduled throughout any given school year, it being important that the teachers have time to work with children on their own between the in-service workshop sessions.

In many ways teachers in these workshops responded very similarly to the way the children themselves responded in the sessions with them. It took a good deal of time before the teachers began to work as a group, to understand what was being asked of them, to believe that we were asking for *their own* responses to problems. The initial response of the teachers, as of the children, was always to seek the "right" way to solve any problem presented.

Principles on Which the Program Is Based

At the outset of our program, a set of principles was agreed upon. (The importance of this first step is even more clear now that all concerned can, after several years, look back at the experience.) The success of the program in many ways hinged upon the following principles:

1. THE PROGRAM MUST BE A PROGRAM OF DOING

The first principle was that this program needed to be a program of doing, the key theme of which was involvement. Children who are having difficulty are in some ways inadequately involved in the learning experience. Further, if our program was to change teaching, teachers, too, needed to be involved. Those responsible for the program also needed to be involved—involved in working with children in the classroom setting.

2. THE PROGRAM MUST WORK IN THE CLASSROOM

The second main principle agreed upon was that the program must deal with children in the classroom. To be realistic, it had to work in the ordinary classroom, with approximately twenty-five children and one teacher per classroom. While it would be desirable to have smaller groups and different physical plants, the program should be effective within the structure of classrooms *as they now exist.*

Since the program was an attempt to reach more children in the schools, to effect desired changes and to maximize the possibilities of effecting changes in children and their learning skills, in teachers and their teaching methods, and in what goes on in classrooms, it had to take place in the actual classroom.

3. THE PROGRAM MUST BE A COOPERATIVE EFFORT

The third principle was that the program should be a cooperative effort. It could not be a Gesell program imposed on schools and teachers. All involved had something to contribute, and in some ways the end product could not completely be defined or predicted at the start.

The program itself had to be consistent with what it was attempting to accomplish in the classroom. The presentation to teachers should employ the same methods and orientation being encouraged between teachers and students. If the program were to have any success in allowing children to express their styles of learning, their individual needs and goals, it had likewise to recognize individual teachers' styles and goals.

4. THE PROGRAM SHOULD BRING ABOUT AN EDUCATION–CHILD DEVELOPMENT UNION

The fourth basic principle was that we must bring into better than usual union information and ideas from the two separate fields of child development and education. Each had information and experience which could be beneficial to the other. Likewise, each lacked certain information and experience in the other's field.

The proposed program should ideally make the total educational experience more human and more personal. *The needs of all too many children are not being met in the traditional classroom. The educational experience must change in order to serve more of the needs of children in terms of what is and will be important in their total lives. The purpose of school as we see it is to help each child develop his or her potentials as a human being.*

The Gesell staff has information, ideas, and experiences in child development, perceptual development, and emotional development. These all relate to the very areas where education shows its greatest needs and weaknesses. On the other hand, educators in general and, more importantly, involved teachers, have special information, ideas, and experience in teaching, teaching methods, and teaching content. All that is going on in schools is by no means bad. Education has achieved a great deal, and its values should not be discarded. At the same time, traditional teaching often falls short of serving all children. In fact, in some cases it probably produces or intensifies problems.

The goal of our program was to unify the information from these two different fields. To the degree that this can be successful, it should change the viewpoints of *both* groups.

5. THE PROGRAM MUST BE SELF-PROPAGATING

If this kind of program is to survive and grow, it must do so by its own force. The Gesell staff could be intensively involved for a period of time, but educators must eventually assume the responsibility of directing the program without outside support. If we continued to be needed, the approach would not appear to have life-sustaining qualities, at least at this time. The program, then, must outgrow a dependence upon us and become an independent educationally directed program. This, fortunately, has been accomplished in that most in-service training in Cheshire is now being conducted by classroom teachers originally trained by us and experienced in this approach.

6. THE PROGRAM SHOULD EXPAND TO INCLUDE ALL CHILDREN IN THE CLASSROOM

To make a preliminary test of the effectiveness of our approach, the initial experience was directed toward children with known problems. Our first experience (in 1966) was thus with two groups of second-grade children who had been diagnosed (by means of the Bender Gestalt test) as having perceptual problems. The program at this time (1972) has been expanded to include all children in the Cheshire Public Schools, Cheshire, Connecticut, from kindergarten through fifth grade.

Some Considerations in Our Attempt

DEFINING GOALS

This first consideration was very basic. The question was asked, "Why should children go to school? What do we hope to accomplish by having them go to school?" Rather than answering this question ourselves, we asked teachers. The reasons given seem to be universal throughout the United States. The list of teachers' goals, on pages 233–234, is a complete list collected from many different groups of teachers. While the language of expressing these goals may be somewhat different from one teacher to another, or from one part of the country to another, the list from any given group of teachers pretty well matches that of another.

As one examines this list of teacher goals, it becomes difficult to reconcile it with what actually takes place in the usual classroom— if indeed these really are the true goals. Too often, the typical classroom exercise becomes just that—an exercise or attempt either to get the children to score better, to cover a given curriculum, or to get ready for the next grade. In other words, what one hopes will go on in the classroom becomes bogged down in the nuts and bolts of getting children to score or perform in such a way that the teacher can be certain that his (or her) superiors will give him credit for doing his job.

The system locks in on producing higher test scores to prove that the child is ready for the next step and that the teacher indeed has covered the required work. Too little attention is paid to what learning has actually taken place, or to what has really happened to the children as they pass through the treadmill. To reach necessary goals the most efficient way has been to line desks up in rows, to restrict the children to their desks, and to suppress communication unless it comes from the teacher or is teacher directed. The major involvement is through language, through words either spoken or written. Answers and conforming to the system are made substitutes for obtaining true skill and knowledge, and success is judged mainly in terms of written or spoken productions.

Probably the most damnable aspect of all is the subtle communication that such a system projects. The child is made to feel, or at least comes to feel, that the only way to be "right" is to conform to some predetermined standard. It may not be the best way, but it is the way that is being asked. Even more disturbing, to do well is identified with being on the top—above everyone else. It doesn't make too much difference how you get there, but if you can score higher than anyone else you are top dog. This system puts a premium on beating everyone else, doing better, trampling others down. It's good to be a winner, but how one wins is too often made unimportant in the present system.

VALUE SYSTEM

Our second consideration, after determining our goals, was to find ways to change value systems. How do you teach in such a way that children can come to recognize the great reward that comes from helping someone else, a reward perhaps greater than making your own discoveries? As with so many other things in life, one does not learn this kind of thing by words. Rather, the program must structure itself in such a way as to offer children opportunities to learn the value of helping others.

To do this, it is necessary first to admit that everyone has problems. Next, it is important to recognize that the very things that seem easiest to some may be very difficult for others. This becomes believable only when interchange can take place among children themselves—among members of a peer group. Situations *can* be structured so that children can learn from other children, and the atmosphere must be open enough so that a child is willing to express or in some way state his or her problems. Answers or solutions should be judged in terms of whether or not they work, not just of whether they are "right" or "wrong."

An example of one such experience shows clearly this aspect of value change. Jimmy, a youngster in a second-grade class, was having difficulty with spelling. The class had progressed far enough so that the children could talk about their problems. The teacher asked them what they could suggest to help Jimmy. After trying several approaches, such as tracing the words with a finger, tracing them on the child's back, etc., one of the children came up with a suggestion of "tracing the words with your tongue in your mouth as you write them." He said he knew it sounded foolish, but it had worked for him.

That week Jimmy scored a 90 on his spelling test. The next week he scored 95. After school one day in the second week, three boys, completely on their own and without the teacher's knowledge, appeared at Jimmy's house. When his mother came to the door they gave her the following report. "You don't have to worry about Jimmy. He's not dumb any more."

A New Kind of Program

A third basic consideration is the recognition that learning takes place most effectively when a child can work out something for himself, and that the way he works it out, the steps he takes as he does so, are important. Another important consideration is whether or not the solution works. The activities used should present "real" problems in a believable situation. They should encourage the development of all the sensory-motor systems and should also be oriented as far as possible to total body involvement.

The selection of particular activities is not as important in our approach as it seems to be in many programs. In other words, we did not make up and do not offer a list of prescribed activities, although initially we found it necessary to supply the teachers with some suggested activities and problems in order to get them started. Furthermore, we did not make up a rigid sequence even for some of our suggested activities.

We found that, with each new workshop we held, the teachers responded similarly in relation to the activities. During the early weeks or even months, they kept asking for more prescribed activities. They were reluctant to try their own ideas, and were even more reluctant to capitalize upon problems that came up in the classroom, either during the special half hour of the program or during the rest of the day. (The children, on the other hand, mostly view the activities as games, and recognize the value of these "games" in terms of learning and thinking. When a class really catches on, they often expand a given activity into more new "games" of their own.)

245

Activities Oriented to Movement and Communication

The activities used in a program of this kind are mostly away-from-the-desk activities. As much as possible, activities should attempt to bridge the gap between doing and representational or coding systems. Understanding concepts and verbalizing them are two different things. When we teach mainly through language, we cannot be sure the child understands a concept even when he has the words. Our idea was to give children the opportunity for going from action to representation, to codes and code systems.

Before children come to school, they all have experience in the use of action as a representation system. Much of preschool learning is gained through active participation, through playing and being active in experiences that are motoric in nature. Even when language and symbols are involved they usually occupy less of a role than does other motor movement.

Since movement and action are more nearly the universal language of young children, it is only natural to introduce representation in terms of an action component. *Footprints* have been found to be one useful example in a way of working with some concepts of representation. Children using the footprints have named the use of them as "reading" footprints and "writing" footprints. Reading footprints for the children has consisted of looking at a footstep pattern, then matching the pattern in action. Writing with footprints, a more difficult task, consists of watching a person do something and then picturing his movement as a series of footprints.

The use of footprints is one method of letting children deal with representation in terms of sequencing place, form, number, right, left, likes and differences, coding, decoding and encoding, and, most importantly, communication. The communication of a coding system through footprints encourages involvement of the student. Children can try their code "reading" or code "writing" to see if

246

it works. Can the next child travel the pattern you place? Can you tell what the last child did or had in mind by his footprint pattern? Can you do it? Can you match the footprint pattern and yet do something differently?

Teachers have asked, Why not use geometric forms instead of footprints? The answer is obvious. When we move we make footprints, not geometric forms. Geometric forms are at least one further level of abstraction removed from the actual task. Furthermore they provide an arbitrary step that is removed from the motor act of doing. When we have asked children to code sounds or actions in any way they want, somehow within their code system they have related the code to what was done to make the sound or the movement. They produce a picture of the action, the body part, the result of the action, the spatial aspect or some other pertinent aspect of producing either the sound or the movement. A first-grade class asked to code the three sounds of (1) a foot stamping on the floor, (2) clicking of the two heels together while seated, and (3) slapping the desk with an open hand resulted in the following codes:

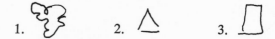

The first is very much like water splashing as one stamps into it; the second represents the movement of the lower legs; and the third, the movement of the hand.

One of the more difficult aspects of footprint coding is recognizing the right-left differences in the footprints. Normally when children begin using the prints, they will match a foot to each print, but will pay little attention to either the form or color that differentiates right and left. They match number and placement, so that, if a right footprint is in front of the left foot, they will probably step with the left foot. It is only after they have used the system for a short time that they really begin to be able to attend to the more subtle and complex clues or color and form. (Red and blue were selected for the color codes by the children. They explained that there was a sound match: red-right and blue-left. This choice of colors has been quite consistent with different groups of children.)

The footprint activity can quite naturally lead into related activities. It can, for instance, be used in conjunction with a large number line in the form of a flat ladder on the floor. It may be used in conjunction with a walking rail to designate a way to walk the rail. It might be used in conjunction with a map of the classroom floor to tell where someone stood in the room while the child reading the map was outside the class.

Footprints are also valuable in helping the child discover how many different ways one can move to match the same coded pattern. A simple right-left-right-left pattern could be matched by walking forward, walking backward from the other end, hopping forward on one foot and backward on the other, hopping on both feet, one ahead of the other. This helps children recognize the limitations of coding systems as well as the need for accepted conventions and rules.

One significant advantage of activity in movement is that this approach throws light on the child's process. It helps reveal his or her approach, style, and problems. Not only can the teacher understand these things more clearly, but also the teacher and other children are more likely to deal with any difficulties *at the time they occur.* They do not have to wait for feedback on the appropriateness of a response. On paper tasks, this evaluation of and dealing with any difficulty usually occurs hours later or even on the next day.

A Demonstration Session

The best way to get the flavor of the kind of program we propose is to take part in it. Since it is not possible to arrange this in a book, it may be helpful to the reader for us to give a recounting of a single, typical session. The following account describes one of the kinds of activities often used to demonstrate to educators some of the ideas of our perceptual training and problem-solving program.

The setting varies depending upon what is available. The session might start with walking into a kindergarten or first- or second-grade classroom as a stranger, along with fifteen to twenty-five other adults, who will be observing. In that event, the first thing that usually takes place is that the chairs, tables and desks are moved to the edges of the room. Or it might be that the children come into a large, strange room with twenty or more adults standing around the room. At other times, the children might come into a room where there are TV cameras set up for closed circuit viewing by an audience. The main requirement is that there be a fairly large space available on the floor of the room.

As I (JWS) am introducing myself to the children, I will sit on the floor. Usually without a word this produces an automatic response from the children. They, too, will sit on the floor, but usually not too close to me. I at this point (and not the children) am the one who is trying to get answers, namely to guess the names of children in the group. (If they are wearing name tags, the only fair way is to cover my eyes.) After I have made several guesses of boys' and girls' names, the children soon become aware that I am correct in naming some of the group, but that I usually also have given at least an equal number of names that are not in the group. (This method seems a much more convincing way to tell the children that in what we are going to do there is no stigma attached to being "wrong," than merely to make such a statement. In all probability they have already been told in the past that it isn't bad to be wrong, but then have ended up by either being penalized or ridiculed for their efforts if they turn out to be wrong.)

By this time the children are usually pretty well ignoring the other adults (or the TV cameras) in the room. Two children are asked to volunteer to help me make a "road" on the floor by putting down two ten- or twelve-foot-long strips of masking tape, the two strips separated by about one and one-half feet.

With this accomplished, the children are asked if they think they can read my mind. A chorus of Nos always goes up. In spite of the Nos, when I have given them the clue that "I am thinking of a form, a geometric form, one that has no corners," I always fail to get any further before voices from the group cut me off with "Circle."

At this point the rules of the game must be stated. The first question children ask in most cases is, "What is the game?" They may not do this verbally, but watch them in their actions—they want to know the name of the game. And the name of our game is to travel the road in some way, any way they want, but somehow to make a circle as they travel the road.

There is usually a short pause, which to me always seems like ages. All of the hand-raising volunteers for helping make a road suddenly have forgotten how to raise their hands. I really used to fear that everything might bog down right at this point. (And this would be happening in front of from fifteen to fifty or more educators.) Always during this pause, I want to say, "Go ahead, do it this way, do it that way," or even to go up and demonstrate myself.

More and more I have realized this same feeling in different situations, and it always reflects my lack of trust in children's abilities. This is the time to bite one's tongue, give some encouragement, but above all give the children time. They always come through. The furthest I have had to go to giving an answer was to read some child's expression well enough to know that he had an idea and then to ask him to *show* what he had in mind.

Often the first child to volunteer travels the road much like a slowly spinning top. The other children's eyes all move to me—to seek my reaction. "Was that right?" Rather than right or wrong at this point, we discuss briefly *how* what the child did was making a circle and traveling the road. The feedback is given that the execution did match the rules of the game, and while that was one way to do what was asked, I suggest that there are many *different* ways to travel the road and make circles. The next volunteer, and this time it *is* a volunteer, usually modifies in some way the slowly spinning top—or whatever the first child did.

Now we have *two* ways to travel the road and make circles. This allows a discussion of how the two ways were different. How were they alike? By the time this has taken place, faces are lighting up and hands are in ready position to be raised. The rules of the game have been better defined and now greater chances are taken.

Invariably at about this time in the activities, some boy who is usually thought of as the class cutup (sometimes it might even be a girl) volunteers and does a forward roll down the road. At times it appears to surprise such a child that he or she can get credit this one time for being a cutup. For certainly this is a different but acceptable way to travel the road and make circles. As the children discuss it they can describe how it was like yet different from the other ways—and in the process they thus better define what makes a circle.

Usually even the more cautious children are now ready to volunteer. And when they do, they usually find some small, less committing kind of way to meet the rules. One youngster may make the circle with both thumbs and index fingers held together as he goes down the road. Another will walk and trace small circles on the road with an index finger. Another holds her mouth in a circle. But as they are given credit for finding unusual ways that even I had never thought of, they, too, become more involved and then take even bigger chances.

Invariably, one child will walk down one tape line almost to the end and then round out the end and walk back on the other tape, rounding out the starting end to the place of origin. This usually brings forth some comment that that was not a circle. Even kindergarten children as a rule get around to the concept that it is circular, and thus somewhat like what has gone before, but that it made something different from a circle. Someone then will bring up the word *oval,* which allows for some talk on how ovals and circles are like and yet different.

When each child has had at least one turn, one may then expect such variations as rolling down the road, rolling the head as the child walks down the road, running down the road twirling, hopping and twirling, waving arms in circles, and even waving pigtails in circles. Someone might even come up with starting from the other end of the road, either because it is closer or because it is seen as a different possibility.

When this does happen, and when it can be one of the differences that children can recognize, then we talk about how many different ways have suddenly opened up. If we had ten before, how many now? It is important for children to recognize that not all learning necessarily takes place just one tiny step at a time, but that sometimes there are leaps in learning. Sometimes there comes an insight that doubles possible solutions. But a word of warning. This different orientation of having a different place to start may not emerge for a week, or two weeks, or even longer in this kind of activity. It admittedly is tempting to tell the children this marvelous insight and thus take away somebody's discovery of it.

Usually the noise level is getting higher by this time. Children are becoming involved and are even being given credit for odd ideas. Faces have become alive, and with life goes excitement and raising of voices. It is time to put some new direction into the life of the situation, a more direct social interaction and cooperation.

To signal a change, I will sit on the floor again and ask them to sit down. It is interesting to note that they now crowd in much closer to me. Also, they usually sit in a circular formation or in a semicircular formation, maybe two deep. The next activity is to divide into smaller groups of four, five, or six children in a group (depending on how many children are involved) so that the numbers in each group can come out even. I have always been amazed at how even kindergarten children can divide into groups of even numbers, when they supposedly have no concept of division. After they get into groups, they are asked to figure out ways that the *groups* can make circles and move at the same time.

This activity requires cooperation and agreement among the members of the group. Usually the first group to come up with an idea holds hands and walks in a circle (though at times this is not the first way or even a way any of the groups come up with). Other groups will execute a mere embellishment of whatever the first one does. But soon new and original ideas evolve. A group may interlink arms in circular formation and walk in a circle. A group may spin on their knees, or more likely on their bottoms, while kneeling or sitting in a circle. A group may hold hands and spiral themselves into a tight circle or they may lie on their backs with feet up to meet at a common center and at the same time hold their hands extended, looking much like a ferris wheel flat on the floor. Interestingly enough, it is often the group of boys who are called the nonachievers in the classroom who come up with the most novel ideas. (I have yet to try this activity without there appearing at least one *original* version of circles within the groups.)

During this group circle making, the decibel level certainly rises in the room. But, in spite of the high decibel level, the *noise* level is low, for the sounds made are almost completely related to the task at hand. When I have had the opportunity of observing some of these sessions on TV tape after the session took place, when I could be enough removed so that I didn't feel it was my responsibility to keep the quiet, I have been surprised to note that what I took for noise while with the groups was really constructive working. The "noise" might have been some disagreement among members of a group trying to arrive at a common idea, or some child trying to relate an idea at the same time three or four others were trying to do the same thing.

At first I was concerned about groups that were so silent that it seemed they could be doing nothing. When their turn came to perform I was often surprised, not only that they did have an idea and plan, but that often it was very complex and unique. It really is difficult to trust children at times, especially when they are turned loose without much adult supervision! But the mistrust usually comes from a fear that *we* will not look good, and that they might let us down. Because of experience, I will place my bet with children any day over an equal-size adult group when called upon to carry out some unusual instruction!

Now that the children have experienced making circles by themselves and within a group, they are again asked to change the game. The tables and desks around the room do have some use in learning, even though ideally it should be for a much smaller part of the day than is usually the case. For placed on these tables and desks now are supplies: paper of different colors, crayons, pencils, art yarn or heavy colored cord, scissors, Scotch tape, and staplers. The activity now becomes to use any of this material to make circles in any way that they would like.

One of my best experiences with children occurred at this point in the sequence of activities. I was passing out art yarn to the children, a kindergarten class in California. During the earlier part of the activity, I became the victim of something that all teachers dread. I lost a boy from the class. Bobby crawled under a desk and refused to participate. I attempted to get him to join the group, and only succeeded in losing another of the group who decided to join Bobby, since he was getting attention. I did halt that tactic, mainly because of the fear of losing the whole class.

I dropped a piece of yarn below the desk for Bobby as I walked by. The yarn immediately popped right out in front of me. As I walked, I kicked the yarn back with my foot and went on. After some time, as the children were working, I heard from under the desk, "I've got it! I've got it!"

Out popped Bobby with a knot tied in his art yarn. Bobby got credit for making the smallest circle, and there was no longer any fear of losing him from the group. To convince the other children that a knot was a circle, Bobby had to demonstrate how he made the knot. Several children and several adults gained a new definition of a knot! But more than that, Bobby had succeeded in solving his problem and had come to trust a little more in himself.

This description of a typical demonstration session is not given to set up a blueprint for the way somebody else should carry out an activity session. As we have noted, it is not our aim to prescribe certain set activities that should be carried out. The more creative the leader of such a workshop or activity session turns out to be, the more varied and different the activities proposed will be.

This description is merely intended to give an idea of what the program we propose is like, and the footprint idea has, in practice, proved to be a good way to get started. But as such a program goes on during the year, teachers will be surprised to find that many things they have actually been doing in their own teaching and with their own classes actually lend themselves to our *kind* of presentation.

Further Suggested Activities

To get a better feeling of what our program involves, it might be fun to try one of our usual activities with your own family or with a group of adults. For instance, you might try an activity that demonstrates how difficult it is to use language accurately and effectively. This is a game called "Robot." One person serves as the "robot" and is blindfolded. The robot's job is to follow word instructions from the group. The group's job is to direct the robot to perform some specific task, such as picking up a pencil and putting

A New Kind of Program

it down in some different place. The instructions are given by telling the robot *exactly* what to do.

A good robot will obey the words, but may do so too literally. If the command is "Turn," the robot may start spinning like a top. The instruction did not limit the turn or tell the direction. Thus, clearly, it is important that instructions be given very effectively and specifically.

When third- and fourth-graders play this game, they often take it one step further. Before they start a session they decide on a word program. This may include twenty or forty words, but once the program is made up these are the *only* words they can use. After a trial run with a program, it is fair to allow them to change the program by substituting words to make it work better. This activity is not only a problem-solving activity that children enjoy, but one that will also challenge most adult groups.

Summary

As teachers work with a problem-solving program of this kind, they need to realize that children's answers are in one sense invariably correct, for children answer the question they hear, see, understand. It is true that sometimes the question heard may be different from the one we thought we had asked, for the child's understanding of the question may have been different from our intent. But there tends to be logic, reason, and above all information about the child within the context of his answer, whatever it may be.

And when the answer is not what we had looked for, it is important to help the child solve the problem he or she *understands,* as the first order of business. The next step is to help him see the problem as you meant and asked it. Often this does lead to what may seem like side issues. But more often than not, these side issues may provide more fertile ground for learning than would some preplanned lesson. These side issues are real problems, too, not merely simulated exercises.

Our program, obviously, does not advocate the abolishment of order and discipline. Admittedly children who have been taught traditionally do tend to get a bit "high" when this kind of program is first introduced, since it does allow for more talking and movement than they are accustomed to. When behavior and noise interfere with learning, this fact can be presented to the children. It then becomes *their* problem, a problem *they* must solve. This solution will take time, and the rules and regulations of courtesy they make up will change as they prove effective or ineffective. With this new freedom, it is important that children learn that they also have new responsibilities. Discipline and order are not just the teacher's problem but, first and foremost, the children's problem.

Most teachers find it useful to include class evaluative sessions in the program. These seem to work best as a class circle. Problems can be brought forward and suggested methods of working with them can be raised. The teacher must be prepared to be part of this circle and be willing to attempt some of the changes that the children suggest. This does not mean that the teacher abdicates her position in the class. The difference from the usual situation is that she should be viewed as another human being rather than as *just* a teacher.

We started by saying that we have seen changes in children, teachers, and in what goes on in the classroom as a result of our program. What are these changes? They are *not* reflected in higher scores achieved on academic tests, but rather in changes for the better in tests which measure perception and development (56, 65). The most important changes are seen in the human qualities of the children and teachers involved, in their attitudes, in their values, in their self-confidence, in their social behavior. Probably the most positive result of all is that more children and teachers can look at school as an enjoyable experience. One class involved in our program even wanted to come to school on Saturdays.

Children who have taken part in such a program have shown more self-confidence in approaching school and tasks than formerly. They have become more involved in what is going on in the classroom during the entire day, not just during the program time. They have been more willing to express their differences and to stick up for their beliefs and solutions.

Teachers, too, have changed. They have come to have a greater respect for their own ideas. They have been more willing to try new things. Probably most important, they have become better observers of behavior. One teacher summed up her new attitudes by saying, "It was a lot easier to teach subjects than it is to teach children, but teaching children is a lot more fun."

The classrooms, too, have changed. Chairs are not in neat rows nearly as much, and children are moving around more. Activity centers are being set up. Thus, instead of needing to find excuses to get up, as to sharpen a pencil or to go to the toilet, children find that their activity areas provide positively for times when they need a break.

But the breaks are now not merely for wasting time. They are now used for learning through trying to solve some problem. The child thus may read a code and walk the walking rail to match the code. He may find out how to solve a puzzle problem. Or he may find out how many ways you can balance so that three parts of your body are touching the floor.

We feel that this program has been at least a small step toward helping children turn on to learning, a step toward realizing that changes come from within as well as from outside.

Learning has a good deal to do with the learner. It asks that, in addition to taking in information, he *do something* within his own being. In many ways, a true step in learning is the discovery of something that is within the self and then learning to trust that part of self—yes, trust it even enough to apply what you have learned to another and different situation. When children can approach learning from a self-involved position, they become better prepared

257

to meet tomorrow's questions. We cannot give them tomorrow's answers, for we don't even know the questions. But we *can* help them solve some of the problems of today and thus acquire problem-solving abilities.

CHAPTER 13

SUGGESTIONS FOR PROMOTING SCHOOL SUCCESS

*Hell is hardship, hardship. And you have to go to
school until you are thirty years old.*
—COMMENT BY TEN-YEAR-OLD FIFTH GRADER

How can we make things better and more successful for that large, captive population who must attend our schools, not till they are thirty but at least till they are in their late teens? Here are some suggestions:

1. First and foremost, if your boy or girl is having serious trouble in school, find out, with the help of teacher, principal, guidance worker, child psychologist, or clinic, why he is having this trouble. Appreciate that in most instances diagnosis must precede treatment. Unless you know what is wrong, it's hard to set it right.

2. Never forget that behind every child's behavior there is a physical body. The more you, and others, understand and respect that body, the more effective you, and they, will be in helping him function at his highest level of capacity.

3. Appreciate that one of the tools that specialists use to evaluate your child's personality, intelligence, and behavior level is tests. Try to rise above the currently proposed notion that tests are an invasion of privacy. They invade privacy no more than does a medical examination, and we need them if we are to understand and help your children.

4. Don't delay. If things are wrong in school, don't let months or years go by before you take steps to set them right.

259

5. Keep in mind, when things go wrong, that more likely than not the answer lies in the child's own organism. Chances are that faced with the same problems and lack of money and not always ideal scholastic material, you might not do any better than the school is doing. The many popular books on the market that criticize the schools find it easy to tell what is wrong. They are generally rather weak when they come to the part about how they would set things right.

6. Don't be upset by an occasional, "Do I have to go to school today?" or "I hate school." But, if your child strongly and consistently over a long period of time makes it evident that he really does hate school, find out why.

7. There are many different possible reasons why a child may have trouble in school. Since the most common source of difficulty is overplacement, be as sure as you reasonably can that your child is *ready* before you start him in school. And be as sure as you reasonably can that he is ready for promotion before you have him move on to a next grade.

8. If repeating seems indicated, don't be afraid to have him repeat. If his response to kindergarten was not successful, don't push him on to first grade with the idea that if he fails *that,* he can then repeat. If repeating seems indicated, better to repeat kindergarten than to try first grade, fail that, and *then* repeat.

9. Do everything you can to see that your child gets a good start in school. Kindergarten, to you, may not seem to make all that difference. It *does* make a difference, if only because it comes first. A child's attitude toward school depends a great deal on his own personality and aptitude. But it also depends on the impression he gets about school right at the start.

10. Keep in mind that there are many different ways a child has of telling you that he is in trouble in school. It isn't just a poor report card that should be a warning. Excessive illness, excessive fatigue, or excessive dislike of school can also be warning signs.

Ask yourself, "Is poor health interfering with my child's schooling, or is it the demands of school that may be causing or exaggerating poor health?"

11. Since physical illness *may* lie at the basis of much inadequate or disruptive school behavior, if a child behaves *very* badly in school, at least take the trouble to see to it that he has a *thorough* physical checkup.

12. Consider the possibility that medication might help to slow down an overactive schoolchild to the point where he could respond effectively to the demands of the usual school routine. Or that chemotherapy or endocrine help might aid the child in trouble to respond more effectively.

13. Consider the very real possibility that your child may need visual help—either glasses or visual training or both.

14. Don't worry too much that your child is so bright that he or she will be bored in school and needs to be double promoted. Boredom is not always a sign of brightness, and more than a high I.Q. is needed for a child to be ready for a much higher grade than the one he is in.

15. In fact do not confuse high intelligence with maturity and readiness for even the usual single promotion, let alone double promotion. A child can be unquestionably bright, but at the same time immature. Brightness and maturity develop along separate lines, so a child can be definitely above average in brightness and below average in maturity. The fact that any child is unusually bright does not guarantee that he will be mature enough to start school early. Also do not confuse early reading ability with maturity. The fact that a child is advanced in reading does not guarantee readiness for first grade.

16. If you have a child in the 80 to 90 I.Q. range and the school does not have any special classes for such children, see if such classes cannot be set up in your community. They are needed.

17. Do what you can to provide a stimulating home atmo-

sphere but give up any notion that you are going to make a child smarter or brighter or substantially more intelligent by home drill or training or by having him watch special television programs.

18. Don't confuse issues. If your child is doing poorly in school, don't try to motivate him by removing home privileges. The two things don't equate.

19. Don't think of discipline or punishment as your first recourse when your boy or girl is reported to "behave badly" in school. So-called bad behavior can be as much a warning signal that something is wrong as fever is considered to be in case of illness.

20. Be realistic in your expectations. Not every child is an A or B student. Appreciate, and help your child to appreciate, that there are some instances in which C *is* a respectable grade. Remember that it isn't so much what happens as how it seems to the child that counts.

21. Try to realize that school grades do not always go up or do not always stay up. It is not unusual or abnormal for any child to have an occasional slump.

22. Don't let grades get to be a big issue in your household. Too much emphasis on grades, if the child is a poor scholar, will be too great a strain. If he is a good scholar, it may cause him to see things out of proportion. Use grades, as they should be used, as a clue to you and to your child as to how things are going. Reward, if you wish, for good performance. Let poor performance be a clue to you that some sort of help or adjustment is needed. But don't let grades become a matter of life and death. Don't let your home become "grade-centered."

23. Though tutoring can when needed be really helpful, don't count on tutoring to bridge the gap when as so often the school's demands are far beyond a child's abilities.

24. If homework seems too demanding, don't just rail at the school for giving such long assignments. Be sure that you have provided optimal study conditions for your boy or girl and that you

provide reasonable assistance. However, never do a child's homework for him.

25. Realize that if you have a so-called "underachiever," your problem is complex. To begin with, are you sure he really *is* an underachiever? Just because a child has a relatively high I.Q. or has done well on some achievement test does not guarantee that he will get good grades. So he may *not* be underachieving. He may be doing the best he can.

26. If your child is not reading up to grade level, check carefully to be sure that he really is a problem reader. It may be that he is reading at his true behavior level and that the school is merely pushing too hard and expecting too much. In other words, your problem reader may actually not *be* a problem reader.

27. Try not to get excited about the currently much publicized notion of teaching your preschooler to read. Maybe you can. Maybe you can't. It won't make much difference either way. Forced early reading does not give much advantage later.

28. Try to see to it that your child is doing something more than memorizing at school. Hope that the school is teaching him to think, to use his mind effectively, constructively, and creatively. If it is not, see what you can do along these lines at home. But do it naturally. Don't be self-conscious about it.

In fact, though you will not be able to accomplish this by yourself, you might try through your PTA to give some support to this current notion that it is more important to teach a child to think, to figure things out, to use his mind in constructive ways than merely to memorize and give back specific things he has been taught. Without supporting a complete revolution in the present school system, give support to the notion that school aims and ideals could vary a bit from those which now predominate.

29. Don't believe everything your child tells you about what goes on in school.

30. Though it certainly is possible that a different type of class or different school (private instead of public) may be the an-

swer to your child's school problems, as a rule it is not advisable to move to a different town or part of town just in the hope that you will find a school which will appreciate your child more than his present school does.

31. Don't go down to school to "straighten things out." If things are wrong, try to assume the attitude that you and the school together may be able to set them right. Accept the fact that your own attitude toward school will influence your child's attitude. If you respect the school and the teacher, chances are your child will do the same. Try not to be too quick to criticize the teacher and the school system in general.

32. When things go wrong at school, make at least a superficial check to be sure that it may not be some rather simple thing (trouble in the bus, not understanding the teacher's instructions) that is causing the difficulty.

33. Try not to feel baffled and discouraged if you can't immediately get all the help and advice you want from the school. Communication is sometimes difficult even when both parent and school show full good will.

34. Try to arrange for your school to go back to the old-fashioned idea of half-yearly promotions. There are many children who in June are not ready for a full year's promotion but who do not need to repeat a whole grade. (You cannot make this change all by yourself but possibly it can be arranged for through PTA or school board.)

35. For the very young child, if it should turn out, as it will with many, that all day five days a week is too much school, see if you can make some reasonable effort to lessen this demand. Work for half-day first grade for everybody. And if your child has gone beyond first grade and five days a week is still too much, work with the school to see if an occasional day or half day off can be arranged.

36. Be friendly with the school. Do join the PTA (or PTO). Take part whenever participation is practical.

37. And finally, if things go wrong in school, try not to blame the school. Or the teacher. Or your child. Blaming is not a constructive solution. If you are convinced that a child is doing less well than he "should," you will probably try all the usual things: you will scold, nag, urge, bribe, push, try to motivate. But the likelihood is that it may be the situation, and not the child, that will have to be changed before he will do better.

CHAPTER 14

SUMMARY

At a rough guess two hundred more years may bring the study of human behavior up to the level which physics reached under Newton.

—D. E. BROADBENT

Many parents complain, and justly, that their children are not doing as well as they might in school. Many continue their complaint with the accusation that it is the school's responsibility *to see to it* that all children be given an adequate education. This is less reasonable.

It is easy to criticize the schools. It is equally easy to overlook the tremendous burden we place on them. A democratic form of society holds out many unrealistic expectations to its members. Among these is the unrealistic notion that all children are highly educable and that our schools will be able to deal effectively with all the problems with which schools are faced.

Certainly our schools do try with everybody, but there are many children for whom it is hard to provide good academic answers. One of the reasons is that, as the above quotation suggests, we do not know anywhere near as much as we need to about human behavior.

But we DO know enough to know that behavior has a solid biological basis, and that it develops in as patterned and predictable a way as does the human body. This is a good safe place to start, no matter how ambitious one may be about improving or curing. Keep in mind that behavior *does* make sense. Our problem is to try to find out what sense it makes and what we can do about it.

Much has been written in criticism of the public schools. In our opinion they are doing a tremendous job. Just as many unsung parents in this country are devoting themselves well beyond the call of reason to often difficult and unrewarding children, so are many unsung teachers and school administrators doing the very same thing. The successes are many more than the failures. The efforts expended on the difficult, even when these fail, deserve commendation rather than the unmitigated criticism that is so often their lot.

In our opinion, the majority of schools are doing remarkably well. Parents often become very angry because they feel that the school is not achieving adequate success with their boy or girl. But think of the task. If we had to start the whole thing over, confronted with the mammoth problems now faced, we just might decide that universal education is too difficult a thing to undertake.

Hopefully, the information in this book may help our schools to do even better in the future than in the past by helping parents understand more clearly what they can and cannot expect, and what they as parents can do to cooperate in solving the problems of those children who now are failing.

This book has told you about schoolchildren in trouble. It has talked about some of the reasons why they have trouble and some of the things you can do to prevent or solve school problems that do arise. If we have written clearly, not too much summary should be needed here, but we do want to emphasize that *there's nearly always a good reason when a schoolchild is in trouble.* And if you and the school can't figure it out, there is nearly always somewhere a specialist who can help you.

If your child is having trouble in school, check with the teacher and if need be with the principal. If they can't solve the problem, hopefully they will refer you to a guidance counselor, psychologist, or clinic. If no such specialist is available, hopefully this book can help you start to figure out what *might* lie at the root of your problem. Whatever you do, don't waste time following along with the same old incorrect clichés: "Your child could do the work if he would," or, "Emotional factors in the home lie at the basis of his school difficulty."

Do appreciate that sometimes we never find out *all* the answers but do believe that there are answers to be found.

It is not reasonable to suppose that every parent will be able either to find or to afford a behavior clinic or a psychologist in private practice who will examine his child (if he is in trouble) and tell exactly what is wrong and what should be done about it. Our purpose in writing this book is chiefly to tell you that such services *are* available, and that when they are not you can at least ask yourself some of the questions the professional person *would* ask were he to see your child.

Thus, you can ask yourself if your child is placed correctly with respect to the grade he is in. You can ask if he is of average or better intelligence, or if perhaps he needs to be in a special class. Is his visual functioning adequate to meet the demands of his age and grade or does he need glasses or even a certain amount of visual or perceptual training? Is he of a more or less normal personality endowment or does he have special problems along personality lines for which he may need help? Is he suited to meet the demands of the ordinary classroom situation? Is there something physically or medically wrong with his body that can be corrected?

If there is a question about any of these things, this may be the area in which his problem lies. Try to get the school to help you if no specialist is available to do so.

If absolutely no outside help is offered, you may have to do that hardest thing of all—try to motivate him. How do you do this? Nobody can tell you for sure, but it will help if you can arrange that he be put into situations where he can experience at least some success. It may be academic success or it may be athletic or social success. Any success helps.

Many parents quite naturally harbor the hope that there are relatively simple, easy things they themselves can do at home to solve their children's school problems. If these problems are extremely minor, their hope may be justified.

Thus, there are, indeed, children who have been helped or encouraged to better school performance by more attention from Mother or Father, by a greater expression of interest, by help with homework, by encouragement to study, by reward or praise for work well done. This kind of thing goes on quite naturally in many responsible homes, and many parents give these kinds of help quite routinely. But when children are in real trouble, when they cannot read, cannot study, cannot respond to minimal school demands, when they are, as many are, functioning a grade or two below the one they are in, it takes more than a little help from Mother or Father to set things right.

This book has alerted you to some of the kinds of problems customarily met with and some of the kinds of help you can reasonably seek. And it has stressed throughout that, before we can correct school problems, we do in most instances need a diagnosis (your own or that of a professional person) as to what is wrong.

There should be a school situation for every schoolchild that will make him comfortable and that will permit him to function effectively and be at least reasonably successful and happy. Let's all work hard to try to find it.

Some parents are extremely casual and easygoing about the whole thing and if, as often is the case, they are at the same time blessed with children who like school and do well there, they have it made. There are other parents who by nature are worriers, or who have children they really need to worry about. For them there should be a school situation that can, within reason, meet their needs. We have found that even parents of extremely difficult children, children with problems that are truly hard to solve or even to face, do as a rule respond with remarkable cooperation and calm if somebody only takes the time to explain clearly, and in a friendly and positive manner, just exactly where the child's problem lies and how they can go about helping him.

If children are to be school captives (as they are) for so many years early in life, we should at least make things comfortable for them. Some, of course, will love learning. Others will not, but can manage it. For others, school is not a good situation unless we take very special pains and keep our hopes very modest. And, as we have suggested, hopefully the schools themselves may in the near future be willing at least to consider different kinds of teaching, which will emphasize the importance not of right and wrong answers but rather of learning to think things out and to solve problems for oneself. Facts and information can always be found in books. Using one's own mind is a skill or ability that so far has not always been taught in our schools.

And since more often than any other single factor, overplacement looms large as the most common source of school failure, we end this book with the poem of a friend of ours, psychologist Marlin Spike Werner, which features our favorite theme—that each child should be ready before he enters school:

> What will become of this twelve year old of mine, of mine?
> A twelve year old with a mental age of nine, of nine.
> With an I.Q. of 74 at best
> Who never passed an algebra test
> Must he always go through life depressed
> Then stand in a welfare line?
>
> At the age of six the law can be so cruel, so cruel.
> With a mental age of four and a half he went to school.
> With social promotions, he failed and failed
> As through the primary grades he trailed
> Till now on his heart a sign is nailed
>   "A fool, a fool."
>
> We plant some seeds in early March
> And some we plant in May.
> But kids are planted in school at six
> Right after Labor Day
> Without regard for the varying vine,
> The honeysuckle or pumpkin kind.
> A farmer would never be so inclined
> To plant his seeds that way.

Summary

God has given girls and boys to me and you
To raise in the very finest way we knew, we knew.
We've done our best both day and night
To bring our little boy up right.
But now he has academic blight
What can we do?

TESTS USED AT THE GESELL INSTITUTE

For those readers who would like to know something about the various tests used at the Gesell Institute, and mentioned in Chapter 2, the following detail may be of help. The average parent reader will, perhaps, not care to concern himself or herself with these descriptions.

Developmental (or Behavior) Tests

One of the main themes of this book is that our expectations, academic or otherwise, of any child should depend more on his behavior age (i.e., the age at which he is behaving) than on his birthday age. Even though a child may be legally six years old, if his behavior age is five, we can expect of him only those things which a five-year-old can do, and he should be placed in kindergarten, not in first grade.

Behavior tests are simple tests that tell the age at which a child is behaving. In infancy, for instance, a behavior test might consist of such things as seeing whether a baby can creep or walk, say a few words, pick up an object, place a round block in the round hole of a formboard.

Behavior tests of the preschooler or school-age child are more complex, but not too different. They consist of a simple group of tasks or test situations that the child is asked to perform or respond to. Response is not rated primarily right or wrong. Rather it is matched to a set of norms we have obtained by examining thousands of children at every age level and then determining what the average or usual response is for a child of that age level.

Behavior tests referred to most frequently in this book include:

COPY FORMS TEST

The child is shown, on separate cards in sequence, drawings of a circle, cross, square, triangle, divided rectangle, and diamond. He is asked to copy each in turn on a piece of paper 8½ by 11 inches in size. He may take as long as he wants to on each.

Copying a circle may not seem a particularly telling bit of behavior, and yet from the way a child performs this simple task we can rate his response as falling anywhere from eighteen months to six years or older. Thus an eighteen-monther responds to the request to imitate* a circle by scribbling, usually obliquely. The two-year-old can scribble in a rather circular fashion. By three, however, most are past the scribble stage and can imitate a circular stroke and stop after the first time around.

The child's circle at this time, though large and wobbly, is most often begun at the top and drawn in the same direction in which a right-handed adult draws, that is, counterclockwise. However, from three and a half years on, when the child copies the circular form he tends to start at the bottom and go around in a clockwise direction. And it is not till around five years of age for girls, and five and a half for boys, that the circle is again drawn from the top down and in a counterclockwise direction. (These and similar changes in behavior occur as a result of growth changes that are not fully understood at present.)

Thus, if your five-year-old girl or five-and-a-half-year-old boy, when asked to copy a circle, still starts at the bottom and/or draws clockwise, he is showing that, for this test at least, he is not responding up to his age.

---

* At the earliest ages the child is asked to *imitate* the circle, cross, and other forms he sees the examiner make. At later ages he is asked to *copy* them from a pictured form.

This, or other behavior in which a child is not responding up to his age, is not by any means necessarily a sign of low intelligence or of anything to worry about. But it is a clue that the child is showing an immaturity at least in this special test situation.

The same sort of changes occur in other forms we ask a child to copy. And it is not just the way he copies the individual form, but also the size of the forms and the way he arranges them on the page and in relation to each other, that gives the experienced examiner the clues he needs in determining the age at which the individual child is responding.

Thus, up through four years of age a child may use a whole sheet of paper just to copy the circle. As they get older, even by four and a half years, most get all the forms onto one side of one piece of paper. By seven we expect forms to be arranged horizontally, in correct order, at or near the top of the paper, and by seven many use not more than half a page for all forms.

PRINTING NAME AND ADDRESS, AND NUMBERS

Many children are able to print their first name at five years of age or before, and we expect the child who is developing at an average rate to be able to print his, or her, first name at or soon after five and a half years of age. We expect the six-year-old to be able to print both names. Cursive writing of both names does not come in till eight years of age; size of printed letters is not consistent until seven.

Address, including street, number, city, and state is not accomplished till eight years of age by girls, nine by boys.

INCOMPLETE MAN TEST

One of the most revealing tests we have is the one called the Incomplete Man Test. As figure 14 shows, the Incomplete Man figure as presented to the child consists of the unfinished figure of a man. This includes one arm and hand; one leg and foot; nose,

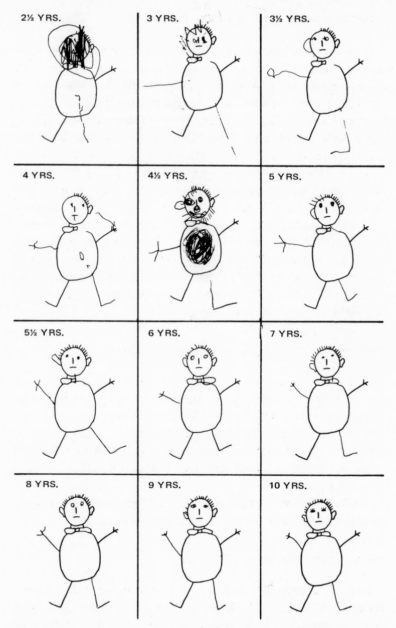

Fig. 14. Expected age changes in response to the Incomplete Man Test

276

mouth; hair, and ear on one side; and half of the neck and tie—that is, it gives a model for all missing parts except the eyes. The child is asked what this is and then asked to finish it.

As a child grows older, he adds an increasing number of parts. However, it is not so much the number of parts he adds as it is the way he draws them that indicates his maturity. As figure 14 shows, the following age changes take place:

The added arm, which at first (around three to three and a half years of age) tends to be placed too low, be pointed downward, and be of too long a length, gradually moves up on the body line, turns so that it points upward, and becomes shorter, till it matches in size, angle, and placement the arm (and hand) already provided.

The leg, too, changes with age. As the child grows older, leg and foot both become shorter, and leg is gradually better placed so as increasingly to match the leg already provided.

Eyes, which at first are scribbles, later become large and round, then small and round, then oval with pupils, and eventually have eyebrows and occasionally lashes. As the child grows older he can make the two eyes of the same size and can place them side by side in good balance.

Hair, which at first is too long and tends to go too far around the head (even, at four and a half years, under the chin) gradually becomes shorter and covers less space. The ear is gradually better placed and of a more accurate shape.

At the neck area, the very young child (of preschool age) often adds nothing or merely continues the body line. By five, many add a slanting line from chin to body (for the neck); by five and a half they make a straight neck, and then a curved line to fit into the (given) body line. By six they struggle to add a tie. By seven most can make a reasonably good tie, as well as making neck and body line.

Around four to four and a half, many children add a belly button. For the five-year-old, a belly button is considered a sign of clear immaturity.

277

And so, not only are more parts added but, as the child matures, the added parts increasingly resemble the parts already provided. From the way the total man looks, once he is completed, an experienced examiner can easily place the age of the total response, whether it is up to, below, or ahead of the child's birthday age.

MONROE VISUAL III

Another developmental test we have mentioned in this book is Marion Monroe's Visual III, a memory for designs test that evaluates the child's power of recall. The test consists of four separate 8½- by 11-inch cards, on each of which are four geometric figures in horizontal alignment. The child is allowed to look at each card, in turn, for ten seconds and then is asked to write down as many of the forms as he can remember on his own sheet of paper. At five years of age we expect that only about one-third of the figures will be reproduced correctly. Even by ten years only 74 percent are, on the average, reproduced correctly, so that this test provides a good evaluation of the power of recall even right up into the teen ages.

RIGHT AND LEFT TESTS, SINGLE AND DOUBLE COMMANDS

A final developmental situation we frequently use is Right and Left Tests, which check the child's spatial orientation, not only to right and left as related to his own body, but also as related to the bodies of others. The children who are poorly oriented as to right and left frequently are also poorly oriented to letters and often have great difficulty in reading. The tests we use are modified from those of Dr. J. Robert Jacobson.

The child is asked to identify the examiner's eye, eyebrow, palm, elbow, thumb, and index finger. He is then asked to identify his own right and left hand, eye, and ear. Single Commands ask him to touch his eye, show his pointer, ring, and middle fingers, close his eyes and bend his head, touch his right ear, show his right thumb, show his right index finger, etc.

In Double Commands he is asked to carry out more complicated instructions such as, "Touch your right thumb with your right little finger," "Place your left hand on your right knee," "Put your left ring finger to your right eyebrow," etc.

The child's speed and accuracy in carrying out such commands help us to know how well or poorly oriented he is to his own body and in space.

BENDER GESTALT

Though not generally classed with the Gesell Behavior Tests, the Koppitz version of the Bender Gestalt is given by us routinely and makes an excellent supplement to our Copy Forms Test. The Bender consists of nine small cards, each of which bears a rather intricate design. The child is asked to copy each in turn on a piece of paper, 8½ by 11 inches in size. This test of perception is especially useful because it has been scored and normed so specifically by Dr. Elizabeth Koppitz. From the number of errors the child makes in copying these designs one can determine his developmental level (that is, the age at which he is performing), whether or not he has emotional problems, and whether or not there is suggestion of possible brain damage.

HEALY II: A PICTORIAL COMPLETION TEST

This test is comprised of a series of eleven pictures (one of which is very simple in idea and is used merely for demonstration purposes). The pictures represent in sequence situations or events occurring in one day in the life of the boy depicted in each picture. From each picture there is a one-inch-square piece cut out and missing. The picture is to be completed by selecting the proper square from sixty accompanying small illustrations, each one an inch square, and only one of which represents the object needed to exactly fulfill the idea of the given picture.

Ideas from which to choose in filling the spaces are represented by the stock of sixty small pictures. Just as one selects verbal ideas from his own mental stock in a language completion test, here one chooses pictures to fill in what has been cut out of the main illustrations.

Of all tests used for measuring apperception, the Healy Pictorial Completion Test is perhaps fairest to children of different backgrounds, since it eliminates to a large degree factors of training and of special ability or disability in language.

THE TREE TEST

The Tree Test is a test just coming into use at the Gesell Institute and elsewhere. The subject is given a white sheet of paper, letter size, and a box of Mongol colored pencils and is asked to draw a tree. Norms for this test are not yet available, but it promises to be a test that gives good clues as to developmental, or behavior, age.

Intelligence Test

Though certainly much more than the I.Q. goes to school, and though we consistently emphasize that being highly intelligent is no guarantee of readiness to begin school (since a child might be highly intelligent and still immature—"superior immature"), it is nevertheless most important to know the intellectual level of any child who is having trouble in school.

Opinions differ as to the extent to which intelligence level can be increased or improved. Our position is that intellectual level is very probably genetically determined. That is, we think each child is born with a certain intellectual potential, even though this may be a *range* rather than any set and exact amount.

In cases of school difficulty it is especially important to know the general intellectual level of the child in question since, if it is *below* a certain level, it may turn out that the academic difficulty the child is experiencing results simply from the fact that academic demands are greater than his intelligence can permit him to accept.

There are many intelligence tests commonly used today. The one we use most routinely is called the WISC (Wechsler Intelligence Scale for Children).* This test has two parts—the Verbal Scale and the Performance Scale. The Verbal Scale consists of questions that determine the level of the child's Information, his Comprehension, Arithmetic ability, ability to spot Similarities, and extent of his Vocabulary. The Performance tests include Picture Completion, Picture Arrangement, Block Design, Object Assembly, and Coding.

This is, obviously, a test with right and wrong answers or ways of putting things together.

The correct score (for each part separately) is divided by the child's age in order to obtain his intelligence quotient. (It is a little more complicated than this, but that's the basic idea.) Thus, if a six-year-old boy or girl gets exactly as many correct answers as a six-year-old is expected to get, you divide 6 by 6 and get (obviously) 1. For reasons best known to psychologists, two zeros are added and the I.Q. is 100, or average. If the child were seven and responding like a six-year-old, you would divide 6 by 7 and get an I.Q. of 85; if he were six and responding like a seven-year-old, you would divide 7 by 6 and get an I.Q. of 116.

Since there are two parts to this test, the examiner may give just the verbal and thus obtain the child's verbal I.Q.; he may give just the performance and obtain the performance I.Q.; or he may use both and thus get a more comprehensive score.

---

* The WPPSI (Wechsler Preschool and Primary Scale of Intelligence) is a very similar test available for use with younger children. Since it is used only rarely, it will not be described in detail.

It is considered significant, and a possible source of difficulty, if there is a wide discrepancy between the verbal and performance scores.

The I.Q. score presumably tells us how intelligent or how bright a child is as compared to others of his age.

Achievement Tests

Achievement tests differ from behavior tests in that what they measure is not so much potential as actual achievement. They determine how much the child has learned in any given subject. Subjects we check are reading and arithmetic. Reading is checked both for single words, and for the reading of paragraphs. The latter is measured by use of a reading test called the Gray Oral.

In testing a child in arithmetic it is first necessary to understand the process the child is using. Some of the basic steps in performance seem first to occur through intuitive understanding (under five years). Gradually the child begins to work from direct concrete experiences (five years). Later he is able to function abstractly.

Most five-year-olds can calculate within 5. Five-and-a-half-year-olds can calculate within 10. Six-year-olds can calculate within 15 or 20. It is important to know exactly where a child is functioning in his ability to weigh facts and to draw conclusions from which he will base judgments.

Problems posed are as follows:

1. Ask how high the child can count. If he says 100, ask, "Any higher?"
2. Check spontaneous counting. (Stop at 40.)
3. Try calculations within 15 or 20.
4. If child cannot calculate, place pennies in a row two inches apart and ask him to count them. Try first four, then ten, then thirteen, then twenty. In each instance after he has counted, ask, "How many altogether?"

Projective Tests

In arriving at the fullest possible understanding of any given boy or girl, we like sometimes to look below the surface in an effort to know more about what this child is "really" like. One of the most effective tools available is the so-called projective test.

A projective test is a test to which there are no right and wrong answers, but which, rather, consists of a supposedly more or less fluid medium onto which the child *projects* his own personality. That is, by his responses to the test material he tells us what he is like and/or what the world is like to him.

There are many such tests available. The four we use most are the Rorschach Inkblot Test, the Lowenfeld Mosaic Test, the Sentence Completion Test, and the Kinetic Family Drawing Test.

RORSCHACH INKBLOT TEST

The Rorschach Inkblot Test consists of a set of ten cards, each one 6½ by 9½ inches in size, each printed with a rather vague, inkblot-type design, some in black and white, some in colors. These blots do not actually represent any person or thing but, like cloud pictures, tend to be interpreted differently by each viewer.

Without explaining the rationale behind the use of this test, suffice it to say that the examiner can determine, from what the subject sees in these blots, a great deal about his basic personality or individuality. Thus we can tell whether he is introversive or extratensive, more influenced by his own inner drives or by outside stimuli, primarily intellectual or primarily emotional. We can tell whether he is of a basically normal and sound temperament or if he is neurotic or psychotic. If he is troubled, it can often be told what is troubling him and how good the possibility of improvement. We can tell how he sees things (whether he primarily sees the whole of a situation or merely the parts) and we can tell whether or not he in general sees the world as others do or merely a distorted version of what we consider to be reality.

And, at least as the test is used at the Gesell Institute, we can tell whether a boy or girl is responding approximately at his age level or, perhaps, above or below his age level.

In short, the Rorschach is generally considered to tell us how the individual experiences reality.

LOWENFELD MOSAIC TEST

In contrast, the Lowenfeld Mosaic Test, another of the so-called projective tests to which there are no right or wrong answers, tells us how he functions, how he may be expected to perform. It tells the experienced examiner a good deal about individuality, but as we use it it tells primarily whether the child is responding at his age, below age or ahead of age. The test consists of a box of 456 small plastic pieces, one-sixth of an inch thick. The pieces come in five different shapes—square, diamond, and equilateral, right-angled isosceles, and scalene triangles—and in six different colors—blue, white, red, yellow, green, and black.

The child is asked to take some of the pieces (as many as he chooses and any pieces that he chooses) out of the box and to make something on a piece of white paper covering the surface of a rectangular wooden tray, which is used as a base. The standard size of this working surface is 10¼ by 12⅝ inches. The child may make anything he chooses and may take as long as he chooses.

You don't need to know a great deal about this. Suffice it to say that a two-year-old child just scatters single pieces. By three, he may still scatter but may occasionally combine two squares, two triangles, or any two pieces of the same shape. By four he may combine six of the large triangles into a hexagon. By five he might make a small two-piece house or any other small object, not too much resembling the thing the child presumably has in mind. And so on, up through the older ages. Psychologists who have examined many children can quite easily tell the age level of a child's performance.

SENTENCE COMPLETION TEST

The Sentence Completion Test is one further test to which there are no standard right or wrong answers. Rather, the examiner gives the child (verbally) the beginnings of a number of sentences (there are thirty-three in the set we use), and asks the child to finish each sentence with anything that comes into his head. Simple sentences include: "I like people who . . ."; "It would be fun to be . . ."; "Most boys . . ."; "Sometimes I feel like . . ."

No special psychological finesse is used in interpreting what the child says; we do it in more or less commonsense way. The child, obviously, can reveal quite a good deal about what goes on in his mind and about how he feels by the way in which he completes the given sentences.

KINETIC FAMILY DRAWING TEST

A test which we urge readers to try, though one developed too late to have been applied to cases described in this present book, is Burns' and Kaufman's *Kinetic Family Drawing Test* (16). In using this test the child is merely instructed to "Draw a picture of everyone in your family, including you, doing something. Try to draw whole people, not cartoons or stick people. Remember, make everyone doing something—some kind of action." Readers are referred to Burns and Kaufman for pictured examples of the lively and often extremely revealing drawings which children produce. Often this one drawing, which usually takes not more than five minutes, can reveal more about the child and his relation to his family than could be discovered in any other way.

285

Measures of Physical Status

TEETHING

One of the easiest and most effective measures of any child's developmental status is made by checking his teething. Since we believe that in general behavior is a function of structure—that is, any child tends to behave as he does because of the kind of body he has and the stage it has reached—a good measure of a child's physiological status or the age his body has reached is his level of teething.

Many child specialists feel that one of the best measures of physiological (or body) age is an X ray of the wrist bones, but this is a measure that cannot always easily be made. We use, instead, a check on the child's teething.

We know how far the average child of five, six, or seven has come in losing his first teeth and in acquiring his second. Usually the first teeth the child loses are his lower central incisors (the two lower middle front teeth). These on the average are lost, and replaced with second teeth, when the child is from five and a half to six years of age. Next, as a rule, around six years of age, come the six-year molars.

Then the child loses his upper central incisors, and the new ones come in around six and a half years of age. At this age, too, many get their lower lateral incisors (the teeth on each side of the two middle ones). At seven the upper lateral incisors erupt.

If teething is markedly ahead of this average, behavior, too, may be advanced. If teething is substantially slower than this, it is fair to assume that the child is immature in his bodily development and thus may be immature in his behavior as well.

SOMATOTYPING

We include here a brief description of our somatotyping procedure because of the fact that all children, both research and clinical cases, who come to the Gesell Institute are routinely somatotyped.

A child's somatotype is a physical measure of his body's structure. Following the theory and methods of Dr. William H. Sheldon's constitutional psychology, an approach to human behavior that holds that behavior is a function of structure and that people behave as they do largely because of the way their bodies are built, we photograph each child, without clothing, in three positions (front, back, and side) in standardized poses.

Then the photograph is measured to determine in what proportion the child expresses each of Sheldon's three components: endomorphy, mesomorphy, ectomorphy. The child in whom endomorphy predominates tends to be fat and round; he in whom mesomorphy predominates is broad-shouldered, squarely built, muscular, and athletic; he in whom ectomorphy predominates is thin, fragile, angular, flat-chested, stoop-shouldered, and has pipe-stem arms and legs.

Achilleometer Test for Thyroid Dysfunction*

This is a very simple and easy to use test which takes the place of the earlier PBI (Protein-bound iodine) test of endocrine function. The Medco *Achilleometer* is a solid state (transistorized) direct reading computer for the determination of Achilles Reflex Test. It is battery operated. In using this instrument, the child is asked to kneel on a low chair surface, grasping a metal bar with his hands. A "remote sensor" connected by cord with the Achilleometer is strapped onto the plantar surface of the child's shoe, and his Achilles tendon is tapped sharply, causing a sharp reflex kick.

The timing of this kick, that is, the time interval between the first stimulus of the reflex hammer and the end of the muscle contrac-

---

* Medco Products Co., Inc., 3601-F East Admiral Place, Tulsa, Oklahoma 84150.

tion, is measured in milliseconds on an easily read scale on the face of the Achilleometer. For the subject with possible hypothyroidism, the time of response is long—from 30 to 40 milliseconds. For the subject with possible hyperthyroidism, reaction time is short—from 10 to 18 milliseconds. Those with no suspected thyroid problem measure between 20 and 28 milliseconds.

A deviant response on this test is merely an indication that further, medical, diagnosis should be sought, but this instrument often picks up hitherto unsuspected problems, and we have found it extremely useful.

Wepman Auditory Discrimination Test

The Wepman Auditory Discrimination Test, developed by Dr. Joseph M. Wepman of the University of Chicago, is an easy-to-administer method of determining a child's ability to recognize the fine differences that exist between the phonemes used in English speech. The test is a simple one. It measures only the ability to hear accurately. No visual ability is necessary, only the ability to respond affirmatively or negatively by saying a single word or even by nodding and shaking the head. The child is asked to listen to the examiner as he reads pairs of words and to indicate whether the words read are the same (a single word repeated) or different (two different words).

Vision Tests

These tests need not be described here, since they are technical tests given by a vision specialist. However, one warning is in order. Since most of the schoolwork the child does is carried out at his desk, every parent should try to make certain that his child's vision and vision performance are tested within arm's distance (ten to sixteen inches) and not just at the usual farther distance.

REFERENCES

1. Ames, Louise B. Predictive value of infant behavior examinations. In *Exceptional Infant: The Normal Infant,* vol. 1. Seattle, Wash.: Special Child Publications, 1965, pp. 209–239.
2. ———. Search for children showing academic promise in a predominantly Negro school. *J. Genet. Psychol.* 110 (1967): 217–231.
3. ———. *Is Your Child in the Wrong Grade?* New York: Harper & Row, 1970.
4. ———. Children with perceptual problems may also lag developmentally. *J. Learning Disabilities* 2 (1969): 205–208.
5. ———. *Child Care and Development.* Philadelphia: Lippincott, 1970.
6. Ames, Louise B., and Ilg, Frances L. *Parents Ask,* a syndicated daily newspaper column. New York: Publishers Hall Syndicate, 1950 to date.
7. Aukerman, Robert C. The right to read—where do we go from here? *New England Reading Association Journal* 5 (1970): 3–5.
8. Austin, John J., and Lafferty, J. Clayton. *Ready or Not? The School Readiness Checklist.* Muskegon, Mich.: Research Concepts, 1963.
9. Axline, Virginia. *Dibs in Search of Self.* Boston: Houghton Mifflin, 1964.
10. Beadle, Muriel. *A Child's Mind: How Children Learn during the Critical Years from Birth to Age Five.* New York: Doubleday, 1970.
11. Beck, Joan. *How to Raise a Brighter Child.* New York: Trident Press, 1967.
12. Berecz, John M. Phobias of childhood: Etiology and treatment. In *Annual Progress in Child Psychiatry and Child Development,* ed. Stella Chess and Alexander Thomas, 1969, pp. 558–601. (Special emphasis on school phobia.)

13. Blaine, Graham B., Jr. *Patience and Fortitude: The Parents' Guide to Adolescence.* Boston: Atlantic–Little, Brown, 1962.
14. Brenton, Myron. *What Happened to Teacher?* New York: Coward-McCann, 1970.
15. Briggs, Dorothy Corkille. *Your Child's Self Esteem.* New York: Doubleday, 1970.
16. Burns, Robert C., and Kaufman, S. Harvard. *Kinetic Family Drawings (K-F-D).* New York: Brunner/Mazel, 1970.
17. Carner, Richard L. Learning disabilities: Ethics and practice. *J. Learning Disabilities* 2 (1969): 448–450.
18. Chall, Jeanne. *Learning to Read: The Great Debate.* New York: McGraw-Hill, 1968.
19. Chase, Joan A. A study of the impact of grade retention on primary school children. *J. Psychol.* 70 (1968): 169–177.
20. DeHirsch, Katrina; Jansky, Jeannette J.; and Langford, William. *Predicting Reading Failure.* New York: Harper & Row, 1966.
21. Dodson, Fitzhugh. *How to Parent.* Los Angeles: Nash Publishing Co., 1970.
22. Douglass, Malcolm P. Laterality and knowledge of direction. *Elem. School Journal* 66 (1965): 68–74.
23. Drucker, Peter. *The Age of Discontinuity.* New York: Harper & Row, 1970.
24. DuPress, David. Pills for learning. *Wall Street Journal,* January 28, 1971, p. 1.
25. Edgington, Ruth. *Helping Children with Reading Disability.* Chicago: Developmental Learning Materials, 1968.
26. Ellingson, Careth. *The Shadow Children.* Chicago: Topaz Books, 1967.
27. Flesch, Rudolf. *Why Johnny Can't Read.* New York: Harper & Bros., 1955.
28. Frankel, Herman. Five suggestions: An approach to the identification and management of children with learning disabilities. *J. Learning Disabilities* 1 (1968): 750–755.
29. Freeman, Roger A. The alchemists in our public schools. In *Ashe: Human Learning.* Orange City, Fla.: American Society of Humanistic Education.
30. Furth, Hans G. *Piaget for Teachers.* Englewood Cliffs, N.J.: Prentice-Hall, 1970.
31. Gardner, Richard A. *Therapeutic Communication with Children: Mutual Storytelling Technique in Child Psychiatry.* New York: Science House, 1971.

290

32. Gartner, Alan, ed. *New Human Services Newsletter.* New York University School of Education, February, 1971.

33. Gesell, Arnold. The documentation of infant behavior in relation to cultural anthropology. In *Proceedings Eighth American Scientific Congress, Anthropological Sciences,* vol. 2, pp. 279–291. Washington, D.C., 1942.

34. Gesell, Arnold, and Gesell, Beatrice C. *The Normal Child and Primary Education.* Boston: Ginn & Company, 1912.

35. Gesell, Arnold, and Ilg, Frances L. *The Child from Five to Ten.* New York: Harper & Bros., 1946.

36. Gesell, Arnold; Ilg, Frances L.; and Ames, Louise B. *Youth: The Years from Ten to Sixteen.* New York: Harper & Bros., 1956.

37. Gesell, Arnold; Ilg, Frances L.; and Bullis, Glenna. *Vision: Its Development in Infant and Child.* New York: Hoeber, 1949.

38. Ginott, Haim. *Between Parent and Child.* New York: Macmillan, 1965.

39. ————. *Teacher and Child.* New York: Macmillan, 1972.

40. Glasser, William. *Schools Without Failure.* New York: Harper & Row, 1969.

41. Goodlad, John I. Thought, invention and research in the advancement of education. In Committee for Economic Development, *The Schools and the Challenge of Innovation,* 1969.

42. Goodlad, John I., and Anderson, Robert H. *The Nongraded Elementary School.* New York: Harcourt, Brace & World. Rev. ed., 1969.

43. Gordon, Sol. Quoted in *Behavior Today* 2 (February 8, 1971): 2.

44. Gray, William S. *Standardized Oral Reading Paragraphs.* Indianapolis: Bobbs Merrill.

45. Greenwald, Sheila. My life story. *Harper's Magazine,* July 1966.

46. Hallahan, Daniel P. Cognitive styles: Preschool implications for the disadvantaged. *J. Learning Disabilities* 3 (1970): 5–9.

47. Healy, William. *Pictorial Completion Test II.* Chicago: C.H. Stoelting Co.

48. Hechinger, Fred. Open door help to open up the children. *New York Times,* February 7, 1971.

49. Heimgartner, Norman. Developmental age as a predictor of reading success. Unpublished paper. University of Northern Colorado, 1971.

50. Holt, John. *How Children Fail.* New York: Pitman, 1964.

51. ————. *How Children Learn.* New York: Pitman, 1968.

52. ———. *What Do I Do Monday?* New York: Dutton, 1970.

53. ———. Big Bird, Meet Dick and Jane: A critique of Sesame Street. *Atlantic Monthly* 227 (May 1971): 72–78.

54. Hunt, J. McV. How children develop intellectually. *Children* 11 (1964): 89–91.

55. Ilg, Frances L., and Ames, Louise B. *Child Behavior.* New York: Harper & Bros., 1955.

56. ———. *School Readiness.* New York: Harper & Row, 1965.

57. Ilg, Frances L.; Ames, Louise B.; and Scranton, Joan. *Incomplete Man Playing Cards.* Lumberville, Pa.: Programs for Education, 1969.

58. Ilg, Frances L.; Ames, Louise B.; and Haines, Jacqueline. *Copy Forms Playing Cards.* Lumberville, Pa.: Programs for Education, 1971.

59. Jackson, Philip W. *Life in Classrooms.* New York: Holt, Rinehart & Winston, 1968.

60. Jensen, Arthur R. How much can we boost I.Q. and scholastic achievement? *Harvard Educational Review* 39 (Winter 1968): 1–123.

61. ———. *Understanding Readiness: An Occasional Paper,* Urbana, Illinois: University of Illinois Press, 1969.

62. *Journal of Learning Disabilities* (1971) *4,* 4, note on page 203; and entire issue for November, 1971, *4, 9,* pp. 466–543.

63. Kirkendall, Lester A. The school psychologist and sex education. In *Professional School Psychology,* ed. Monroe G. and Gloria B. Gottsegen, vol. 3. New York: Grune & Stratton, 1969, pp. 148–171.

64. Knox, G. E. Classroom symptoms of vision difficulty. In Clinical Studies in Reading, ed. Helen H. Robinson. *Supplementary Education Monograph* 77 (1953), University of Chicago Press.

65. Koppitz, Elizabeth M. *The Bender Gestalt Test for Young Children.* New York: Grune & Stratton, 1964.

66. ———. *Children with Learning Disabilities.* New York: Grune & Stratton, 1971.

67. Krippner, Stanley. On research in visual training and reading disability. *J. Learning Disabilities* 4 (1971): 65–76.

68. Kruger-Smith, Bert. *Your Non-Learning Child: His World of Upside Down.* Boston: Beacon Press, 1968.

69. Leonard, George. *Education and Ecstasy.* New York: Delacorte, 1968.

References

70. Lubchenco, Lula O., *et al.* Sequelae of premature birth. *Amer. J. Dis. Child.* 106 (1963): 101–115.
71. Mawhinney, Paul E. Why we gave up on early entrance. *Michigan Education Journal* 41 (1964): 25.
72. Mayer, Jean. *Overweight: Causes, Cost and Control.* Englewood Cliffs, N.J.: Prentice-Hall, 1966.
73. McGaugh, James. Biological bases of memory. *Mental Health Program Report No. 4.* Chevy Chase, Md.: U.S. Department of Health, Education and Welfare, 1970.
74. Meier, John H. Prevalence and characteristics of learning disabilities found in second grade children. *J. Learning Disabilities* 4 (1971): 1–16.
75. *Miller-Unruh Specialists' Newsletter: The Special Teacher of Reading* 1 (Winter 1969): 3.
76. O'Donnell, Patrick A., and Eisenson, Jon. Delacato training for reading achievement and visual-motor integration. *J. Learning Disabilities* 2 (1969): 441–447.
77. Piaget, Jean. Lecture given at University of Miami's Mailman Center for Child Development. Reported in *Behavior Today* 2 (March 29, 1971): 1.
78. *The Porter Sargent Handbook of Private Schools.* Boston: Porter Sargent, 1970.
79. *Private Independent Schools: The Bunting and Lyon Bluebook.* Wallingford, Conn., Bunting and Lyon, 1970.
80. Radler, D. H., and Kephart, Newell C. *Success through Play.* New York: Harper & Row, 1960.
81. Rosenthal, Robert. *Pygmalion in the Classroom.* New York: Holt, Rinehart & Winston, 1968.
82. Rossi, Albert O. The slow learner. *New York State Journal of Medicine* 68 (1968): 3123–3128.
83. ———. Genetics of higher level disorders. *J. Learning Disabilities* 3 (1970): 387–390; and personal communication, 1970.
84. Schulman, Irving. Report in *J. Learning Disabilities* 4 (1971): 203.
85. Scott, Betty, and Ames, Louise B. Improved academic personal and social adjustment in selected primary school repeaters. *Elem. School Journal* 69 (1969): 431–439.
86. Selye, Hans. *The Stress of Life.* New York: McGraw-Hill, 1956.
87. Sheldon, William H. *Varieties of Temperament.* New York: Harper & Bros., 1942.

293

88. Siegel, Ernest. *Helping Your Brain Injured Child.* New York: New York Association for Brain Injured Children, 1961.

89. ———. *Special Education in the Regular Classroom.* New York: John Day, 1969.

90. Silberberg, Norman E., and Silberberg, Margaret. Myths in remedial education. *J. Learning Disabilities* 2 (1969): 209–217.

91. ———. The bookless curriculum: an educational alternative. *J. Learning Disabilities* 2 (1969): 302–307.

92. Silberman, Charles E. *Crisis in the Classroom.* New York: Random House, 1970.

93. Smith, Lendon H. *The Children's Doctor.* Englewood Cliffs, N.J.: Prentice-Hall, 1969.

94. Smith, Marion F., and Burks, Arthur J. *Teaching the Slow Learning Child.* New York: Harper & Row, 1960.

95. Streff, John W. Vision: A developmental approach. *New England J. Optometry* 21 (1970): 92–99.

96. Von Hilsheimer, Rev. George. *How to Live with Your Special Child: A Handbook for Behavior Change.* Washington, D.C.: Acropolis Books, 1970.

97. ———. Personal communication, December 30, 1970.

98. ———. Reading achievement as a function of maturity, diet, and manipulation of chronic states of high arousal. Lecture given at the ACLD 8th Annual International Conference, Chicago, March 19, 1971.

99. Wechsler, David. *Wechsler Intelligence Scale for Children.* New York: The Psychological Corporation, 1949.

100. ———. The I.Q. IS an intelligent test. *New York Times,* June, 1966, pp. 12, 13.

101. Wees, W. R. *Nobody Can Teach Anyone Anything.* New York: Doubleday, 1971.

102. Wepman, Joseph M. *Auditory Discrimination Test.* Chicago: University of Chicago Press.

103. White House Conference on Children and Youth. Report of the Right to Read Forum, 1970.

104. Williams, Roger J. *You Are Extraordinary.* New York: Random House, 1967.

105. ———. The biology of behavior. *Saturday Review,* January 30, 1971: 17–19, 61.

106. Wunderlich, Ray C. Personal communication, 1967.

References

107. ————. *Kids, Brains and Learning*. St. Petersburg, Fla.: Johnny Reads Press, 1970.
108. ————. A pediatrician's view of the learning disabled child (in press).
109. Young, Francis A. The effect of restricted visual span on the refractive error of the young monkey eye. *Investigative Ophthal.* 2 (1963): 571–577.
110. Young, Francis A., Baldwin, William, *et al.* The transmission of refractive errors within Eskimo families. *Am. J. Optom. & Archives of A.A.O.* 46 (1969): 676–685.
111. Young, Milton A. *Buttons Are to Push: Developing Your Child's Creativity*. New York: Pitman, 1970.

INDEX

Index

307

72 73 74 75 10 9 8 7 6 5 4 3 2 1